COMPUTER TECHNOLOGY AND COMPUTER PROGRAMMING

New Research and Strategies

COMPUTER TECHNOLOGY AND COMPUTER PROGRAMMING
New Research and Strategies

James L. Antonakos

Distinguished Professor of Computer Science,
Broome Community College, State University of New York,
Binghamton; Online Instructor and Faculty Advisor, Excelsior College,
Albany, New York and Sullivan University, Kentucky, U.S.A.

Apple Academic Press

Computer Technology and Computer Programming: New Research and Strategies

This book contains information obtained from authentic and highly regarded sources. A wide variety of references are listed. Reasonable efforts have been made to publish reliable data and information, but the editors and the publisher cannot assume responsibility for the validity of all materials or for the consequences of their use.

First Published in the Canada, 2011
Apple Academic Press Inc.
3333 Mistwell Crescent
Oakville, ON L6L 0A2
Tel. : (888) 241-2035
Fax: (866) 222-9549
E-mail: info@appleacademicpress.com
www.appleacademicpress.com

> **The full-color tables, figures, diagrams, and images in this book may be viewed at www.appleacademicpress.com**

First issued in paperback 2021

ISBN 13: 978-1-77463-254-3 (pbk)
ISBN 13: 978-1-926692-96-8 (hbk)

James L. Antonakos

Cover Design: Psqua

Library and Archives Canada Cataloguing in Publication Data
CIP Data on file with the Library and Archives Canada

CONTENTS

INTRODUCTION

What I find most remarkable about the field of computer science is its vast scope. Practically any topic you might imagine falls in some way under the umbrella of computer science. Many topics may seem to naturally belong there, such as research into advanced computer architectures, distributed and cloud computing (and their associated high-speed networking components), computer forensics, operating systems, and the details of many different programming languages. But these areas are just a few of a wider array of topics and activities found in computer science. Computer scientists spend a great deal of time and energy studying compression algorithms for images, video, and data; encryption techniques; efficient hardware computation pipelines; computer gaming and its associated artificial intelligence; networking protocols that enable secure and reliable transmission of information; image processing; database technologies; and new ways of sharing information over the Internet.

Of course, many areas of computer science require a good foundation in mathematics. Here it is remarkable to know that we use mathematics to prove that some things are possible and that other things are impossible. Some concepts or problems have not yet been proved either way, even with a great many researchers looking into them. When and if these open problems are eventually solved, the solutions will usher in a new age in computer science and also new challenges. For example, if we gain a deeper insight and understanding of random numbers, what will be the effect on the security algorithms we use every day to encrypt our private communication over the Internet?

Let us also take note of the astounding visual reality now available, of computer graphics algorithms so complex they render stunning visual effects in video games in real time and produce "Is it real or computer generated?" effects in motion pictures. Again, here the computer scientist must have programming skills, knowledge of mathematics, physics, optics, and the hardware details of the processor or processors rendering the image. We can see for ourselves the fruits of many researchers' labors over the years.

The time spent by computer scientists examining arcane topics that appear to have little practical application is very misleading. Advances in medical imaging, understanding biological processes, recognizing human speech, mining data and distinguishing patterns, and exploring the nature of memory via neural networks have all been made possible by computer scientists toiling away in their labs.

Today the line between software and hardware is becoming blurred. A computer scientist crafting a new optimizing compiler must have detailed knowledge of the internal hardware workings of a processor in order to efficiently schedule instructions and generate code that utilizes the processor pipeline, registers, and cache memory to provide maximum performance. Even something as simple as extending the life of the battery in a laptop computer is a combined effort between the hardware designers and the software writers.

Perhaps the most important quality a computer scientist can possess is curiosity, a constant desire to understand how things work. When this curiosity is coupled with determination, the end result is often useful in ways that were not originally intended. Keep this curiosity in mind as you read the papers on *Computer Technology and Computer Programming* contained within this book.

— **James L. Antonakos**

Novel FTLRNN with Gamma Memory for Short-Term and Long-Term Predictions of Chaotic Time Series

Sanjay L. Badjate and Sanjay V. Dudu

ABSTRACT

Multistep ahead prediction of a chaotic time series is a difficult task that has attracted increasing interest in the recent years. The interest in this work is the development of nonlinear neural network models for the purpose of building multistep chaotic time series prediction. In the literature there is a wide range of different approaches but their success depends on the predicting performance of the individual methods. Also the most popular neural models are based on the statistical and traditional feed forward neural networks. But it is seen that this kind of neural model may present some disadvantages when long-term prediction is required. In this paper focused time-lagged recurrent neural network (FTLRNN) model with gamma memory is developed for different prediction horizons. It is observed that this predictor performs re-markably well for short-term predictions as well as medium-term predictions. For coupled partial differential equations generated chaotic time series such as Mackey Glass and Duffing, FTLRNN-based predictor performs consis-tently well for different depths of predictions ranging from short term to long term, with only slight deterioration after k is increased beyond 50. For real-world highly complex and nonstationary time series like Sunspots and Laser, though the proposed predictor does perform reasonably for short term and me-dium-term predictions, its prediction ability drops for long term ahead pre-diction. However, still this is the best possible prediction results considering the facts that these are nonstationary time series. As a matter of fact, no oth-er NN configuration can match the performance of FTLRNN model. The authors experimented the performance of this FTLRNN model on predict-ing the dynamic behavior of typical Chaotic Mackey-Glass time series, Duff-ing time series, and two real-time chaotic time series such as monthly sunspots and laser. Static multi layer perceptron (MLP) model is also attempted and compared against the proposed model on the performance measures like mean squared error (MSE), Normalized mean squared error (NMSE), and Cor-relation Coefficient (r). The standard back-propagation algorithm with mo-mentum term has been used for both the models.

Introduction

Predicting the future which has been the goal of many research activities in the last century is an important problem for human, arising from the fear of unknown phenomenon and calamities all around the infinitely large world with its many variables showing highly nonlinear and chaotic behavior. Chaotic time series have many applications in various fields of science, for example, astrophysics, fluid me-chanics, medicine, stock market, weather, and are also useful in engineering such as speech coding [1], radar modeling of electromagnetic wave propagation and scattering [2]. The chaotic interconnected complex dynamical systems in nature are characterized by high sensitivity to initial conditions which results in long-term unpredictability. The dynamical reconstruction seems to be extremely dif-ficult, even in developing era of super computers, not because of computational complexity, but due to inaccessibility of perfect inputs and state variables. Many different methods have been developed to deal with chaotic time series prediction. Among them neural networks occupy an important place being adequate model of the nonlinearity and nonstationarity.

Inspired from the structure of the human brain and the way it is supposed to operate, neural networks are parallel computational systems capable of solving number of complex problems in such a diverse areas as pattern recognition, computer vision, robotics, control and medical diagnosis, to name just few [3]. Neural networks are an effective tool to perform any nonlinear input output mappings and prediction problem [4]. Predicting a chaotic time series using a neural network is of particular interest [5]. Not only it is an efficient method to reconstruct a dynamical system from an observed time series, but it also has many applications in engineering problems like radar noise cancellation [6], radar [7] demodulation of chaotic secure communication systems [8], and spread spectrum/code division multiple access (CDMA) systems [9, 10]. It is already established that, under appropriate conditions, they are able to uniformly approximate any complex continuous function to any desired degree of accuracy [11]. Later, similar results were published independently in [12]. It is these fundamental results that allow us to employ neural network in time series prediction. Since neural networks' models do not need any a priori assumption about the underlying statistical distribution of the series to be predicted, they are commonly classified as "data-driven" approach, to contrast them with the "model-driven" statistical methods. Neural networks that are the instruments in broad sense can learn the complex nonlinear mappings from the set of observations [13]. The static MLP network has gained an immense popularity from numerous practical application published over the past decade, there seems to be substantial evidence that multilayer perceptron indeed possesses an impressive ability [14]. There have been some theoretical results that try to explain the reasons for the success in [15, 16]. Most applications are based on feed-forward neural networks, such as the back-propagation (BP) network [17] and Radial basis function (RBF) network [18, 19]. It has also been shown that modeling capacity of feed-forward neural networks can be improved if the iteration of the network is incorporated into the learning process [20].

Several methods with different performance measures have been attempted in the literature to predict the chaotic time series. It is has been predicted for Mackey-Glass chaotic time series for short-term ahead prediction with a percentage error of 20% [21]. A new class of wavelet network was developed with a standard deviation of 0.0029 for short-term ahead prediction of Mackey-Glass chaotic time series and annual sunspots for 1 step ahead prediction [22]. By using recurrent predictor neural network for monthly sunspots chaotic time series for 6 months ahead prediction with E_{PA} (Prediction accuracy) equals 0.992 and E_{RMSE} (Root mean squared error) equals 4.419, for 10 months ahead prediction with E_{PA} of 0.980 and E_{RMSE} of 7.050, for 15 months ahead prediction of E_{PA} equals 0.9222 and E_{RMSE} equals 13.658, and 20 months ahead prediction with E_{PA} of 0.866 and E_{RMSE} of 16.79323 [23]. Also by using radial basis function with orthogonal least square Fuzzy model for monthly sunspots with prediction error +6 to -4 and for Mackey-Glass chaotic time series with E_{RMSE} of 0.0015 [24]. It is also attempted with Hybrid network for Mackey-Glass time series with iterative prediction and

Normalized Mean Square Error NMSE of 0.053 [25]. By using Elman neural network for yearly sunspots for 1 year ahead prediction with E_{RMSE} equals 30.2931 and prediction accuracy of 0.9732 [26].

From the scrupulous review of the related research work, it is noticed that no simple model is available for long-term prediction of chaotic time series so far. It is necessary to develop a simple model that is able to perform short-, medium- and long-term predictions of chaotic time series with reasonable accuracy. In view of the remarkable ability of neural network in learning from the instances, it can prove as a potential candidate with a view to design a versatile predictor (forecaster) for the chaotic time series. Hence in this paper a novel focused time-lagged recurrent neural network model with gamma memory filter is proposed as an intelligent tool for predicting the two non linear differential equation Mackey-Glass and Duffing time series and two real-time monthly sunspots and Laser chaotic time series not only for short-term but long-term prediction also because they acquire temporal processing ability through the realization of short-term memory and information about the preceding units, which is important when the long-term prediction is required. The Mackey-Glass chaotic time series was first proposed as a model for white blood cell production, the Duffing chaotic time series describes a specific nonlinear circuit or the hardening spring effect observed in many mechanical problems, monthly sunspots number is a good measure of solar activity which has a period of 11 years, so-called solar cycle. The solar activity has a measure effect on earth, climate, space weather, satellites, and space missions, and a highly nonlinear laser time series. These chaotic time series are the good benchmark for the proposed model. The various parameters like number of hidden layers, number of processing elements in the hidden layer, step size, the different learning rules, the various transfer functions like tanh, sigmoid, linear-tan-h, and linear sigmoid, different error norms L_1, L_2, L_3, L_4, L_5, and L_∞, the different memories TDNN, Laguarre and gamma filter, and different combination of training and testing samples are exhaustively varied and experimented for obtaining the optimal values of performance measures as mentioned in the flow chart. The obtained results indicate the superior performance of estimated dynamic FTLRNN-based model with gamma memory over the MLPNN in various performance measures such as Mean Square Error (MSE), Normalized Mean Square Error (NMSE), and correlation coefficient (r) on testing as well as training data set. The proposed network is attempted for training up to 20 000 numbers of epochs for obtaining the improved values of performance measures. The experimentation process is demonstrated in flow chart of Figure 1. This paper is organized as follows in Section 2 the static MLP model is presented, and the learning procedure is explained. In Section 3 the proposed FTLRNN model is explained. In Section 4 the performance measures and their importance are discussed. Section 5 explains about the significance of the benchmark chaotic time series. Section 6 explains the experimental procedure and analysis. Section 7 summarizes the evaluation results and analyses for the proposed model. Finally concluding remarks on empirical findings are provided in Section 8.

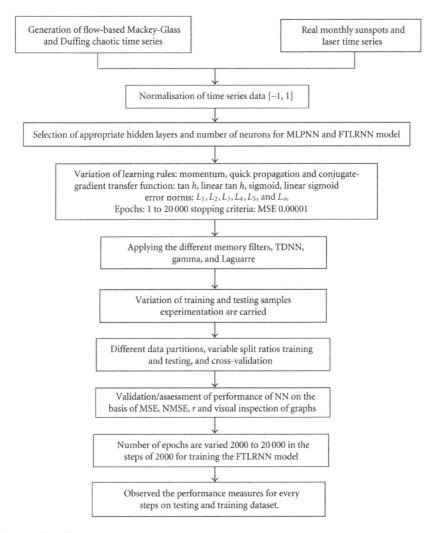

Figure 1. Flow Chart.

Static NN-Based Model

Static Neural networks typically use Multilayer perceptron MLP as a backbone. They are layered feed-forward networks typically trained with static back propagation.

MLP solid-based model has a solid foundation [27, 28]. The main reason for this is its ability to model simple as well as complex functional relationships. This has been proven through a number of practical applications [29]. In [11] it is shown that all continuous functions can be approximated to any desired accuracy, in terms of the uniform norm, with a network of one hidden layer of sigmoid or (hyperbolic tangent) hidden units and a layer of linear or tanh output unit to include in the hidden layer. The paper does not explain how many units to include in the hidden layer. This is discussed in [30], and a significant result is derived approximation capabilities of two layer perception networks when the function to be approximated shows certain smoothness. The biggest advantage of using MLP NN for approximation of mapping from input to the output of the system resides in its simplicity and the fact that it is well suited for online implementation. The objective of training is then to determine a mapping from a set of training data to the set of possible weights so that the network will produce predictions y(t), which in some sense are close to the true outputs y(t). The prediction error approach is based on the introduction of measure of closeness in terms of mean square error (MSE) criteria:

$$V_N(\theta, Z^N) = \frac{1}{2N} \sum_{t=1}^{N} \left[y(t) - y(t^\wedge|) \right]^T \left[y(t) - y(t^\wedge|\theta) \right] \tag{1}$$

$$= \frac{1}{2N} \sum_{t=1}^{N} \varepsilon^2(t, \theta).$$

The weights are then found as

$$\hat{\theta} = \arg \min_{\theta} V_N(\theta, Z^N), \tag{2}$$

by some kind of iterative minimization scheme:

$$\theta^{(i+1)} = \theta^{(i)} + \mu^{(i)} f^{(i)}, \tag{3}$$

where $\theta^{(i)}$ specifies the current iterate (number "i"), $f^{(i)}$ is the search direction, and $\mu^{(i)}$ is the step size.

When NN has been trained, the next step is to evaluate it. This is done by standard method in statistics called independent validation [31]. It is never a good idea to assess the generalization properties of an NN-based on training data alone. This method divides the available data sets into two sets, namely, training data set and testing data set. The training data set are next divided into two partitions: the first partition is used to update the weights in the network and the second partition is used to assess (or cross-validate) the training performance. The testing data set are then used to assess how the network has generalized. The learning and generalization ability of the estimated NN-based model is assessed on the basis of certain performance measures such as MSE, NMSE, and the regression ability of the NN by visual inspection of the correlation coefficient characteristics for different outputs of system under study.

FTLRNN Model

Time-lagged recurrent networks (TLRNs) are MLPs extended with short-term memory structures. Here, a "static" NN (e.g., MLP) is augmented with dynamic properties [14]. This, in turn, makes the network reactive to the temporal structure of information bearing signals. For an NN to be dynamic, it must be given memory. This memories may be classified into "short-term" and "long-term" memories. Long-term memory is built into an NN through supervised learning, whereby the information content of the training data set is stored (in part or in full) in the synaptic weights of the network [32]. However, if the task at hand has a temporal dimension, some form of "short-term" memory is needed to make the network dynamic. One simple way of building short-term memory into the structure of an NN is through the use of time delays, which can be applied at the input layer of the network (focused). A short-term memory structure transforms a sequence of samples into a point in the reconstruction space [33]. This memory structure is incorporated inside the learning machine. This means that instead of using a window over the input data, processing elements (PEs) created are dedicated to store either the history of the input signal or the PE activations.

The input PEs of an MLP are replaced with a tap delay line, which is followed by the MLPNN. This topology is called the focused time-delay NN (TDNN). The focused topology only includes the memory Kernels connected to the input layer. This way, only the past of the input is remembered. The delay line of the focused TDNN stores the past samples of the input. The combination of the tap delay line and the weights that connect the taps to the PEs of the first hidden layer is simply linear combiners followed by a static nonlinearity. Typically, a gamma short-term memory mechanism is combined with nonlinear PEs in restricted topologies called focused. Basically, the first layer of the focused TDNN is a filtering layer, with as many adaptive filters as PEs in the first hidden layer. The outputs of the linear combiners are passed through a nonlinearity (of the hidden-layer PE) and are then further processed by the subsequent layers of the MLP for system identification, where the goal is to find the weights that produce a network output that best matches the present output of the system by combining the information of the present and a predefined number of past samples (given by the size of the tap delay line) [32]. Size of the memory layer depends on the number of past samples that are needed to describe the input characteristics in time. This number depends on the characteristics of the input and the task. This focused TDNN can still be trained with static back propagation, provided that a desired signal is available at each time step. This is because the tap delay line at the input layer does not have any free parameters. So the only adaptive parameters are in the static feed-forward path.

The memory PE receives in general many inputs $x_i(n)$ and produces multiple outputs $y = [y_0(n),..., y_D(n)]^T$, which are delayed versions of $y_0(n)$ the combined input,

$$y_k(n) = g(y_{k-1}(n)), \qquad y_0(n) = \sum_{j=1}^{P} x_j(n), \qquad (4)$$

where $g(\cdot)$ is a delay function.

These short-term memory structures can be studied by linear adaptive filter theory if $g(\cdot)$ is a linear operator. It is important to emphasize that the memory PE is a short-term memory mechanism, to make clear the distinction from the network weights, which represent the long-term memory of the network.

There are basically two types of memory mechanisms: memory by delay and memory by feedback. We seek to find the most general linear delay operator (special case of the Auto Regressive Moving Average model), where the memory traces yK(n) would be recursively computed from the previous memory trace yK-1(n). This memory PE is the generalized feed-forward memory PE. It can be shown that the defining relationship for the generalized feed-forward memory PE is mentioned

$$g_k(n) = g(n)^* g_{k-1}(n), \qquad k \geq 1, \qquad (5)$$

where, * is the convolution operation, $g(n)$ is a causal time function, and K is the tap index. Since this is a recursive equation, $g_0(n)$ should be assigned a value independently. This relationship means that the next memory trace is constructed from the previous memory trace by convolution with the same function $g(n)$, the memory Kernel yet unspecified. Different choices of $g(n)$ will provide different choices for the projection space axes. When we apply the input $x(n)$ to the generalized feed-forward memory PE, the tap signals $y_K(n)$ become

$$y_K(n) = g(n)^* y_{K-1}(n), \qquad (6)$$

the convolution of y_{k-1}(n) with the memory Kernel. For k=0, we have

$$y_0(n) = g_0(n)^* x(n), \qquad (7)$$

where g0(n) may be specified separately. The projection x(n) of the input signal is obtained by linearly weighting the tap signals according to

$$x(n) = \sum_{k=0}^{D} w_k y_k(n). \tag{8}$$

The most obvious choice for the basis is to use the past samples of the input signal x(n) directly, that is, the Kth tap signal becomes yK(n)=x(n-K). This choice corresponds to

$$g(n) = \delta(n-1). \tag{9}$$

In this case $g_0(n)$ is also a delta function δ(n) (delta function operator used in the tap delay line). The memory depth is strictly controlled by D, that is, the memory traces store the past D samples of the input. The time delay NN uses exactly this choice of basis.

The gamma memory PE attenuates the signals at each tap because it is a cascade of leaky integrators with the same time constant gamma model. The gamma memory PE is a special case of the generalized feed-forward memory PE, where

$$g(n) = \mu(1-\mu)^n, \qquad n \geq 1, \tag{10}$$

and g0(n)=δ(n). The gamma memory is basically a cascade of low-pass filters with the same time constant 1-μ. The over all impulse response of the gamma memory is

$$g_p(n) = \binom{n-1}{p-1} \mu^P (1-\mu)^{n-p}, \qquad n \geq p, \tag{11}$$

where (:) is a binomial coefficient defined by

$$\binom{n}{p} = \frac{n(n-1)\cdots(n-p+1)}{p!}. \tag{12}$$

For integer values of n and p, the overall impulse response $g_p(n)$ for varying p represents a discrete version of the integrand of the gamma function, hence the name of the memory.

The gamma memory PE has a multiple pole that can be adaptively moved along the real Z-domain axis, that is, the gamma memory can implement only low-pass (0 < μ < 1) or high-pass (1 < μ < 2) transfer functions. The high-pass transfer function creates an extra ability to model fast-moving signals by alternating the signs of the samples in the gamma PE (the impulse response for 1 < μ < 2 has alternating signs). The depth in samples parameters (D) is used to compute the number of taps (T) contained within the memory structure (s) of the network.

Performance Measures

Three different types of statistical performance evaluation criteria were employed to evaluate the performance of these models developed in this paper. These are as follows.

MSE: the mean square error is given by:

$$MSE = \frac{\sum_{j=0}^{P} \sum_{i=0}^{N} (dij - yij)^2}{N \times P},\qquad(13)$$

where P = number of output PEs, N = number of exemplars in the data set, y_{ij} = network output for exemplar i at PEj, and d_{ij} = desired output for exemplar i at PEj.

NMSE (normalized mean square error). The normalized mean square error is defined by the following formula, where P = Number of output PEs, N = Number of exemplars in data set,

$$NMSE = \frac{P \times N \times MSE}{\sum_{J=0}^{P} \left(\left(N \sum_{i=0}^{N} d_{ij}^2 - \left(\sum_{i=0}^{N} d_{ij} \right)^2 \right) / N \right)}.\qquad(14)$$

MSE=Mean square error, d_{ij} = desired output for exemplar i at PEj (jth element of PEs) Correlation Coefficient (r). The mean square error (MSE) can be used to determine how well the network output fits the desired output but it does not necessarily reflect whether the two sets of data move in the same direction. For instance by simply scaling the network output, we can change the MSE without changing the directionality of the data. The correlation coefficient solves this problem. By definition, the correlation coefficient between a network output x and a desired output d is

$$r = \frac{\sum_i \left((xi - \bar{x})(di - \bar{d}) / N \right)}{\sqrt{\sum_i \left((di - \bar{d}) / N \right)} \times \sqrt{\sum_i \left((di - \bar{d}) / N \right)}}.\qquad(15)$$

The correlation coefficient is confined to the range [-1,1].

Benchmark Chaotic Time Series

In science, chaos is used as a synonym for irregular behavior, whose long-term prediction is essentially unpredictable. Chaotic differential equations exhibit not only irregular behavior but they are also unstable with respect to small perturbations of their initial condition. Consequently it is difficult to forecast the future of time series based on chaotic differential equations; they are the good benchmark for a neural network design algorithm.

Mackey-Glass Time Series

The Mackey-Glass equation is time delay differential equation, which was first proposed as model of white blood cells production [34]. It is often used in practice as a benchmark set because of its nonlinear chaotic characteristics. Chaotic time series do not converge or diverge in time, and their trajectories are highly sensitive to initial conditions. Data are generated by using fourth order Runge-Kutta method. The equation is given by:

$$\frac{dx}{dt} = \frac{ax(t-\tau)}{1+x(t-\tau)^c} - bx(t),\tag{16}$$

where a, b, c are constant coefficients and t is time delay, the coefficient we are selected: a=0.2, b=0.1, c=10, τ=17. The Mackey-Glass time series is shown in Figure 2.

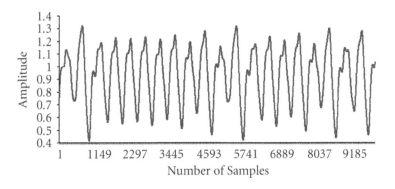

— MG

Figure 2. Mackey-Glass time series.

Duffing Time Series

Duffing time series describes a specific nonlinear circuit or the hardening spring effect observed in many mechanical problems [35]. The Duffing equation is time delay differential equation which is given as

$$\frac{dy}{dt} = y,$$

$$\frac{dy}{dt} = \left\{ F^x Cos(\tau) - x^3 - b^x y \right\},\qquad(17)$$

$$\frac{d\tau}{dt} = w,$$

where driving force F = 7.5, X_0=initial position 1.0, damping constant (b = 0.05), frequency w = 1.0, Delay time = 0.001. The chaotic time series is as shown in Figure 3.

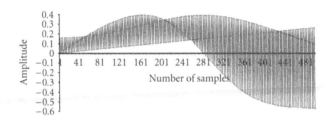

—— Duffing

Figure 3. Duffing time series (first 500 samples).

Sunspot Time Series

A sunspot number is a good measure of solar activity which has a period of 11 years, so-called solar cycle. The solar activity has a measure effect on earth, climate, space weather, satellites, and space missions, thus is an important value to be predicted. But due to intrinsic complexity of time behavior and the lack of a quantitative theoretical model, the prediction of solar cycle is very difficult. Many prediction techniques have been examined on the yearly sunspots number time series as an indicator of solar activity. However, in more recent studies the international monthly sunspot time series, which has a better time resolution and accuracy, has been used. In particular, a nonlinear dynamics approach has been developed in [36], and prediction results are compared between several prediction techniques from both statistical and physical classes. There has been a lot of work on controversial issue of nonlinear characteristics of the solar activity [36–39]; several recent analyses have provided evidence for low-dimensional deterministic nonlinear chaotic behavior of the monthly smoothed sunspot time series [36–38] which has intense. The data considered the monthly variations from January 1749 to December 2006. The total samples are 3096 considered and demonstrated in Figure 4. The series is normalized in the range of -1 to +1. The monthly smoothed sunspot number time series is downloaded from the SIDC (World Data Center for the Sunspot Index) [40].

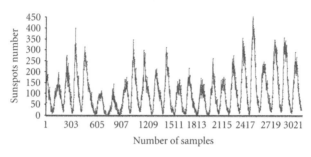

Figure 4. Monthly Sunspot time series.

Laser Time Series

The laser data were recorded from a Far Infrared-laser in a chaotic state. The measurements were made on an 81.5-micron 14 NH_3 cw (FIR) laser, pumped optically by the P (16) line of an N_2O laser, via the vibrational aQ(8, 7) NH_3 transition. The basic laser setup can be found in [41]. The intensity data was recorded by an Le Croy oscilloscope. It was made available worldwide during a time series prediction competition organized by Santa Fe Institute and a highly nonlinear data set, since then, it has been used in benchmark studies. The time series has 1000 samples points which has been rescaled to the range of [-1,1]. The time series is shown in Figure 5.

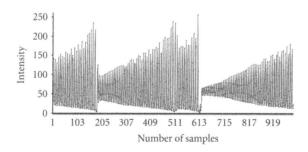

Figure 5. Laser time series.

Experimental Results

The choice of the number of hidden layers and the number of hidden units in each hidden layers is critical [42]. It has been established that an MLPNN that has only one hidden layer, with sufficient number of neurons, acts as a universal approximators of nonlinear mappings [43]. The tradeoff between accuracy and complexity of the model should be resolved accurately [44]. In practice, it is very difficult to determine a sufficient number of neurons necessary to achieve the desired degree of approximation accuracy. Frequently the number of units in the hidden layer is determined by trial and error. To determine the weight values, one must have a set of examples of how the output should relate to the inputs. The task of determining the weights from these examples is called training or learning and is basically a conventional estimation problem. That is, the weights are estimated from the examples in such away that the network, according to metric, models the true relationship as accurately as possible. Since learning is a stochastic process, the learning curve may be drastically different from run to run. In order to compare the performance of a particular search methodology or the effects of different parameters have on a system, it is needed to obtain the average learning curve over the number of runs so that the randomness can be averaged out. An exhaustive and careful experimentation has been carried to determine the configuration of the static MLP model and the optimal proposed FTLRNN model with gamma memory for short-term and long-term ahead predictions for the benchmark chaotic time series for 60% training, 15% cross-validation and 25% testing samples for the considered benchmark chaotic time series. It is found that the performance of the selected model is optimal for 38, 21, 15, and 43 neurons in the hidden layer with regard to the MSE, NMSE, and the correlation coefficient r performance for the testing data sets for Mackey-Glass, Duffing, Monthly Sunspots, and Laser time series, respectively, and the different parameters like transfer function, Learning rule, step size, and momentum values are mentioned in Table 1 for Mackey-Glass and Duffing chaotic time series and in Table 2 for monthly sunspots and Laser time series.

Table 1. Optimal Parameters of FTLRNN for both time series.

Sr. no.	Parameters	Hidden layer for MG	Hidden layer for Duffing	Output layer for MG	Output layer for Duffing
1	Number of PEs	38	21	1	1
2	Transfer function	Tanh	Tanh	Tanh	Lin tanh
3	Learning rule	Momentum	Momentum	Momentum	Momentum
4	Step size	1	1	0.1	0.1
5	Momentum	0.8	0.8	0.8	0.8

Table 2. Optimal Parameters of FTLRNN for both real-time series.

Sr. no.	Parameters	Hidden layer for sun spot time series	Hidden layer for laser time series	Output layer for sunspot time series	Output layer for laser time series
1	Number of PEs	15	43	1	1
2	Transfer function	Tanh	Tanh	Tanh	Tanh
3	Learning rule	Momentum	Momentum	Momentum	Momentum
4	Step size	1	1	0.1	0.1
5	Momentum	0.8	0.8	0.8	0.8

When we attempted to increase the number of hidden layer and the number of processing element in the hidden layer, the performance of the model is not to seen to improve significantly. On the contrary it takes too long time for training because of complexity of the model. As there is single input and single output for the given system, the number of input and output Processing Elements is chosen as one. Now the NN models are trained three times with different weight initialization with 1000 iterations of the static back-propagation algorithm with momentum term for these two models. All the possible variations for the model such as number of hidden layers, number of processing elements in each hidden layer, different transfer functions like tanh, linear tanh, sigmoid, linear sigmoid in output layer, the different supervised learning rules like momentum, conjugant gradient, and quick propagation are attempted for 10-step ahead prediction for Mackey-Glass, Duffing, and Laser time series, and 6 months ahead prediction for the monthly sunspots time series. The results are placed in Table 3 for Mackey-Glass and Duffing time series and in Table 4 for real-time monthly sunspots, and Laser time series for different learning rules on testing data set.

Table 3. Learning rules variations for the Mackey-Glass and Duffing time series.

Learning rule	Mackey-Glass time series (K = 10 step ahead prediction)			Duffing time series (K = 10 step ahead prediction)		
	MSE	NMSE	r	MSE	NMSE	r
Conjugate gradient	0.00545	0.09321	0.94965	0.12332	0.80365	0.77838
Momentum	0.004475	0.07940	0.9596	0.00335	0.02185	0.98910
Quick propagation	0.00534	0.09486	0.9481	0.00660	0.04305	0.97821

Table 4. Learning rules variations for the real sunspots and Laser time series.

Learning rule	Real sunspots time series (K = 6 months ahead prediction)			Real Laser time series (K = 10 step ahead prediction)		
	MSE	NMSE	r	MSE	NMSE	r
Conjugate gradient	0.00624	0.1135	0.9450	0.1450	0.511140	0.79772
Momentum	0.00554	0.1008	0.95528	0.009563	0.337	0.8302
Quick Propagation	0.00866	0.15757	0.92256	0.01787	0.62995	0.64371

Also the various error norms L_1, L_2, L_3, L_4, L_5, and L_∞, are varied, and FTL-RNN model is trained and tested for the optimum transfer function. The results are obtained and placed in Table 5 for artificial Mackey-Glass and Duffing time series and in Table 6 for real-time monthly sunspots and Laser time series. It is clear from Table 5 that for L2 error norm and tanh transfer function the value of MSE is minimum and correlation coefficient r is maximum for the Mackey-Glass chaotic time series. For Duffing chaotic time series the optimal values of MSE, NMSE, and correlation coefficient r is obtained for linear tanh transfer function and L1 error norm can be seen from Table 5.

Table 5. Error norms variations for the Mackey-Glass and Duffing time series for FTLRNN model on testing data set.

Error norms	Mackey-Glass time series (K = 10 step ahead prediction) Transfer function tanh			Duffing time series (K = 10 step ahead prediction) Transfer function linear tanh		
	MSE	NMSE	r	MSE	NMSE	r
L_1	0.00455	0.08077	0.94576	0.00335	0.02185	0.98910
L_2	0.00447	0.07940	0.9596	0.00389	0.02747	0.9831
L_3	0.00484	0.08595	0.9345	0.0488	0.02756	0.9821
L_4	0.00577	0.1024	0.93823	0.01624	0.02756	0.96108
L_5	0.00629	0.1117	0.9332	0.01656	0.09354	0.95725
L_∞	0.00544	0.0887	0.94990	0.00341	0.01901	0.9810

Table 6. Error norms variations for the real Sunspots time series and laser time series for FTLRNN model on testing data set.

Error norms	Monthly sunspots time series (K = 6 months ahead prediction) Transfer function tanh			Laser time series (K = 10 step ahead prediction) Transfer function tanh		
	MSE	NMSE	r	MSE	NMSE	r
L_1 (tanh)	0.02016	0.36673	0.85915	0.006171	0.2174	0.9014
L_2 (tanh)	0.00554	0.1008	0.95528	0.009563	0.337	0.8302
L_3 (tanh)	0.00571	0.10387	0.94882	0.0279	0.98417	0.3038
L_4 (tanh)	0.00956	0.17388	0.91375	0.2430	1.18040	0.2430
L_5 (tanh)	0.01618	0.29439	0.85462	0.02168	0.7641	0.5541
L_∞ (tanh)	0.00653	0.11889	0.92482	0.01536	0.5393	0.7887

Similarly, for real-time monthly sunspots time series, the minimum value of MSE and maximum value correlation relation coefficient r are obtained for L_2 error norm and tanh transfer function. For Laser time series the minimum value of MSE and maximum value of correlation coefficient r resulted for L1 error norm and tanh transfer function.

Then on these resulted optimal parameters the FTLRNN model is trained and tested for short-term (1, 5, 10) and long-term (20, 50, and 100) step ahead prediction. The FTLRNN structure is the MLP extended with the short-term memory structures. So these optimal parameters obtained for FTLRNN model are used for training and testing the MLPNN. Then on the same optimal parameters the static MLPNN model was attempted, and the performance measures like MSE, NMSE, and correlation coefficient r for the short-term (1, 5, and 10) and long-term (20, 50, and 100) step ahead prediction were obtained as stated in Table 7 for Mackey-Glass chaotic time series, in Table 8 for Duffing chaotic time series, in Table 9 for laser time series, and in Table 10 for monthly sunspots time series. It is obvious from Tables 7, 8, 9, and 10 that for all the time series considered for short-term and long-term ahead predictions, the performance of this FTLRNN model is optimal on the test dataset for the following number of taps = 6, Tap Delay = 1, Trajectory Length = 50 with regards to the value of correlation coefficient r, MSE, and NMSE.

Table 7. Performance of MLPNN and FTLRNN on testing data for Mackey-Glass time series.

K (step)	MLPNN on testing data			FTLRNN on testing data		
	MSE	NMSE	r	MSE	NMSE	r
1	0.007	0.01	0.9933	0.000491	0.00919	0.99542
5	0.0028	0.051	0.9745	0.00227	0.04145	0.97911
10	0.0056	0.1008	0.9485	0.004475	0.07940	0.9596
20	0.0128	0.2159	0.8860	0.00944	0.15861	0.891822
50	0.0411	0.599	0.6406	0.024382	0.35655	0.80849
100	0.08180	0.9988	0.1971	0.05345	0.65267	0.62265

Table 8. Performance of MLPNN and FTLRNN on testing data for Duffing time series.

K (step)	MLPNN on testing data			FTLRNN on testing data		
	MSE	NMSE	r	MSE	NMSE	r
1	0.08750	0.5666	0.66035	0.00113	0.00957	0.99545
5	0.07634	0.55568	0.68434	0.00202	0.01315	0.99356
10	0.08331	0.54275	0.67991	0.00335	0.02185	0.98910
20	0.08580	0.62975	0.63454	0.00632	0.04150	0.97982
50	0.10079	0.74545	0.54593	0.00927	0.06562	0.96663
100	0.11397	0.85011	0.40191	0.00117	0.07870	0.96000

Table 9. Performance of MLPNN and FTLRNN for testing data set for Laser time series.

K (step)	MLP neural network			FTLRNN		
	MSE	NMSE	r	MSE	NMSE	r
1	0.01815	0.681	0.59818	0.00282	0.105	0.94592
5	0.02522	0.918	0.35641	0.00372	0.135	0.93962
10	0.01957	0.689	0.5587	0.00956	0.337	0.9014
20	0.03040	1.009	0.11287	0.01635	0.543	0.71872
50	0.03499	1.039	0.28146	0.03466	1.02971	0.41330

Then training and testing samples are varied from 10% to 80% as training with the increments of 10% samples and 75% to 5% as testing on the proposed optimal FTLRNN model, the number of training and testing samples was as testing samples with the decrements of 10% keeping exemplars for Cross-Validation

(CV) 15% constant. The performance measures were obtained and compared on testing and training datasets and to gauge the performance and robustness of the FTLRNN. The results are obtained and are placed in Table 11 for 1-step ahead predictions, Table 12 for 5-step ahead prediction, Table 13 for 10-step ahead prediction, Table 14 for 20-step ahead prediction, Table 15 for 50-step ahead prediction and Table 16 for 100-step ahead prediction for Mackey-Glass and Duffing chaotic time series.

Table 10. Performance of MLPNN and FTLRNN for testing data set for monthly sunspot time series.

K (month)	MLP neural network			FTLRNN		
	MSE	NMSE	r	MSE	NMSE	r
1	0.00247	0.04533	0.97569	0.002227	0.04162	0.98163
6	0.01229	0.2234	0.8917	0.00554	0.1008	0.9528
12	0.02387	0.43132	0.77184	0.01693	0.30599	0.8550
18	0.03989	0.7174	0.5741	0.02266	0.4075	0.7977
24	0.0538	0.9658	0.3584	0.03059	0.54899	0.71497

Table 11. For K = 1, training and testing samples variation for FTLRNN on testing data set.

Time series		Mackey-Glass time series			Duffing time series		
Training exemplars	Testing exemplars	MSE	NMSE	r	MSE	NMSE	r
10%	75%	0.000315	0.00627	0.99707	0.00230	0.03972	0.98015
20%	65%	0.000247	0.004854	0.99757	0.00101	0.00774	0.99618
30%	55%	0.000405	0.007732	0.99628	0.00104	0.00707	0.99671
40%	45%	0.000371	0.00691	0.99663	0.00103	0.00655	0.99692
50%	35%	0.000371	0.007283	0.9964	0.00087	0.00555	0.99733
60%	25%	0.000491	0.00919	0.99542	0.00113	0.00957	0.99545
70%	15%	0.00078	0.01353	0.9933	0.00091	0.00609	0.99712
80%	05%	0.002217	0.03312	0.98337	0.00484	0.03271	0.98827

Table 12. For K = 5, training and testing samples variation for FTLRNN on testing data set.

Time series		Mackey-Glass time series			Duffing time series		
Training exemplars	Testing exemplars	MSE	NMSE	r	MSE	NMSE	r
10%	75%	0.000501	0.01779	0.99122	0.00465	0.08523	0.95975
20%	65%	0.001006	0.019508	0.9902	0.00162	0.01236	0.99388
30%	55%	0.001196	0.02256	0.98875	0.00150	0.00944	0.99552
40%	45%	0.00144	0.02653	0.98675	0.00139	0.00885	0.99578
50%	35%	0.00167	0.0322	0.9838	0.00170	0.01154	0.99435
60%	25%	0.00227	0.04145	0.97911	0.00202	0.01315	0.99356
70%	15%	0.00371	0.06227	0.9684	0.00149	0.00999	0.99524
80%	05%	0.01089	0.1502	0.9226	0.00435	0.02941	0.98926

Table 13. For K = 10, training and testing samples variation for FTLRNN on testing data set.

Time series		Mackey-Glass time series			Duffing time series		
Training exemplars	Testing exemplars	MSE	NMSE	r	MSE	NMSE	r
10%	75%	0.00191	0.03733	0.9812	0.00804	0.15432	0.92405
20%	65%	0.00208	0.03994	0.97985	0.00314	0.02395	0.98796
30%	55%	0.02261	0.04205	0.97888	0.00202	0.01315	0.99356
40%	45%	0.00266	0.04815	0.97581	0.00260	0.01653	0.99185
50%	35%	0.03448	0.06483	0.967219	0.00288	0.01936	0.99014
60%	25%	0.004475	0.07940	0.9596	0.00335	0.02185	0.98910
70%	15%	0.00757	0.12238	0.9373	0.00306	0.02046	0.99001
80%	05%	0.02204	0.27796	0.8537	0.00655	0.04429	0.97835

Table 14. For K = 20, training and testing samples variation for FTLRNN on testing data set.

Time series		Mackey-Glass time series			Duffing time series		
Training exemplars	Testing exemplars	MSE	NMSE	r	MSE	NMSE	r
10%	75%	0.00407	0.07799	0.96028	0.01342	0.30048	0.86374
20%	65%	0.00436	0.08154	0.95852	0.00503	0.03857	0.98132
30%	55%	0.00469	0.08499	0.95721	0.00732	0.04650	0.96982
40%	45%	0.00578	0.10149	0.948802	0.00427	0.02725	0.98192
50%	35%	0.00707	0.127302	0.93491	0.00516	0.03518	0.98270
60%	25%	0.00944	0.15861	0.91822	0.00632	0.04150	0.97982
70%	15%	0.01535	0.23154	0.87938	0.00492	0.03154	0.98420
80%	05%	0.04379	0.47688	0.74082	0.00662	0.04481	0.97861

Table 15. For K = 50, training and testing samples variation for FTLRNN on testing data set.

Time series		Mackey-Glass time series			Duffing time series		
Training exemplars	Testing exemplars	MSE	NMSE	r	MSE	NMSE	r
10%	75%	0.01082	0.19456	0.89823	0.01290	0.79033	0.71021
20%	65%	0.01169	0.20374	0.89309	0.01027	0.08318	0.95984
30%	55%	0.01316	0.22115	0.88438	0.00658	0.04203	0.97902
40%	45%	0.01529	0.24709	0.87032	0.00763	0.05034	0.97470
50%	35%	0.01816	0.29049	0.84538	0.00781	0.05426	0.97271
60%	25%	0.024382	0.35655	0.80849	0.00927	0.06562	0.96663
70%	15%	0.03829	0.48826	0.73543	0.00743	0.05020	0.97567
80%	05%	0.1056	0.87428	0.52529	0.00953	0.06451	0.96811

Table 16. For K = 100, training and testing samples variation for FTLRNN on testing data set.

Time series		Mackey-Glass time series			Duffing time series		
Training exemplars	Testing exemplars	MSE	NMSE	r	MSE	NMSE	r
10%	75%	0.029161	0.47623	0.7294	0.01359	0.54149	0.80092
20%	65%	0.02897	0.45601	0.74595	0.00927	0.07219	0.96339
30%	55%	0.03182	0.48156	0.72938	0.00116	0.07810	0.962300
40%	45%	0.03439	0.50398	0.71524	0.00875	0.05663	0.97196
50%	35%	0.04027	0.54749	0.68781	0.00883	0.06062	0.96947
60%	25%	0.05345	0.65267	0.62265	0.00117	0.07870	0.96000
70%	15%	0.08017	0.81243	0.53108	0.01033	0.06935	0.96570
80%	05%	0.21006	1.47654	0.24862	0.01141	0.07715	0.96069

In a similar way, for real-time monthly sunspots and Laser time series, the number of training and testing samples was varied from 10% to 80% as training with the increments of 10% samples and 75% to 5% as testing samples with the decrements of 10% keeping exemplars for Cross-Validation (CV) 15% constant. The performance measures were obtained and compared on testing and training data sets and to gauge the performance and robustness of the FTLRNN. The obtained results are placed in Tables 17, 18, 19, 20, and 21 for monthly sunspots and Laser time series for the value K in K-step ahead prediction.

Table 17. For K = 1, training and testing samples variation for FTLRNN on testing data set.

Time series		Sunspot time series			Laser time series $K = 1$		
Training exemplars	Testing exemplars	MSE	NMSE	r	MSE	NMSE	r
10%	75%	0.00320	0.08705	0.96121	0.00777	0.24076	0.87475
20%	65%	0.00258	0.6819	0.96605	0.01042	0.30799	0.84821
30%	55%	0.00188	0.04608	0.97791	0.01054	0.32361	0.84657
40%	45%	0.00218	0.05092	0.97928	0.00991	0.39119	0.81057
50%	35%	0.00273	0.05795	0.97837	0.00185	0.09233	0.98836
60%	25%	0.00227	0.04162	0.98163	0.00282	0.10597	0.94592
70%	15%	0.00336	0.07416	0.96799	0.00080	0.02293	0.98873
80%	05%	0.00153	0.05069	0.97512	0.00184	0.04229	0.97872

Table 18. For K = 6, training and testing samples variation for FTLRNN on testing data set for monthly sunspot time series and K = 5 for laser time series.

Time series		Sunspot time series $K = 6$ Months			Laser time series $K = 5$		
Training exemplars	Testing exemplars	MSE	NMSE	r	MSE	NMSE	r
10%	75%	0.00707	0.19197	0.91703	0.00782	0.24068	0.87439
20%	65%	0.00451	0.11888	0.94153	0.00811	0.23969	0.88027
30%	55%	0.00423	0.10308	0.94712	0.00808	0.24814	0.87504
40%	45%	0.00438	0.10197	0.95081	0.00635	0.25307	0.87748
50%	35%	0.00654	0.13744	0.94252	0.00267	0.12898	0.94513
60%	25%	0.00554	0.1008	0.95528	0.00372	0.13558	0.93962
70%	15%	0.00473	0.10259	0.95359	0.00534	0.14838	0.92717
80%	05%	0.00499	0.15725	0.92195	0.01579	0.34297	0.83272

Table 19. For K = 12 , training and testing samples variation for FTLRNN on testing data set for monthly sunspot time series and K = 10 for laser time series.

Time series		Sunspot time series $K = 12$			Laser time series $K = 10$		
Training exemplars	Testing exemplars	MSE	NMSE	r	MSE	NMSE	r
10%	75%	0.01187	0.32145	0.87483	0.01506	0.45940	0.76210
20%	65%	0.01116	0.29307	0.84917	0.01310	0.38332	0.80583
30%	55%	0.00967	0.23485	0.88221	0.00140	0.43507	0.77113
40%	45%	0.00749	0.17299	0.91236	0.01221	0.48119	0.75879
50%	35%	0.00909	0.19003	0.91050	0.00444	0.20709	0.89826
60%	25%	0.01693	0.30599	0.8550	0.00956	0.337	0.9014
70%	15%	0.00841	0.17893	0.92008	0.01047	0.28229	0.87301
80%	05%	0.00871	0.26119	0.86836	0.02631	0.59165	0.71077

Table 20. For K = 18 , training and testing samples variation for FTLRNN on testing data set for monthly sunspot time series and K = 20 for laser time series.

Time series		Sunspot time series $K = 18$			Laser time series $K = 20$		
Training exemplars	Testing exemplars	MSE	NMSE	r	MSE	NMSE	r
10%	75%	0.01804	0.48780	0.74535	0.02676	0.80529	0.58788
20%	65%	0.01853	0.48428	0.75209	0.02361	0.68739	0.67208
30%	55%	0.01287	0.31169	0.82991	0.02569	0.79376	0.56198
40%	45%	0.01403	0.32187	0.83052	0.01659	0.66263	0.65482
50%	35%	0.02792	0.57914	0.73685	0.00703	0.30705	0.85539
60%	25%	0.02266	0.04075	0.7977	0.01635	0.543	0.71872
70%	15%	0.01885	0.39372	0.78804	0.03573	0.37992	0.37992
80%	05%	0.00745	0.21530	0.89769	0.00323	0.59234	0.59234

Table 21. For K = 24, training and testing samples variation for FTLRNN on testing data set for monthly sunspot time series and for laser time series (K = 50).

Time series		Sunspot time series $K = 24$			Laser time series $K = 50$		
Training exemplars	Testing Exemplars	MSE	NMSE	r	MSE	NMSE	r
10%	75%	0.03246	0.37734	0.49224	0.04073	1.18215	0.13264
20%	65%	0.03657	0.58297	0.43616	0.04310	1.23643	-0.00980
30%	55%	0.02280	0.52882	0.69373	0.03018	0.98884	0.27393
40%	45%	0.01839	0.83622	0.77659	0.04425	1.87215	-0.22273
50%	35%	0.04066	0.41935	0.53973	0.02534	0.94845	0.26601
60%	25%	0.03019	0.54899	0.71497	0.03466	1.02971	0.41330
70%	15%	0.02834	0.95150	0.75528	0.03447	0.89215	0.44330
80%	05%	0.02339	0.57734	0.8012	0.08839	0.96548	0.28132

Next for the optimum values of performance measures obtained from the combinations data partition as training and testing samples for the chaotic time series as mentioned in Tables 11 to 16 for the Mackey-Glass chaotic time series for all the cases of multistep ahead prediction and Duffing time series all the step ahead prediction. Similarly, for the real-time monthly sunspots and Laser time series for all the multistep ahead prediction.

Then for the optimal data partition of training and testing samples combination resulted for the K-step ahead prediction for the cases of K-value in K-step ahead prediction for all the considered time series. For those combinations, the number of epochs is varied from 2000 to 20,000 in a step of 2000, and again the proposed FTLRNN model is trained to observe the more prominent values of performance measures for all the chaotic time series and for all the steps ahead prediction.

Discussion

It can be clearly observed that dynamic FTLRNN model with gamma memory clearly outperforms the static MLP not only for short-term prediction but also for long-term prediction for testing data as well as training data set. From the results of Table 7, for Mackey-Glass chaotic time series, it is noticed that up to the 20-step ahead prediction the Performance measures values of MLP and dynamic FTLRNN are slightly deviating but for long 50- and 100-step ahead prediction the Performance measures values of MSE, NMSE, and correlation coefficient (r) for FTLRNN model are significantly improved as compared to the static MLP. For the Duffing time series from Table 8 it is observed that for short- and long-step ahead predictions the proposed dynamic FTLRNN with gamma memory filter clearly outperforms well as compared to the static MLP with regards to the performance metrics like MSE, NMSE, and correlation coefficient r.

Also for the real monthly sunspots time series, it is observed from Table 9 that for the 1, 6, 12, months ahead predictions the performance metrics values of MLP and dynamic FTLRNN are slightly deviating but for 18 and 24 months ahead prediction, the performance metrics values for FTLRNN are significantly improved as compared to the static MLP. For the Laser time series from Table 10 it is observed that for short- and long-term ahead (K=1, 5, 10, 20, 50) prediction the proposed dynamic FTLRNN with gamma memory filter clearly outperforms well as compared to the static MLP for the values of MSE, NMSE, and correlation coefficient r.

Next for the resulted optimal parameters the FTLRNN model is trained for different training and testing samples combinations varying from 10% to 80% as a training sample and 75% to 5% as a testing sample and Keeping cross-validation samples constant equal to 15% for short-term and long-term step ahead predictions for finding robustness of model and obtaining the significant results of performance measures for training and testing samples combinations. Tables 11 to 16 show the performance metrics values for one-step ahead to 100-step ahead predictions for different combination of training and testing samples for the equation generated Mackey-Glass and Duffing time series.

Similarly for real-time series the training and testing samples are varied in combination as mentioned in Tables 17 to 21 for one month ahead to twenty four months ahead predictions for monthly sunspot time series and for one-step to fifty-step ahead predictions for Laser time series.

For which training and testing samples the values of MSE NMSE are minimum, and correlation coefficient is closed to unity for short-term and long-term predictions for the chaotic time series for that training and testing samples the FTLRNN with gamma filter is trained for 2000 to 20,000 epochs in the steps of 2000 for obtaining more significant values and observing the network performance with regards to the performance measures. The results are plotted in Figure 6 for 1- and 5-step ahead predictions, Figure 7 for 10- and 20-step ahead predictions and Figure 8 for 50- and 100-step ahead predictions for performance on MSE and NMSE due to epochs variation, and Figure 9 for performance on regression due to epochs variation for 1-, 5-, 10-, 20-, 50- and 100-step ahead predictions for Mackey-Glass chaotic time series. It is observed that up to 50 steps ahead prediction the performance metrics are slightly deviating but for long-term 100-step ahead predictions above the values of 12 000 epochs training the performance measure like MSE and NMSE values are decreased, and the correlation coefficient r is substantially increased.

Also it can be visually inspected closely from Figures 10, 11, 12, and 13 that the output of the proposed FTLRNN model closely follows the desired output for 1-, 5-, 10-, 20-step ahead predictions.

From Figure 14 and Figure 15, it is clear that, the output of the network is slightly deviating from the desired output for long 50-step and 100-step ahead predictions.

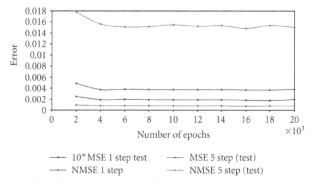

Figure 6. Performance of epoch's variation on Errors for 1 and 5 step for Mackey-Glass time series.

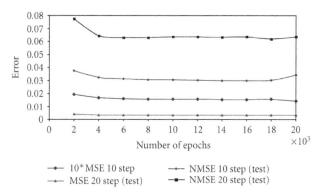

Figure 7. Performance of epoch's variation on Errors for 10 and 20 step for Mackey-Glass time series.

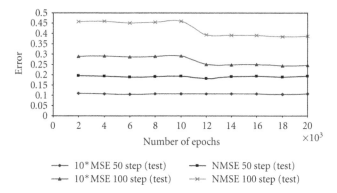

Figure 8. Performance of epoch's variation on Errors for 50 and 100 step for Mackey-Glass time series.

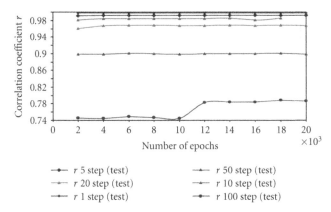

Figure 9. Performance of epochs variation on Correlation Coefficient r for 1, 5, 10, 20, 50, and 100 step for Mackey-Glass time series.

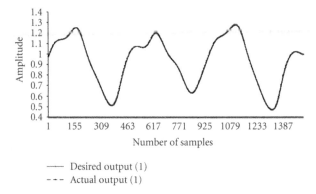

Figure 10. Desired output and network output for 1-step ahead Prediction for Mackey-Glass time series.

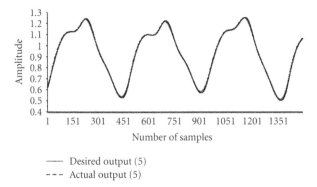

Figure 11. Desired output and FTLRNN output for 5-step ahead prediction for Mackey-Glass time series.

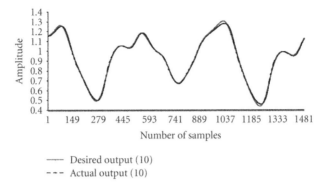

Figure 12. Desired output and FTLRNN output for 10-step ahead prediction for Mackey-Glass time series.

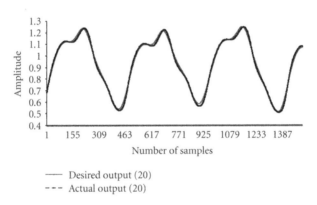

Figure 13. Desired output and FTLRNN output for 20-step ahead prediction for Mackey-Glass time series.

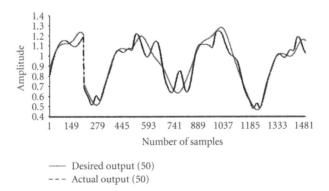

Figure 14. Desired output and FTLRNN Output for Testing data set 50-step ahead prediction for Mackey-Glass time series.

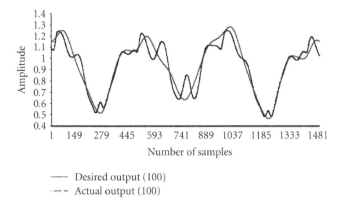

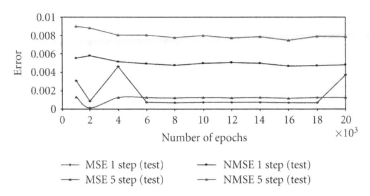

Figure 15. Desired output and FTLRNN Output for testing data 100-step ahead prediction for Mackey-Glass time series.

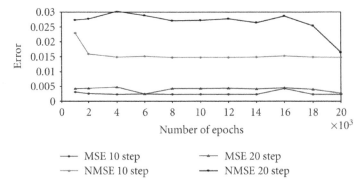

Figure 16. Epochs variation performance on errors for K = 1 and K = 5 for Duffing time series.

Figure 17. Epochs variation performance on errors for K = 10 and K = 20 for Duffing time series.

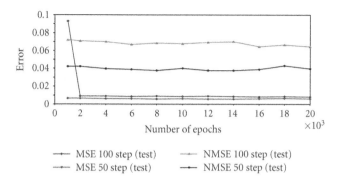

Figure 18. Epochs variation performance on errors for K = 50 and K = 100 for Duffing time series.

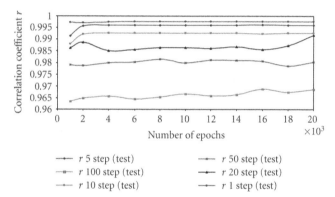

Figure 19. Performance of epochs variation on Correlation Coefficient r for 1, 5, 10, 20, 50, and 100 step for Duffing time series.

For the Duffing time series the results are shown in Figure 16 for 1- and 5-step ahead predictions, Figure 17 for 10- and 20-step ahead predictions and Figure 18 for 50- and 100-step ahead predictions for performance on MSE and NMSE due to epochs variation, and Figure 19 for Correlation coefficient for 1-, 5-, 10-, 20-, 50- and 100-step ahead predictions. It is observed that for short-term prediction and up to 50-step ahead predictions the results are not deviating much. But for 100-step ahead prediction, the performance measures values are improved well.

From the close inspection of Figure 20 and Figure 21 for 1- and 5-step ahead predictions the output of the FTLRNN closely follows the desired output. From Figure 22 and Figure 23 for 10- and 20-step ahead predictions, up to the first 20 samples the FTLRNN output is slightly deviating and after that the actual output closely follows the desired output. Similarly from the Figure 24 and Figure 25 the FTLRNN output follows the desired output for long-term 50- and 100-step ahead predictions.

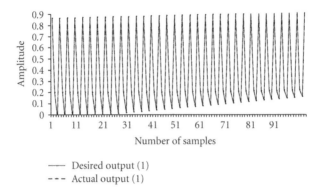

Figure 20. Desired and FTLRNN Outputs for Testing data for 1-step ahead prediction for Duffing time series.

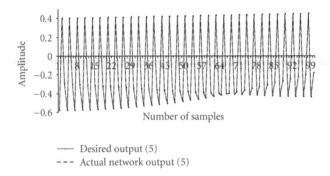

Figure 21. Desired and FTLRNN Outputs for Testing data for 5-step ahead prediction for Duffing time series.

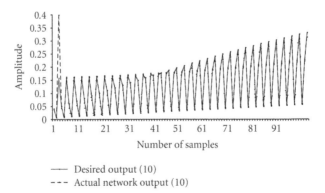

Figure 22. Desired and FTLRNN Outputs for testing data for 10-step ahead prediction for Duffing time series.

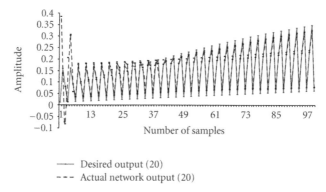

Figure 23. Desired and FTLRNN Outputs for testing data for 20-step ahead prediction for Duffing time series.

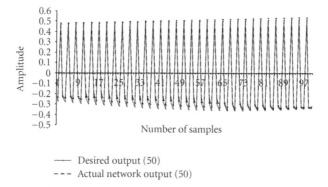

Figure 24. Desired and FTLRNN Outputs for Testing data for 50-step ahead prediction for Duffing time series.

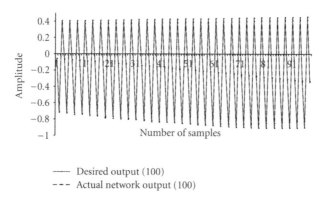

Figure 25. Desired and FTLRNN Outputs for Testing data for 100-step ahead prediction for Duffing time series.

Similarly for real monthly sunspots time series the results are plotted in Figure 26 and Figure 27 for performance on MSE and NMSE, respectively, due to epochs variations for 1 and 6 months ahead prediction, Figure 28 and Figure 29 for due to epochs variations for 12, 18, and 24 months ahead prediction and Figure 30 for the correlation coefficient (r) for all the month ahead prediction. For short-term 1 and 6 months ahead prediction the performance values are slightly improved. Also for 12 and 18 months ahead prediction the results are slightly deviating but for 24 months ahead prediction for 10,000 epochs training the values of MSE , NMSE, and Correlation Coefficient r are significantly improved that is, MSE of 0.00824 and NMSE of 0.23236, respectively, and the value of Correlation Coefficient r is 0.88460 where as for the 1000 epochs training the value of MSE and NMSE is 0.0339, 0.57734, and r is 0.8012.

Also from the close inspection of Figure 31 , Figure 32 and Figure 33 for short-term 1, 6, and 12 months ahead prediction the FTLRNN output closely follows the desired output and from Figure 34 and Figure 35 for long-term 18 and 24 months ahead prediction the FTLRNN output is slightly deviating from the desired output.

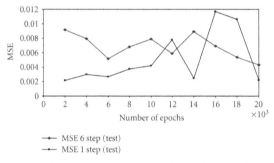

Figure 26. Epochs variation performance on MSE for 1 month and 6 months ahead prediction for sunspot time series.

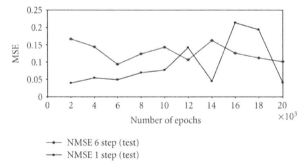

Figure 27. Epochs variation performance on NMSE for 1 month and 6 months ahead prediction for sunspot time series.

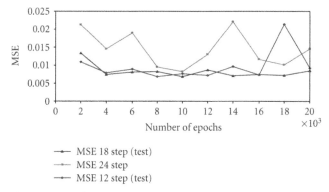

Figure 28. Epochs variation performance on MSE for 12, 18, and 24 months ahead prediction for sunspot time series.

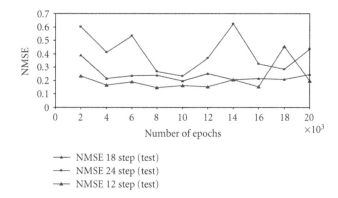

Figure 29. Epochs variation performance on NMSE for 12, 18, and 24 months ahead prediction for sunspot time series.

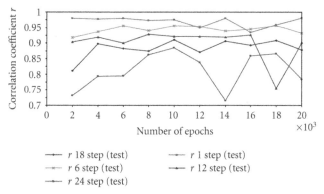

Figure 30. Epochs variation performance on Correlation Coefficient r for 1, 6, 12, 18, and 24 months ahead prediction for sunspot time series.

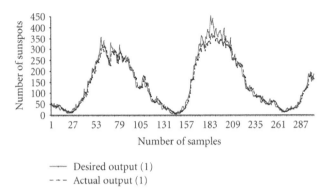

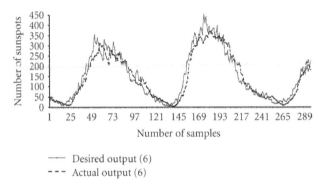

Figure 31. Plot between Desired versus Actual FTLRNN outputs for 1 month ahead prediction for FTLRNN model

Figure 32. Plot between Desired versus FTLRNN Outputs for 6-month ahead prediction for FTLRNN Model.

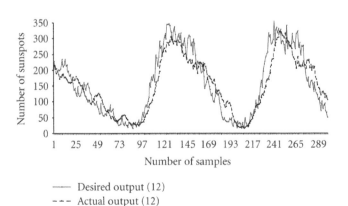

Figure 33. Plot between Desired versus Actual FTLRNN Outputs for 12 month ahead prediction for FTLRNN Model.

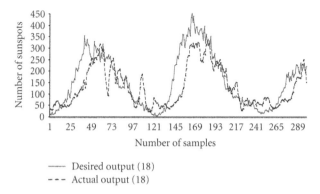

Figure 34. Plot between Desired versus Actual FTLRNN Outputs for 18 month ahead prediction for FTLRNN Model.

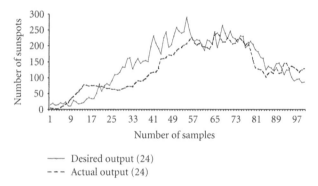

Figure 35. Plot between Desired versus Actual FTLRNN Output for 24 months ahead prediction for FTLRNN Model.

For Laser time series the results are plotted in Figure 36 and Figure 37 for 1-, 5-, and 10-step ahead prediction and Figure 38 and Figure 39 for 20- and 50-step ahead prediction for performance on MSE and NMSE due to epochs variations, and Figure 40 for the performance on Correlation coefficient r due to epochs variation for all the step ahead predictions. It is observed that for short-step ahead prediction the performance metrics are slightly deviating but for 50-step ahead prediction, the error values MSE and NMSE and correlation coefficient r are improved substantially. For 1000 epochs training the values of MSE and NMSE are 0.03447 and 0.89215, and value of r is 0.44330 and when the number of epochs for training is increased to 20,000 the values of MSE and NMSE are 0.154 and 0.412, and the value of r is significantly improved to 0.789.

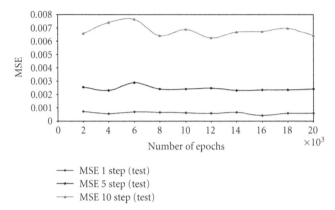

Figure 36. Epochs variation performance on MSE for 1, 5, 10, step ahead prediction for laser time series.

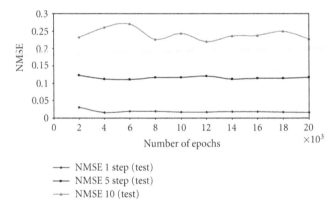

Figure 37. Epochs variation performance on NMSE for 1, 5, 10, step ahead prediction for laser time series.

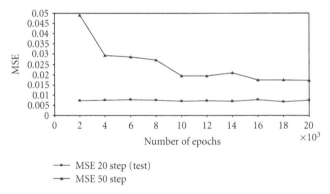

Figure 38. Epochs variation performance on MSE for 20- and 50-step ahead prediction for laser time series.

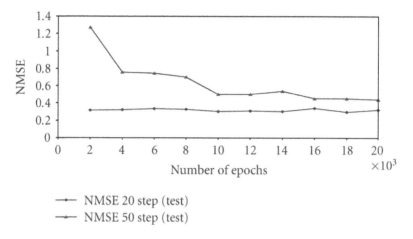

Figure 39. Epochs variation performance on NMSE for 20- and 50-Step ahead prediction for laser time series.

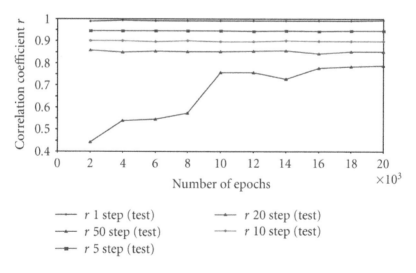

Figure 40. Epochs variation performance on Correlation Coefficient r for 1-, 5-, 10-, 20-, and 50-Step ahead predictions for laser time series.

Also from the close inspection Figures 41, 42 and 43 for short-term 1-, 5-, and 10-step ahead prediction the FTLRNN output closely follows the desired output and from Figure 44 and Figure 45 for long-term 20- and 50-step ahead predictions, it is clear that the FTLRNN output is slightly deviating from the desired output.

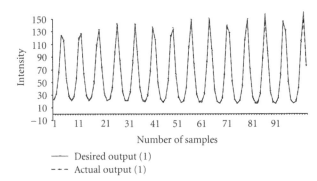

Figure 41. Plot between Desired versus Actual FTLRNN outputs for 1-step ahead predictions for FTLRNN Model.

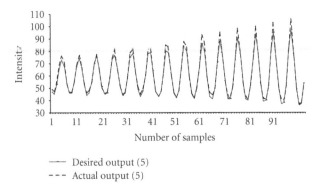

Figure 42. Plot between Desired versus Actual FTLRNN Outputs for 5-step ahead prediction for FTLRNN Model.

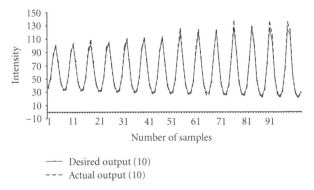

Figure 43. Plot between Desired versus FTLRNN Outputs for 10-step ahead prediction for FTLRNN Model.

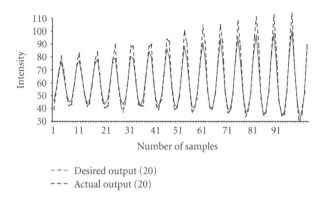

Figure 44. Plot between Desired versus FTLRNN Output for 20-step ahead prediction for FTLRNN Model.

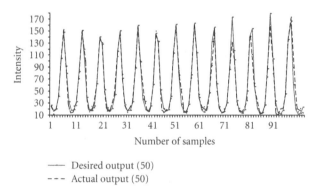

Figure 45. Plot between Desired versus Actual FTLRNN Output for 50-step ahead prediction for FTLRNN Model.

Conclusions

It is seen that focused time-lagged recurrent network with gamma memory is able to predict the differential equation generated Mackey-Glass and Duffing time series and real-world monthly sunspots and laser time series quite elegantly in comparison with the Multilayer perceptron (MLP). Static NN configuration such as MLPNN-based model fails to cope up with the underlying nonlinear dynamics of the all the time series for short-term and long-term ahead predictions. It is observed that MSE NMSE of the proposed focused time-lagged recurrent neural network (FTLRNN) dynamic model for testing data set as well as for training data set are significant better than those of static MLP NN. In addition, it is also observed that the correlation coefficient of this model for testing and training exemplars is much higher than that of MLPNN for the short-term and long-term ahead predictions for the chaotic time series considered. The FTLRNN is trained for different combination of training samples and tested on testing data sets to find the robustness and sustainability of FTLRNN model for all the step ahead predictions for the differential equation generated and real-time chaotic time series. Also for the proposed FTLRNN model, the output closely follows the desired output and learned the true trajectory for short-term prediction. For long-term prediction the output is slightly deviating for the considered benchmark chaotic time series as discussed.It is inferred from the experiments that the FTL-RNN model with gamma memory has learned the dynamics of chaotic time series quite well as compared to multilayer perceptron network for testing data set (data set not used for training) with reasonable accuracy. On the contrary, it is observed that static MLP performs poorly bad, because on the one hand it yields much higher MSE and NMSE on testing data sets and on the other hand the correlation coefficient for testing data set is far less than unity. Hence the focused time-lagged recurrent neural network with gamma memory filter has outperformed the static MLP-based neural network better for short-term and for long-term ahead predictions. Then the number of epochs is varied from 2000 to 20,000 in the steps of 2000, and the network is trained for finding out the performance of the model for epoch's variation.

References

1. B. Townshend, "Nonlinear prediction of speech signals," in Nonlinear Modeling and Forecasting, M. Casdagli and S. Euban, Eds., pp. 433–453, Addison-Wesley, Reading, Mass, USA, 1992.

2. P. G. Cooper, M. N. Hays, and J. E. Whalen, "Neural networks for propagation modeling," Atlantic Research Corporation Repot, Electromagnetic Environmental Test facility, Fort Huachuca, Ariz, USA, 1992.

3. S. HayKin, Neural Networks: A Comprehensive Foundation, Pearson Education, Delhi, India, 2nd edition, 2006.

4. A. S. Weigend and N. A. Greshenfeld, Time Series Prediction: Forecasting the Future and Understanding the Past, vol. 15 of Santa Fe Institute Studies in the Sciences of Complexity, Addison-Wesley, Reading, Mass, USA, 1993.

5. M. Casdagli, "Nonlinear prediction of chaotic time series," Physica D, vol. 35, no. 3, pp. 335–356, 1989.

6. H. Leung and T. Lo, "Chaotic radar signal processing over the sea," IEEE Journal of Oceanic Engineering, vol. 18, no. 3, pp. 287–295, 1993.

7. H. Leung, "Applying chaos to radar detection in an ocean environment: an experimental study," IEEE Journal of Oceanic Engineering, vol. 20, no. 1, pp. 56–64, 1995.

8. K. M. Short, "Steps toward unmasking secure communications," International Journal of Bifurcation and Chaos, vol. 4, no. 4, pp. 959–977, 1994.

9. G. Heidari-Bateni and C. D. McGillen, "A chaotic direct-sequence spread-spectrum communication system," IEEE Transactions on Communications, vol. 42, no. 234, pp. 1524–1527, 1994.

10. Y. Fu and H. Leung, "Narrow-band interference cancellation in spread-spectrum communication systems using chaos," IEEE Transactions on Circuits and Systems I, vol. 48, no. 7, pp. 847–858, 2001.

11. G. Cybenko, "Approximation by superpositions of a sigmoidal function," Mathematics of Control, Signals, and Systems, vol. 2, no. 4, pp. 303–314, 1989.

12. K. Hornik, M. Stinchcombe, and H. White, "Multilayer feedforward networks are universal approximators," Neural Networks, vol. 2, no. 5, pp. 359–366, 1989.

13. S. V. Dudul, "Prediction of a Lorenz chaotic attractor using two-layer perceptron neural network," Applied Soft Computing, vol. 5, no. 4, pp. 333–355, 2005.

14. S. V. Dudul, "Identification of a liquid saturated steam heat exchanger using focused time lagged recurrent neural network model," IETE Journal of Research, vol. 53, no. 1, pp. 69–82, 2007.

15. A. R. Barron, "Universal approximation bounds for superpositions of a sigmoidal function," IEEE Transactions on Information Theory, vol. 39, no. 3, pp. 930–945, 1993.

16. A. Juditsky, H. Hjalmarson, A. Benveniste, et al., "Nonlinear black-box models in system identification: mathematical foundations," Automatica, vol. 31, no. 12, pp. 1725–1750, 1995.

17. R. Bakker, J. C. Schouten, C. L. Giles, F. Takens, and C. M. van den Bleek, "Learning chaotic attractors by neural networks," Neural Computations, vol. 12, no. 10, pp. 2355–2383, 2000.

18. Z. Zhaocoui and D. Yurong, "Chaotic time series analysis based on radial basis function network," Chinese Journal of Chongqing University, vol. 22, no. 6, pp. 113–120, 1999.

19. H. Leung, T. Lo, and S. Wang, "Prediction of noisy chaotic time series using an optimal radialbasis function neural network," IEEE Transactions on Neural Networks, vol. 12, no. 5, pp. 1163–1172, 2001.

20. G. Deco and M. Schurmann, "Neural learning of chaotic system behavior," IEICE Transactions Fundamentals, vol. E77-A, no. 11, pp. 1840–1845, 1994.

21. U. Thissen, R. van Brakel, A. P. de Weijer, W. J. Melssen, and L. M. C. Buydens, "Using support vector machines for time series prediction," Chemometrics and Intelligent Laboratory Systems, vol. 69, no. 1-2, pp. 35–49, 2003.

22. S. A. Billings and H.-L. Wei, "A new class of wavelet networks for nonlinear system identification," IEEE Transactions on Neural Networks, vol. 16, no. 4, pp. 862–874, 2005.

23. M. Han, J. Xi, S. Xu, and F.-L. Yin, "Prediction of chaotic time series based on the recurrent predictor neural network," IEEE Transactions on Signal Processing, vol. 52, no. 12, pp. 3409–3416, 2004.

24. A. Gholipour, B. N. Araabi, and C. Lucas, "Predicting chaotic time series using neural and neurofuzzy models: a comparative study," Neural Processing Letters, vol. 24, no. 3, pp. 217–239, 2006.

25. H. Inoue, Y. Fukunaga, and H. Narihisa, "Efficient hybrid neural network for chaotic time series prediction," in Proceedings of the International Conference on Artificial Neural Networks (ICANN '01), vol. 2130 of Lecture Notes in Computer Science, pp. 712–718, Springer, Vienna, Austria, August 2001.

26. M. Han, M. Fan, and J. Xi, "Study of nonlinear multivariate time series prediction based on neural networks," in Proceedings of the 2nd International Symposium on Neural Networks (ISNN '05), vol. 3497 of Lecture Notes in Computer Science, pp. 618–623, Chongqing, China, May-June 2005.

27. S.-Z. Qin, H.-T. Su, and T. J. McAvoy, "Comparison of four neural net learning methods for dynamic system identification," IEEE Transactions on Neural Networks, vol. 3, no. 1, pp. 122–130, 1992.

28. K. S. Naraendra and K. Parthasarathy, "Identification and control of dynamic systems using neural networks," IEEE Transactions on Neural Networks, vol. 1, no. 1, pp. 4–27, 1990.

29. Demuth and M. Beale, "Neural network tool box for use with MATLAB," Users Guide, Version 4.0, The MathWorks, Inc., Natick, Mass, USA, 2004, http://www.mathworks.com.

30. G. F. FranKlin, J. D. Powell, and M. L. WorKman, Digital Control of Dynamics Systems, Addison-Wesley, Reading, Mass, USA, 3rd edition, 1998.

31. F. M. Ham and I. Kostanic, Principles of Neurocomputing for Science and Engineering, Tata McGraw-Hill, New Delhi, India, 2002.

32. B. de Vries and J. C. Principe, "The gamma model—a new neural model for temporal processing," Neural Networks, vol. 5, no. 4, pp. 565–576, 1992.

33. J. C. Principe and N. R. Euliano, Neural and Adaptive Systems: Fundamental through Simulations, John Wiley & Sons, New York, NY, USA, 2000.

34. M. C. Mackey and L. Glass, "Oscillation and chaos in physiological control systems," Science, vol. 197, no. 4300, pp. 287–289, 1977.

35. H. Nijmeijer and H. Berghuis, "On Lyapunov control of the Duffing equation," IEEE Transactions on Circuits and Systems I, vol. 42, no. 8, pp. 473–477, 1995.

36. S. Sello, "Solar cycle forecasting: a nonlinear dynamics approach," Astronomy and Astrophysics, vol. 377, no. 1, pp. 312–320, 2001.

37. J. K. Lawrence, A. C. Cadavid, and A. A. Ruzmaikin, "Turbulent and chaotic dynamics underlying solar magnetic variability," Astrophysical Journal, vol. 455, p. 366, 1995.

38. Q. Zhang, "A nonlinear prediction of the smoothed monthly sunspot numbers," Astronomy and Astrophysics, vol. 310, pp. 646–650, 1996.

39. T. Schreiber, "Interdisciplinary application of nonlinear time series methods," Physical Reports, vol. 308, no. 1, pp. 2–64, 1998.

40. http://sidc.oma.be/index.php3.

41. U. Hübner, N. B. Abraham, and C. O. Weiss, "Dimensions and entropies of chaotic intensity pulsations in a single-mode far-infrared NH3 laser," Physical Review A, vol. 40, no. 11, pp. 6354–6365, 1989.

42. I. V. Turchenko, "Simulation modeling of multi-parameter sensor signal identification using neural networks," in Proceedings of the 2nd IEEE International Conference on Intelligent Systems (IS '04), vol. 3, pp. 48–53, Varna, Bulgaria, June 2004.

43. G.-B. Huang, Y.-Q. Chen, and H. A. Babri, "Classification ability of single hidden layer feedforward neural networks," IEEE Transactions on Neural Networks, vol. 11, no. 3, pp. 799–801, 2000.

44. K. W. Lee and H. N. Lam, "Optimal sizing of feed-forward neural networks: case studies," in Proceedings of the 2nd New Zealand Two-Stream International Conference on Artificial Neural Networks and Expert Systems (ANNES '95), pp. 71–82, Dunedin, New Zealand, November 1995.

Flexible Interconnection Network for Dynamically and Partially Reconfigurable Architectures

Ludovic Devaux, Sana Ben Sassi, Sebastien Pillement,
Daniel Chillet and Didier Demigny

ABSTRACT

The dynamic and partial reconfiguration of FPGAs enables the dynamic placement in reconfigurable zones of the tasks that describe an application. However, the dynamic management of the tasks impacts the communications since tasks are not present in the FPGA during all computation time. So, the task manager should ensure the allocation of each new task and their interconnection which is performed by a flexible interconnection network. In this article, various communication architectures, in particular interconnection networks, are studied. Each architecture is evaluated with respect to its suitability for the paradigm of the dynamic and partial reconfiguration in FPGA implementations. This study leads us to propose the DRAFT network that supports the communication constraints into the context of dynamic reconfiguration. We also present DRAGOON, the automatic generator of networks, which allows to implement and to simulate the DRAFT topology. Finally, DRAFT and the two most popular Networks-on-Chip are implemented in several configurations using DRAGOON, and compared considering real implementation results.

Introduction

Steady technological evolutions, increasingly complex applications, can be supported by reconfigurable architectures. This is particularly true into the framework of complex signal processing applications. However, when the number of tasks constituting an application exceeds the available hardware resources, designers have two options: increasing the number of resources (which increase the complexity of the systems) or implementing only the tasks that should be executed at a given time. In the latter case, tasks are swapped at the end of their execution by freeing logical resources for the others. However, this concept is relevant only if a new task can be implemented instead of a former one without disrupting the execution of other tasks. This concept of hardware preemption of the tasks is called Dynamic and Partial Reconfiguration (DPR).

The objective of the FOSFOR research project (Flexible Operating System for Reconfigurable devices) [1] is to specify and to implement an Operating System (OS) that provides an abstraction of technology for future applications. For this purpose, the FOSFOR OS operates the DPR in order to support complex applications that cannot be statically implemented due to physical restrictions. Several services of the OS are implemented in hardware whereas others are computed in software. Physical implementation of some services allows the OS to efficiently manage hardware and software tasks. In this direction, the FOSFOR project focuses on the hardware implementation of the main services: the task placer and scheduler, the memory manager, and the communication service.

In this work, the communication service is investigated. The objective is to define and to implement in an FPGA a generic interconnection architecture which should support the diversity of applications and the dynamic management of the tasks. For this purpose, the architecture takes into account the constraints imposed by the DPR. Through the physical interconnection architecture and its control, the communication service provides a flexible way for transferring data between every Communicating Element (CE) in an FPGA. Since an application task can be implemented in hardware or processed in software by a hardware processor, CEs are defined as the hardware elements which exchange data. So, a CE can be the hardware implementation of a task (static or dynamic), a shared element (memory, input/output), or a hardware processor running software tasks.

The paper is organized as follows. Assumptions induced by the DPR that should be supported by an interconnection architecture are presented in Section 2. Then, current interconnection architectures are detailed and reviewed in Section 3. The interconnection network called Dynamic Reconfiguration Adapted Fat-Tree (DRAFT), which is specifically designed to support the DPR requirements in FPGAs, is presented in Section 4. Dynamically Reconfigurable Architectures compliant Generator and simulatOr Of Network (DRAGOON), the automatic generator of networks supporting the DRAFT topology is introduced in Section 5. Then, the comparison between DRAFT and the two more popular Networks-on-Chip (NoC) topologies is presented with respect to implementation costs and network performances in Section 6. Finally, an implementation of the DRAFT network into the framework of an application from the FOSFOR project is detailed in Section 7.

Assumptions on Considered Interconnection Architectures

Keeping in view of a large range of applications, an interconnection architecture should support several constraints into the framework of an implementation in FPGAs. Current applications are very complex and their task graphs exhibit a large degree of parallelism. Thus, from the interconnection point of view, the architecture must provide the possibility to realize several communications in parallel. Furthermore, dynamic placement and scheduling of CEs in an FPGA require a high level of flexibility, since the placement and the scheduling of the CEs are dynamic. So, neither the location of CEs nor the data traffic (uniform, all to one, etc.) can be predicted at compile time. These requirements of flexibility should be considered by the network topology, the routing protocol, and the available network performances (bandwidth and latency). An application is typically split into dynamic and static tasks, and there are no reason for every task to be implemented in homogeneous hardware CEs. This point differs from approaches like [2] where CEs are supposed to be homogeneous so that the interconnection topology can be dynamically reconfigured into an FPGA in order to fit the application. Heterogeneous hardware CEs are considered in this work. Hence, a single interconnection topology compliant with this heterogeneity is preferred to dynamically reconfigurable topologies considering their placement constraints as the placement of the CEs themselves.

Considering current FPGAs, Altera devices provide abundant programmable resources but do not support the partial reconfiguration of everyone of them [3, 4]. Atmel series AT40K5AL to AT40K40AL are compliant with the DPR of their resources but do not provide more than 50 K gates which are few when considering complex applications [5]. Hence, Xilinx FPGAs (especially the Virtex 2Pro, Virtex 4, Virtex 5, and Virtex 6) are the only ones that both provide sufficient programmable resources to implement complex applications and support the DPR paradigm [6]. Xilinx architectures offer a column-based distribution of their resources, as shown Figure 1. In a Virtex family (except in Virtex 2Pro), the center column is very specific because it contains not only Input/Output (IO) banks, but also clock managers and DPR ports (ICAP). So, despite their column-based structure, FPGAs are very heterogeneous. Consequently, the interconnection should support the heterogeneity of the FPGAs.

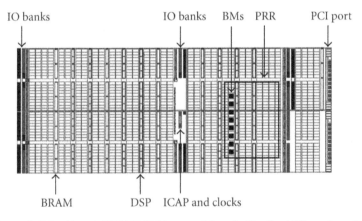

Figure 1. View of a Xilinx Virtex5 5VSX50T FPGA captured from the PlanAhead Xilinx software [7].

Xilinx DPR takes place in specific reconfigurable regions called Partially Reconfigurable Regions (PRRs), which hence constitute the dynamic parts of a system. Dynamic CEs are allocated in these regions. Static CEs (static hardware tasks, memories, processors, etc.) are implemented all around the PRRs and constitute the static part of the system. Communications between dynamic and static regions are performed through interfaces called Bus Macros (BMs) in Xilinx architectures [8]. Since PRRs and BMs are defined statically at compile time, every CE is connected to the interconnection architecture through static interfaces (despite the dynamic locations of the CEs). So, the interconnection architecture can be static if it provides sufficient flexibility to support the DPR paradigm.

Interconnection Architectures: State of the Art

In this section, several interconnection architectures, suitable for supporting the paradigm of the DPR, are analyzed and evaluated. The main constraints are the parallelism of the communications, the flexibility, and the compliance with the connection of heterogeneous CEs in heterogeneous FPGAs.

Bus-Based Architectures

Buses are interconnection architectures which are simple to implement and control, while requiring few hardware resources.

Main-Bus-Based Architectures

One of the first bus-based approaches designed for DPR was Core Unifier [9]. Core Unifier is a tool that allows connecting on the fly dynamic CEs on a bus. For this, the tool adds 3-states buffers to the bus on which dynamic CEs are connected. However, at compile time, Core Unifier needs the knowledge of when and where the CEs should be allocated. So, this approach is not compliant with systems in which scheduling and placement are dynamic.

The Bus-Macro-based architecture [10] and Recobus [11] are the most recent bus-based dynamic interconnection architectures. The communication interfaces of the Recobus approach require less logical resources than the Bus-Macro-based architecture. However, both approaches are based over a horizontal bus connecting vertically placed CEs. CEs are implemented using all the logical resources of a column. So, those approaches are only compliant with the 1D placement (CEs are allocated using several columns of resources of the FPGA) of the dynamic CEs. It is the major limitation of these architectures because it leads to a waste of hardware resources, depending on the size of the CEs. Furthermore, current FPGAs (except the Xilinx Virtex 2Pro series) are compliant with the 2D placement (rectangular region based) of CEs. So, none of these approaches seems suitable to implement a system using DPR in latest FPGAs. Another architecture is the HoneyComb [12], which is a static interconnection architecture connecting static CEs but differing from other bus-based structures. This network, made of regular hexagonal cells linked together through bidirectional buses, allows data routing. HoneyComb offers flexibility at the data path level while using few hardware resources. However, the regular structure is not compliant with current FPGAs nor with dynamic and heterogeneous CEs. So, Honeycomb brings more flexibility than other bus-based architectures but it does not support the DPR paradigm due to its regular structure.

Limitations of Buses

Buses exhibit several drawbacks when considering an application using the DPR. A major constraint for the bus-based interconnection architecture is the necessity to support several data transfers in parallel. One bus supports only a single transfer at a time. There are two solutions for this problem. One is to use several communication lines (multiple buses [13]); the other is to split a bus into a set of independent segments interconnected through several bridges (GALS approach [14]). However, either solution implies an increase of the required hardware resources: the connection of two buses generates a need of buffers (synchronous or asynchronous FIFOs). In order to estimate the size of these buffers, the knowledge of the data traffic is required to avoid bottleneck risks. In a dynamic system where the locations of CEs and the data traffic are unknown at compile time, buffers should be designed to support the worst cases of communication. For instance, the RMBoC approach [15] uses multiple and segmented buses for DPR compliance. However, despite the estimation of buffer sizes, this approach requires a lot of hardware resources to connect the CEs.

To date, the bus-based architectures have not been implemented efficiently to answer the DPR paradigm. Poor flexibility and scalability also with placement limited to 1D are the main drawbacks of bus-based approaches which motivated many researchers to consider the Network-on-Chip (NoC) paradigm [16].

Network-on-Chip Based Architectures

A NoC can be seen as a set of routers, links and network interfaces. The communication topologies and routing protocols (including data flow control, scheduling policies, etc.) are key domains of research [17]. Nowadays, there are a lot of NoCs which can be classified in a few basic families, depending on their topology. Hence, we shall concentrate on the meshes, the application-dependent topologies, the rings and the trees (Figure 2).

Mesh Topology

A mesh topology offers a simple connection scheme (Figure 2(a)), based on a matrix of routers interconnecting regularly implemented CEs. Many meshes were implemented such as HERMES [18]. If the number of connected CEs is N and if D is the radix of the mesh, then the number of routers needed to build a square mesh is

$$R_{mesh} = \left\lceil \sqrt{N} \right\rceil^2 = D^2.$$

$$(1)$$

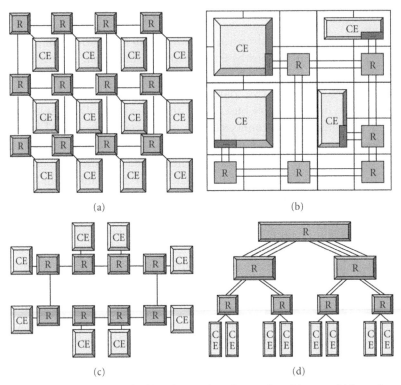

(a)   (b)

(c)   (d)

Figure 2. Network topologies: (a) mesh, (b) application-dependent topology, (c) ring, and (d) tree. Routers are denoted with "R" and communicating elements with "CE."

Whereas the number of needed communication links is

$$L_{mesh} = N + 2(D_2 - D).\qquad(2)$$

The connection of heterogeneous CEs to a regular matrix based network may be problematic. A solution consists in considering that tasks are implemented using one or several homogeneous CEs [19] which are interconnected regularly by the mesh. This solution is used, for example, by the DyNoC approach [20]. Unfortunately, logical resources could be wasted when a small task is executed by a large CE. When a large task is implemented using several CEs, some logical resources are also wasted depending on the granularity of the CEs (Figure 3).

When a task is implemented using several CEs, then CEs can communicate in two ways. The first one is to consider that the communications between the CEs are performed through the network. However, this solution constrains the design of the tasks because each internal communication should be designed to be performed by the network. So, with this solution, the complexity of the tasks increases and the number of required resources too. Thus, this solution is impractical for designers. Another solution is to consider that a task is implemented with dedicated links between the CEs. However, the compliance between the task and the technology becomes difficult due to the limited (and reduced) number of available communication links.

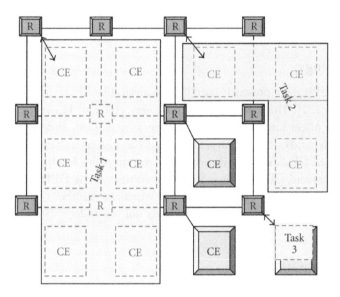

Figure 3. Implementation of three different tasks (executed by one or several CEs) using a mesh network.

A truly regular mesh is based on the assumption that the FPGA is intrinsically homogeneous. So, every CE presents the same hardware properties for task implementation. Considering the heterogeneous structure of available FPGAs, it seems quite difficult to implement a truly regular mesh. Finally, another problem of the mesh structure lies in the connection of shared elements like memories or IOs. Indeed, the communication requirements between tasks (hardware or software) and shared elements induce the creation of hot-spots, which could increase the likelihood of livelock and deadlock.

Application-Dependent Topology

CoNoChi (Figure 2(b)) shows an example of network which topology differs depending on the application [21]. In this approach, the FPGA is divided into regular dynamically reconfigurable regions, with each being defined dynamically as a router, a set of interconnection links, or a CE.

Despite many advantages, the concept of dynamic topology is impractical since PRRs are statically defined in current FPGAs. Hence, their use for link implementation implies wasting a lot of logical resources. Moreover, considering the resulting topology of CoNoChi which differs with the application, the design time can be important to obtain optimal network performances. Indeed, the routing protocol should take into account the network topology which is application-dependent. Keeping in mind these drawbacks, static and generic topologies are preferred to dynamic ones in order to limit the design times and to increase the predictable nature of the network performances.

Ring Topology

Rings (Figure 2(c)) are presently used by industrials like IBM with the Cell Broadband Engine [22]. This architecture can be very efficient. However, in some applications, it offers lower performances than a mesh [23]. Indeed, the available bandwidth depends on the characteristics of the routers and on the number of interconnected CEs. Another drawback of the rings lies in the dependence between latencies and CE locations. So, in the context of the DPR, rings should be interesting if bandwidth did not decreased when the number of connected CEs increases, and furthermore if the latency was not dependent with the placement of the CEs.

Fat-Tree Topology

Trees, and more precisely fat-trees (Figure 2(d)), are indirect interconnection networks. Some routers are only used for data transfers and do not connect directly the CEs. A fat-tree is based on complete binary tree. Every CE is connected to a router located at the base-level of the tree. Each hierarchical level of the fat-tree is linked to upper and lower levels through bidirectional links [23]. The main characteristic of a fat-tree is the aggregative bandwidth (offered by all the links located at the base of the tree) which remains constant between each hierarchical level all the way to the root. A fat-tree offers many advantages compared with other topologies, two of which are a large bandwidth and a low latency [24]. A fat-tree can also simulate every other topology at the cost of the appropriate control [25].

Since every CE is connected to a base-level router of the fat-tree, they are not distributed into the network structure. This point is important because CEs can be heterogeneous from the resource consumption point of view. Indeed, the resource heterogeneity does not impact the transfer times like in a mesh. Furthermore, the structure of the tree does not need to be implemented regularly. So, a fat-tree is compliant with current FPGAs.

Thanks to its constant bandwidth between every hierarchical level, the fat-tree avoids deadlock risks which exist in other topologies without an appropriate control [26].

However, a fat-tree needs many logical resources for routing purpose when the number of connected CEs increases significantly. If the number of connected CEs is N and the number of communication ports for each router is k, then the number of routers in a fat-tree [26] is

$$R_{fat\text{-}tree} = \frac{2N}{k}(\log_{k/2} N).$$

(3)

In this formula, assuming that the fat-tree is complete in terms of connected CEs, N is expressed by $N=2^x$ where x is an integer and $x \geq 1$. When N does not match the previous formula, designers should build the network considering the admissible value of N just higher in order to keep the complete tree-based structure of the network. The number of connection links needed by the fat-tree topology [26] is

$$L_{fat-tree} = N(\log_{k/2} N).$$

(4)

To limit the resource consumption, the XGFT [27] allows the connection of several CEs to only one communication port of a router. Indeed, the fat-tree connects several sets of CEs, which are interconnected by a bus. This approach is very interesting in the context of a static application because this topology optimizes the number of connected CEs in comparison with used resources for routing purpose. However, the XGFT is not optimal into the framework of the DPR. Indeed, the sets of CEs have the same drawbacks as bus-based architectures (control time, one communication at a time without multiple buses, etc.).

Summary of the Interconnection Architectures

The compliance between presented interconnections and the constraints of the DPR paradigm are summarized in Table 1.

Table 1. Compliance between current interconnection structures and DPR constraints.

DPR requirements	Buses	Mesh	CoNoChi	Ring	Fat-tree
Dynamic scheduling	NO	OK	OK	OK	OK
2D placement	NO	OK	OK	OK	OK
Heterogeneous CEs	OK	NO	OK	OK	OK
Heterogeneous FPGAs	OK	NO	NO	OK	OK
Resource consumption	OK	OK	NO	OK	NO
Routing flexibility	NO	OK	—	NO	OK
Communication parallelism	NO	OK	OK	OK	OK
Bandwidth	—	NO	—	NO	OK
Latencies	NO	NO	—	NO	OK

From Table 1, a fat-tree is best adapted to the DPR paradigm and applicative requirements. However, its resource consumption remains the main drawback for an implementation into an FPGA. Thereby, this study of current interconnections leads to the Dynamic Reconfiguration Adapted Fat-Tree (DRAFT) network.

Flexible Interconnection: DRAFT

From the comparison of current NoCs, the fat-tree appears to be the most suitable interconnection architecture to support the DPR paradigm and applicative requirements. DRAFT is a fat-tree-based network whose main characteristic lies in the reduction of needed resources for routing purpose. Like a fat-tree, DRAFT interconnects several CEs, which could be implementations of hardware tasks (static or dynamic), processors running software tasks, and shared elements like shared memories.

DRAFT Topology

The concept proposed in DRAFT is to directly connect half of the CEs to the root-level routers of a fat-tree (Figure 4). This concept reduces a lot the number of hardware resources used for routing purpose compared with the number of connected CEs. Indeed, for the same number of connected CEs, the number of routers is divided by two when compared with the fat-tree topology.

Figure 4. The DRAFT topology. Communicating elements "CEs" are connected to the root and base-levels of a fat-tree network.

Concerning network performances, the distances between the root and base-level CEs are constant whatever their locations. So, the minimal latencies of these communications are constant. However, for the effectiveness of this topology, it is necessary that the CEs connected to the root communicate only with the base-level connected ones. This assumption avoids the creation of hotspots in the root-level router. Communications between the CEs connected to the root would require additional hierarchical levels (leading to the fat-tree topology) in order not to increase the load on the root-level router. However, the base-level connected CEs can freely communicate with every other CE. This assumption is very important and while it is observed, there is no limitation concerning the nature of the CEs. A designer is free to connect its shared elements to the root-level of DRAFT, but also some hardware tasks (static or dynamic) or even processors. So, at the cost of this assumption, DRAFT is completely flexible.

Hardware Requirements

The hardware resources required by DRAFT should be considered first. If the number of connected CEs is N and the number of communication ports for each router is k, then the number of routers in DRAFT is

$$R_{DRAFT} = \frac{N}{k}\left((\log_{k/2} N)-1\right). \tag{5}$$

In this formula, assuming that DRAFT is complete in terms of connected CEs, N should be in the form of $N=2^x$ where x is an integer and $x \geq 2$. If the number of CEs does not match previous formula at design time, then designers should build the network considering the just higher admissible value of N. Similarly, the number of connection links needed by DRAFT is

$$L_{DRAFT} = \frac{N}{2}\left(\log_{k/2} N\right). \tag{6}$$

From this last formula, DRAFT uses two times less connection links than a fat-tree. This is an advantage for the implementation in current FPGAs.

There are several ways to see a fat-tree and so is DRAFT. Thereby, the two fat-trees presented in Figures 4 and 5 have the same properties regarding the CEs. Indeed, a router in Figure 4 can be broken up into a set of several unitary routers called fat-node (Figure 5). This permits to build the network by using a single router type, which is generically defined, and makes the automatic generation of DRAFT easier. However, the latter structure is not fully compliant with the connexion of the CEs to the root-level, since there is only one admissible data path between base- and root-level CEs. The router-based structure (Figure 4) is more flexible due to multiple data paths. If a communication link is already used, data can be transferred through another one to the same destination. This traffic adaptive approach is not possible in the fat-node-based structure for the communications between CEs from the root and base-levels. However, in both structures, a traffic adaptive routing can be implemented for the communications between two base-level connected CEs. So, the fat-node-based structure is less flexible than the router-based one but more generic. Furthermore, it allows to demonstrate the viability of DRAFT even if it constrains the data paths. In a first time, the focus is over the fat-node-based structure due to the generic routers. In future works, the structure will be switched to the router-based one in order to support applications requiring multiple data paths between elements from the base and root-levels.

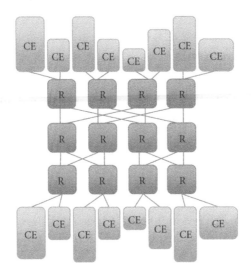

Figure 5. Fat-node view of DRAFT architecture. A fat-node is a set of unitary routers.

Principles of Connection of Various CEs

Since many applications require data transfers between static and dynamic CEs, they should be connected to DRAFT. For this purpose, designers can connect the static CEs directly to the routers, or with a bus-based sub-network (multiple buses e.g.,) connected to a single router, like for the XGFT network. In the latter structure, while CEs are static, the sub-network can be optimally designed for their communication needs. Then, the sub-network and its connected CEs (statically implemented tasks, processors, shared elements, etc.) are viewed by DRAFT as a single CE. On the other hand, the static CEs which do not exchange data with dynamic ones should be interconnected through a separate network optimally designed for this purpose. Similarly, the shared elements which do not communicate with dynamic CEs but only with static ones should be connected to a sub-network rather than to DRAFT. These principles are advised to reduce the size of DRAFT and so its resource consumption. Doing so, DRAFT can be seen as an independent core of network or even as an Intellectual Property (IP) block connecting each part of the application, while providing the flexibility required by the DPR paradigm.

For applications using the DPR, DRAFT does not directly connect the tasks through their network interfaces, but through the Bus Macros (BMs). So, BMs are the interfaces between DRAFT and the dynamic CEs (including their network interfaces (NIs)) as presented in Figure 6.

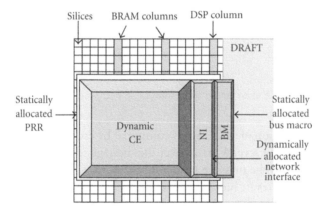

Figure 6. PRR receiving a dynamic CE connected to DRAFT through the dynamic NI and the static BMs.

This concept of dynamically reconfigurable NIs is important because they can be designed optimally for their corresponding CEs. This allows to reduce the hardware cost of the NIs when a CE does not have the same interface as the others. So during the dynamic reconfiguration of a given PRR, DRAFT interface remains the same even if the newly allocated CE presents a specific interface. So, this concept makes DRAFT more generic and more flexible considering the location of the CEs.

Hardware Characteristics of the Routers

The router architecture (Figure 7) is based over four bidirectional communication ports, each including an asynchronous FIFO. FIFO sizes are defined by the designer depending on the flit width (data are fractioned into several small sets of bits called flits), and on the number of flits to store, according to the data flow and the livelock management protocol (credit based, priority, round robin, etc.). A crossbar, controlled by a routing manager which protocol is based on a Turn-Back algorithm [28], performs the routing of data.

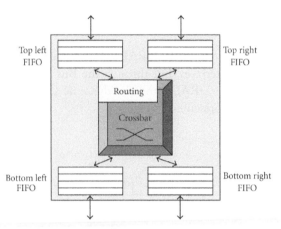

Figure 7. View of the DRAFT unitary router architecture.

The next destination of a message is computed by each router receiving it. The decision is made using several masks over the message source and destination addresses included into the message header. Each router is identified by an internal address which indicates its hierarchical level and its location into this level. Similarly, every CE connected to DRAFT is identified by an internal address which is used to specify the source and the destination of a message. This addressing of the CEs and routers is presented in Figure 8.

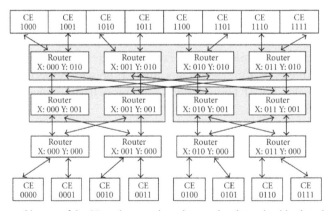

Figure 8. Generic addressing of the CEs and routers depending on their hierarchical levels and their locations into these levels.

Thanks to these addresses, each router uses a hierarchical level dependent mask to determine if a flit should be routed toward an upper hierarchical level in order to reach a different part of the tree. So, each data is routed toward the high until it is able to go down to the desired half (or subpart) of the tree. This lowering routing is directly applied to the CEs connected to the root-level of DRAFT. Destination addresses are sufficient to determine toward which part of the tree a data should be routed. This algorithm, presented in Algorithm 1, provides a minimal distance to the data transfers and the guaranty that there is no deadlock risk [27]. In this algorithm, the source and destination addresses of a data are called, respectively, CEsrc and CEdest. The mask is directly calculated from the Y address of the router corresponding to its hierarchical level. As an example, for router X:0010 Y:0001, the corresponding mask is 0011. The Mshift parameter is the mask previously calculated shifted right of one bit set to 1. Thus, in this example, Mshift is 1001. Similarly, the RXshift is calculated from the X address of the router shifted left of one bit, that is, 0100 in the example.

```
IF("data from port West or South")
// data arrived from a lower level
            IF((RXshift AND mask) XOR (CEdest AND mask) = 0)
            // is the aimed subpart of DRAFT reachable from this router ?
                        "Yes: routing toward lower level"
            ELSE
                        "No: routing toward upper level depending on CEsrc"
            END IF
ELSE
// data arrived from an upper level
            IF((RXshift AND Mshift) XOR (CEdest AND Mshift) = 0)
            // which subpart of DRAFT is the data destination ?
                        "routing toward the right side"
            ELSE
                        "routing toward the left side"
            END IF
END IF
```

Algorithm 1: Routing algorithm implemented into DRAFT routers.

In order to keep static the DRAFT architecture into the framework of the DPR, addressing of the routers and CEs is generic. However, since many CEs are dynamic, it constrains the designer to make sure that the task placer/scheduler keeps up-to-date a routing table. This table is essential for the network interfaces of the CEs to make the correspondence between the internal addresses and the physical elements (implemented task, memory, etc.).

Implementation of DRAFT in a Xilinx FPGA

DRAFT placement is important in the conception of a system using the DPR, because it impacts the use of the reconfigurable resources as well as the network performances. Thus, the concept presented in Figure 9 is to implement DRAFT as a central column into the FPGA. This concept is particularly adapted to current technologies supporting the DPR: Xilinx Virtex 4, Virtex 5, and Virtex 6 FPGAs. CEs are implemented into both halves of the FPGA with the static elements of the application (processor, etc.). Since DRAFT is not distributed into the FPGA, the designer is not constrained by the network for the definition of the CEs in terms of sizes and locations. This is an advantage for the implementation of heterogeneous dynamic CEs. Thus, the implementation of DRAFT is fully compliant with current technology and the DPR requirements.

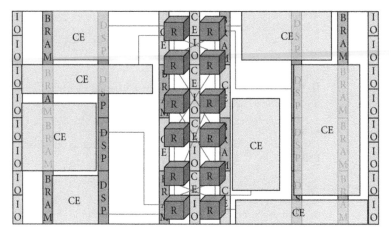

Figure 9. Implementation of DRAFT as a central column interconnecting CEs which are located into both halves of the FPGA.

In present technology, PRRs and BMs are defined statically, but there is no physical obstacle to make them dynamic. The limitation is only due to the design tools which do not support the dynamic definition of the partially reconfigurable regions. Consequently, if the design software allows the definition of dynamically locatable PRRs, then every base- (or roots) level router should be reachable from both halves of the FPGA. Doing so, the dynamic relocation of a PRR from one half of the FPGA to the other will be supported.

In Xilinx FPGAs, shared IOs should be located into the central IO bank column. Similarly, it is recommended to locate the shared memories into the BRAM columns the nearest of the central column. Thereby, the communications between the CEs and the shared elements encounter a minimal latency.

Presentation of DRAGOON

In this section, the design software called Dynamically Reconfigurable Architecture compliant Generator and simulatOr Of Network (DRAGOON) is presented. DRAGOON is a conception environment specifically designed to generate and to simulate the DRAFT topology. It is inspired from ATLAS which was developed to support Hermes NoCs [18]. DRAGOON is also compliant with the fat-tree topology. The conception flow provided by DRAGOON is illustrated Figure 10, in which every step corresponds to a tool.

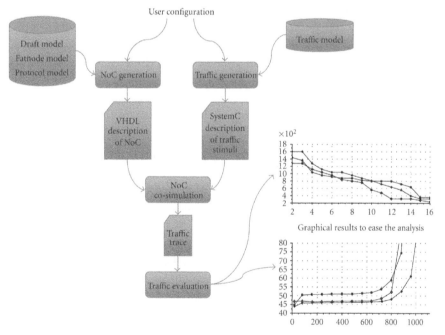

Figure 10. Conception flow of DRAGOON.

The NoC generation tool produces the VHDL description of DRAFT and test benches written on SystemC, according to the configuration chosen by the user. This latter is able to choose the network dimension in terms of connected CEs, and also the flit width or the buffer depth. The flit width parameter determines the length of the data (fractioned into unitary flits) exchanged through the network. Flit width can be set to 16, 32, or 64 bits. The buffer depth indicates how many flits can be stored into one of the four FIFOs of a router. So, a router can store 4, 8, 16, or 32 flits into each of its 4 ports. The number of virtual channels can also be chosen by the user. Using virtual channels, a router is able to support several communications in parallel at the cost of hardware resources. Concerning the data traffic, the type of flow control (credit based or handshake) and the scheduling policy (round robin or priority) are parameterizable. So, the NoC generation tool allows generating DRAFT networks adapted to the requirements of many applications.

The traffic generation tool produces different data traffics (uniform, normal, pareto on/off). Each traffic simulates an application supported by DRAFT. A uniform traffic simulates applications using a constant data flow like video processing. A normal traffic is provided by applications using data dependency like pattern recognition or target tracking. Finally, the pareto on/off traffic simulates the communications between a task and a shared memory where data is transmitted using a burst mode (period of uninterrupted data transmission followed by a period of silence). Furthermore, the traffic generation tool allows the designer to simulate several configurations of the connected CEs. Indeed, the frequencies of the CEs, the targets of data (random or specific), the number of packets to send, and the number of flits in a packet are parameterizable. Designer can also specify the transmission rate of each CE. Using all these parameters, the traffic generator builds input files containing data to be transmitted through the network.

The simulation tool invokes an external VHDL simulator (ModelSim). This simulator was chosen because it supports mixed VHDL and SystemC. Thus, the simulation tool uses the description of the NoC and the generated traffic. This traffic is injected into DRAFT during the simulation phase, which is concluded when the output files are generated.

The evaluation tool provides the interpretation of the results thanks to the previously generated output files. Results are analyzed and presented through graphics and analysis reports. Network performances like latency and throughput are the main results provided by the evaluation tool.

Implementation Results

In this section, DRAFT implementation results are presented. Thanks to the automatic network generator (DRAGOON), DRAFT is compared with the mesh and the fat-tree topologies. This comparison takes into account the use of hardware resources and the network performances. The impacts of the NoC and traffic parameters over hardware and network characteristics are also presented.

Hardware resources are obtained thanks to Xilinx ISE 9.2i tool chain [29], and network performances are measured through ModelSim 9.5c [30] and presented thanks to DRAGOON. From this comparison, the viability and the effectiveness of DRAFT are demonstrated.

For a fair comparison of the three different network topologies, some hypothesis must be considered. Every topology is implemented for maximal network performances. So, both DRAFT and fat-tree architectures are based over a complete binary tree whatever the number of connected CEs. Similarly, every implemented mesh presents a square matrix based structure whatever the number of connected CEs. The mesh topology is implemented and simulated using ATLAS while DRAFT and fat-tree topologies are provided by DRAGOON. Since the fat-tree and DRAFT are generated with a fat-node-based structure, the three networks are implemented with the same router architectures and without virtual channels. The routing algorithm is the only component which differs from a topology to another one, so the topologies are compared independently of their router architecture. Every router is clocked at 100 MHz.

Hardware Resources

DRAFT is defined as a network which supports the DPR requirements and minimizes the hardware resource consumption. In this part, implementation results are investigated, and presented in Figure 11. For this purpose, each router was implemented with a flit width of 32 bits and a buffer depth of 4 flits.

From these implementation results, as expected, a fat-tree needs more hardware resources and more communication links than every other topology. However, using the root-level connection of the CEs, DRAFT needs less hardware resources and less communication links than a mesh when the number of connected CEs is less than 16. When this number increases, resource consumptions are very close but DRAFT needs less resources when the number of connected CEs becomes close to a power of 2. However, DRAFT outnumbers mesh resources in small ranges like from 17 to 25 connected CEs. This point is due to the assumption that DRAFT is implemented as a complete binary tree and the mesh as a square matrix. Hence, DRAFT needs 32 routers to connect from 17 to 32 CEs while a mesh needs only 25 routers to connect from 17 to 25 CEs. Then, this latter needs 36 routers to connect from 26 to 32 routers. The number of routing wires increasingly becomes a limiting factor in FPGAs, so the fact that DRAFT requires less links than a mesh is an important matter for the designers. Using the DRAFT network, designers have more communication links available for the implementation of their tasks.

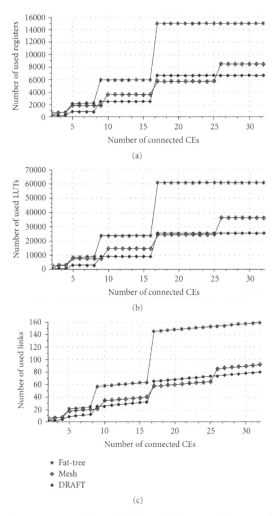

Figure 11. Number of registers (a), LUTs (b), and links (c) used for DRAFT, fat-tree, and mesh implementations in a Xilinx Virtex5 depending on the number of connected CEs.

Network Performances

Usually, latency and throughput results are presented depending on the injection rate. The injection rate corresponds to the percentage of the maximal bandwidth which is used to send data from the CEs point of view. DRAFT and fat-tree to-pologies have two CEs connected to each base- (or roots) level router. However, in a mesh, only one CE is connected to a router, which directly impacts the injection rate. As an example, a 100% injection rate in a mesh corresponds to a data rate of

3200 Mbit/s per CE whereas it corresponds to 1600 Mbit/s per CE in DRAFT or in a fat-tree. The three topologies are simulated connecting 8 CEs with 32 bits flit width and a buffer depth of 4 flits. The frequency of each CE is 100 MHz, and data are sent with a uniform repartition of their sources and destinations. Results are presented in Figure 12. The number of data to transmit is calculated depending on the injection rates for 1ms of continuous data injection.

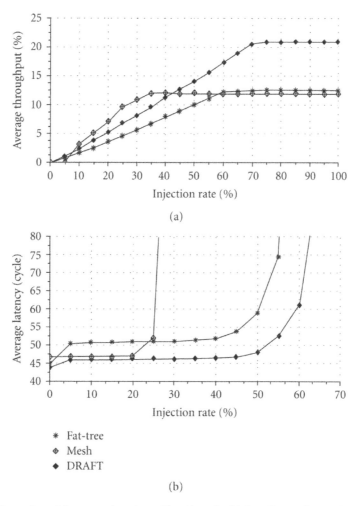

Figure 12. Comparison of the average throughputs (a) and latencies (b) depending on the injection rates for 8 connected CEs.

For a fair comparison of the three topologies, a comparison of the latencies and throughputs depending on the transfer rates is presented in Figure 13.

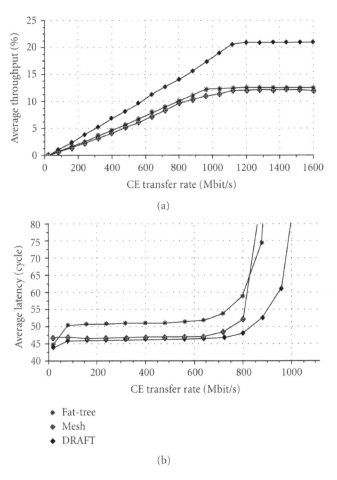

Figure 13. Comparison of the average throughputs (a) and latencies (b) depending on each CE transfer rate.

From these results, if the NoCs are compared depending on the injection rates calculated from their maximal bandwidth, the mesh topology saturates with an injection rate of 25%. The fat-tree and DRAFT saturate, respectively, around 55% and 60% of injection rates. This point is important because it shows that DRAFT supports a higher injection rate than every other topology. Furthermore, with the comparisons depending on the transfer rates, it appears that DRAFT provides a lower average latency while supporting higher transfer rates than the others. This minimal latency is due to the reduction of the number of routers. DRAFT offers also a higher throughput when considering the data rates. This demonstrates a better use of the routing resources than for mesh and fat-tree topologies.

Scalability

From previous implementation results, the lower resource consumption of the DRAFT network was pointed out. However, it is interesting to verify the scalability of the three topologies considering the network performances and the hardware needs. For this comparison, the networks are implemented with the same characteristics as in previous parts. For the network performances, the highest acceptable data rates are chosen in order to place the networks in the worst conditions. So, the data rate is fixed to 800 Mbit/s for each router. Simulations are realized sending 1562 packets of 16 flits each for an injection time of 1ms. Network performances are presented in Figure 14.

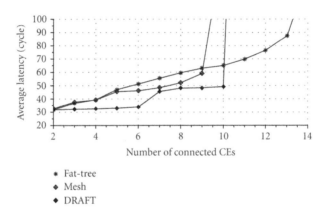

Figure 14. Comparison of the average latencies depending on the number of simultaneously connected CEs.

Thanks to its higher resource consumption, a fat-tree is able to support a higher number of simultaneously connected CEs than other topologies. In these worst transfer conditions, a mesh can manage 9 CEs, DRAFT can handle 10, and the fat-tree supports 13 CEs. Consequently, until 10 simultaneously connected CEs, DRAFT needs less hardware resources and provides a lower latency than other networks. For the connection of more than 10 CEs, the data rates should be restricted or the networks should be adapted for higher network performances at the cost of hardware resources.

The adaptation of the network parameters is now considered in order to improve the network performances. Two parameters are investigated: the flit width and the buffer depth. Results are presented for each parameter considering the required registers and LUTs also with the average latencies. The impact of the flit width is shown Figure 15. The networks are always designed for the connection of 8 CEs, with a buffer depth of 4 flits. The data rate could not be fixed to

800 Mbit/s due to a saturation of the latencies with a flit size of 16 bits. Thus, presented latencies were obtained for a data rate of 400 Mbit/s per CE.

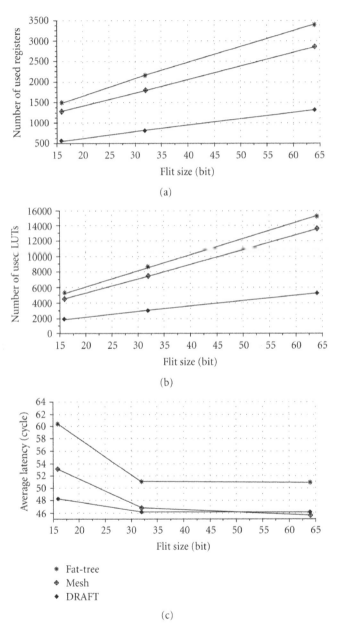

Figure 15. Influence of the flit sizes over the hardware resources (registers (a) and LUTs (b)) and the latencies (c) with a data rate of 400 Mbit/s per CE.

So, the flit size has a great influence over the resource consumption. The impact of this parameter, between 32 and 64 bits, is limited with a data rate of 400 Mbit/s. However, at 800 Mbit/s, it reduces the latencies from 48.05 to 32.31 average cycles, respectively, for 32 and 64 bits in DRAFT. This phenomenon can also be observed for the fat-tree and the mesh. Considering the hardware cost of the flit size, this parameter should be minimized according to the desired performances.

Similarly, the impact of the buffer depth is presented in Figure 16. The presented results were obtained with a flit width of 32 bits and with a data rate of 800 Mbit/s per CE.

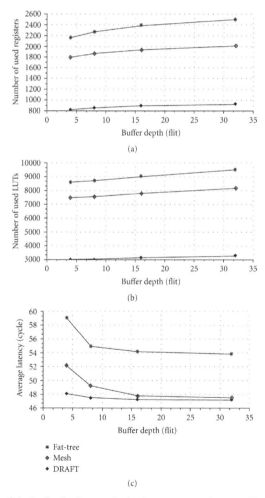

Figure 16. Influence of the buffer depths over the hardware resources (registers (a) and LUTs (b)) and the latencies (c) with a data rate of 800 Mbit/s per CE.

Concerning the buffer depth, an increase of the depths decreases the average latencies, but its impact over the hardware resources is lower than for the flit size. So, if the flit size is set to a minimum, the buffer depth can be increased in order to reach the network performances and the scalability required by the application.

In conclusion over the scalability, every topology can support a relatively low number of simultaneously connected CEs at full network performances. In order to increase this number, the designer should reduce first the data rate of its CEs. This point is particularly true with the DRAFT topology. If it is not possible, the designer should try to increase the flit size and buffer depth parameters. However, these solutions have an important impact on resource overhead. The use of virtual channels can also increase the scalability of the networks, but the impact over hardware resources is impractical for an implementation in an FPGA.

Type of Data Traffic

In this part, the influence of the data traffic is presented. Each network is designed to connect 8 CEs with a flit size of 32 bits and a buffer depth of 4 flits. Three types of traffic are studied. Thus, data are produced with a uniform, a normal, or a "pareto on/off" distribution. This latter is a periodic distribution where a period without any emission of data is followed by a period of emission. Results are presented in Table 2.

Table 2. Influence of the different data traffics over the latency (average clock cycles).

Type of traffic	DRAFT	Fat-tree	Mesh
Uniform (800 Mbit/s)	48.27	58.22	51.91
Normal (800 Mbit/s)	43.40	56.71	49.21
Pareto (800 Mbit/s)	33.11	42.42	38.40
Uniform (400 Mbit/s)	46.20	51.07	46.87
Normal (400 Mbit/s)	35.58	43.28	38.65
Pareto (400 Mbit/s)	31.43	39.83	35.64

From these results, DRAFT appears to better support the different types of traffic, even at maximum data rate. A uniform traffic can be encountered in many applications using an constant flow of data like video processing. The normal repartition of the data rates during computation time is required by applications which depend on the received data like the automatic recognition of a target. The "pareto on/off" corresponds to the traffic between a hardware element and a shared memory using the burst mode, which is the continuous emission of several data during a short period of time. Thus, DRAFT can support all these applications with better performances than other networks.

Implementation of an Application Using DRAFT

In this section, the implementation results (hardware resources and network performances) of an application, designed into the framework of the FOSFOR project, are presented. This application is implemented into a middle size Xilinx Virtex5 FPGA: the XC5VSX50T.

A system using DRAFT to interconnect 4 PRRs and 4 shared IOs is implemented with a MicroBlaze processor to control the DPR [31]. The application realizes a target tracking in a video stream. For this purpose, the application is composed of statically implemented tasks, which transform the video stream, and of dynamically implemented ones, which realize the tracking. Dynamically implemented tasks depend on the dynamic number of targets and on the nature of these targets. Thus, these tasks are very heterogeneous in terms of hardware resource requirements. The four shared IOs are located in the central column of the FPGA. This system operates at 100 MHz with a 32 bits data width. In this Virtex 5, DRAFT needs only 2% of the registers and 10% of the LUTs. So, while including the MicroBlaze processor with its memory and peripherals for the DPR management, 92% of the registers and 85% of the LUTs (also with 88% of the BRAMs) remain free for task implementation. Complete implementation results are shown Table 3.

Table 3. Complete implementation results of DRAFT interconnecting 4 PRRs and 4 shared IOs.

| | Draft alone | | | Global system | | Free space |
	Used	Total	%	Used	%	%
Registers	857	32640	2%	2223	6%	92%
LUT	3470	32640	10%	5150	15%	85%
LUT FLIP FLOP	3497	32640	10%	5560	17%	83%
DSP48E	0	288	0%	3	1%	99%
BRAM36	0	132	0%	16	12%	88%

Concerning network performances, the routers are implemented with a critical path of 9,09 ns (110 MHz). DRAFT presents an average latency of 46 clock cycles. In this implementation without virtual channels, it also offers an aggregative bandwidth of 880 MByte/s. A view of the hardware implementation of the system is presented in Figure 17.

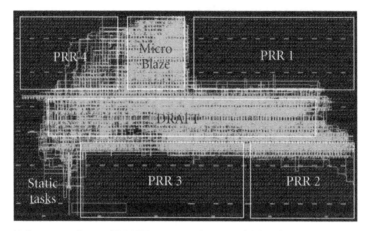

Figure 17. 90-degree rotated view of DRAFT connecting 4 PRRs and 4 shared IOs.

Conclusion

In this article, a flexible interconnection network is described. This network is compliant with applications requiring the DPR, and with current FPGA technologies. Thus, from the comparison of current interconnections, even bus-based or NoC based, the fat-tree appeared as a particularly well suited topology for the compliance with the DPR paradigm. Indeed, this structure offers higher network performances than other topologies in terms of bandwidth and latency. A fat-tree is an indirect network that provides high flexibility at the data path level, and supports the parallelization of the communications. Its structure allows interconnecting heterogeneous CEs in heterogeneous FPGAs. The main drawback of this topology is the hardware resource requirements. Hence, the DRAFT flexible network is proposed. DRAFT is indeed the sum of several concepts concerning the structure and the implementation of a fat-tree. These concepts are proposed in order to significantly reduce the resource consumption, and to obtain a network fully compliant with the DPR paradigm. The main idea of DRAFT consists in connecting half of the CEs directly to the root of a fat-tree. The connection of the static elements and the unshared resources is also presented in order to reduce the number of routers, and so the resource consumption. Then, the way to implement DRAFT as a central column into an FPGA is proposed for taking advantage of current FPGA structures.

The DRAGOON generator is designed to parameterize and to automatically generate the DRAFT topology. DRAGOON also supports the simulation of the network allowing to characterize its performances. According with these concepts and thanks to DRAGOON, the DRAFT viability is demonstrated by the comparison with a fat-tree and a mesh network. DRAFT needs fewer resources and fewer communication links than a mesh and a fat-tree. DRAFT presents a lower average latency than every other topology, and supports higher transfer and injection rates (until 1000 Mbit/s). DRAFT is also less sensitive to the flit sizes and the buffer depths than the others so that it can be implemented minimizing its hardware requirements according with the application. Consequently, DRAFT is very well adapted for an implementation into the framework of applications using DPR where there are around 10 simultaneously connected CEs. Finally, the DRAFT viability in terms of compliance with current applications using DPR, and with current technologies, is demonstrated by the implementation of a target tracking application in a Xilinx Virtex5.

Acknowledgement

This research was supported by the ANR (French National Research Agency) within the framework of the FOSFOR project (Flexible OS FOr Reconfigurable devices), http://www.polytech.unice.fr/~fmuller/fosfor/.

References

1. FOSFOR, http://users.polytech.unice.fr/~fmuller/fosfor/.

2. D. Cozzi, C. Far, A. Meroni, V. Rana, M. D. Santambrogio, and D. Sciuto, "Reconfigurable NoC design flow for multiple applications run-time mapping on FPGA devices," in Proceedings of the 19th ACM Great Lakes Symposium on VLSI (GLSVLSI '09), pp. 421–424, Boston, Mass, USA, May 2009.

3. Altera, "Stratix IV Device Handbook—Volume 1," ver 4.0, November 2009.

4. Altera, "Stratix IV Device Handbook—Volume 2," ver 4.0, November 2009.

5. ATMEL, "AT40K05/10/20/40AL. 5K–50K Gate FPGA with DSP Optimized Core Cell and Distributed FreeRam, Enhanced Performance Improvement and Bi-directional I/Os (3.3 V)," revision F, 2006.

6. Xilinx, "Virtex-5 FPGA Configuration User Guide," v3.5, 2008.

7. "PlanAhead User Guide—version 1.1," Xilinx, 2008.

8. Xilinx, "Difference-Based Partial Reconfiguration, Application Note XAPP290," 2007.

9. F. Moraes, N. Calazans, L. Mller, E. Brio, and E. Carvalho, "Dynamic and partial reconfiguration in FPGA SoCs: requirements tools and a case study," in

New Algorithms, Architectures and Applications for Reconfigurable Computing, pp. 157–168, Springer, New York, NY, USA, 2005.

10. J. Becker, M. Hubner, G. Hettich, R. Constapel, J. Eisenmann, and J. Luka, "Dynamic and partial FPGA exploitation," Proceedings of the IEEE, vol. 95, no. 2, pp. 438–452, 2007.

11. D. Koch, C. Beckhoff, and J. Teich, "Recobus-builder—a novel tool and technique to build statically and dynamically reconfigurable systems for FPGAs," in Proceedings of the International Conference on Field Programmable Logic and Applications (FPL '08), pp. 119–124, Heidelberg, Germany, September 2008.

12. A. Thomas and J. Becker, "Dynamic adaptive runtime routing techniques in multigrain reconfigurable hardware architectures," in Field Programmable Logic and Application, vol. 3203 of Lecture Notes in Computer Science, pp. 115–124, Springer, Berlin, Germany, 2004.

13. S. Winegarden, "Bus architecture of a system on a chip with user-configurable system logic," IEEE Journal of Solid-State Circuits, vol. 35, no. 3, pp. 425–433, 2000.

14. T. Seceleanu, J. Plosila, and P. Liljeberg, "On-chip segmented bus: a self timed approach," in Proceedings of the Annual IEEE International ASIC/SOC Conference—System-on-Chip in a Networked World, pp. 216–220, September 2002.

15. A. Ahmadinia, C. Bobda, J. Ding, et al., "A practical approach for circuit routing on dynamic reconfigurable devices," in Proceedings of the International Workshop on Rapid System Prototyping (RSP '05), pp. 84–90, Montreal, Canada, June 2005.

16. L. Benini and G. De Micheli, "Networks on chips: a new SoC paradigm," Computer, vol. 35, no. 1, pp. 70–78, 2002.

17. E. Salminen, A. Kulmala, and T. D. Hamalainen, "Survey of network-on-chip proposals," http://www.ocpip.org/white_papers.php.

18. F. Moraes, N. Calazans, A. Mello, L. Moller, and L. Ost, "Hermes: an infrastructure for low area overhead packet-switching networks on chip," Integration, the VLSI Journal, vol. 38, no. 1, pp. 69–93, 2004.

19. C. Bobda and A. Ahmadinia, "Dynamic interconnection of reconfigurable modules on reconfigurable devices," IEEE Design & Test of Computers, vol. 22, no. 5, pp. 443–451, 2005.

20. C. Bobda, A. Ahmadinia, M. Majer, J. Teich, S. Fekete, and J. van der Veen, "DyNoC: a dynamic infrastructure for communication in dynamically

reconfigurable devices," in Proceedings of the International Conference on Field Programmable Logic and Applications (FPL '05), vol. 2005, pp. 153–158, Tampere, Finland, August 2005.

21. T. Pionteck, R. Koch, and C. Albrecht, "Applying partial reconfiguration to networks-on-chips," in Proceedings of the International Conference on Field Programmable Logic and Applications (FPL '06), pp. 155–160, Madrid, Spain, August 006.

22. "Cell Broadband Engine Programming Handbook," IBM, version, 1.11, 2008.

23. C. Neeb and N. Wehn, "Designing efficient irregular networks for heterogeneous systems-on-chip," Journal of Systems Architecture, vol. 54, no. 3-4, pp. 384–396, 2008.

24. P. P. Pande, C. Grecu, M. Jones, A. Ivanov, and R. Saleh, "Performance evaluation and design trade-offs for network-on-chip interconnect architectures," IEEE Transactions on Computers, vol. 54, no. 8, pp. 1025–1040, 2005.

25. T. Bjerregaard and S. Mahadevan, "A survey of research and practices of network-on-chip," ACM Computing Surveys, vol. 38, no. 1, pp. 71–121, 2006.

26. J. L. Hennessy and D. A. Patterson, "Appendix E: interconnection networks," in Computer Architecture: A Quantitative Approach, Morgan Kaufmann, San Mateo, Calif, USA, 2006.

27. H. Kariniemi and J. Nurmi, "Reusable XGFT interconnect IP for network-on-chip implementations," in Proceedings of the International Symposium on System-on-Chip, pp. 95–102, Tampere, Finland, November 2004.

28. H. Kariniemi, On-line reconfigurable extended generalized fat tree network-on-chip for multiprocessor system-on-chip circuits, Ph.D. dissertation, Tampere University of Technology, Tampere, Finland, 2006.

29. "Synthesis and Simulation Design Guide—ISE 9.2i," Xilinx, 2008.

30. "ModelSim LE/PE Users Manual 6.5.c," Mentor graphics, 2009.

31. K. Park and H. Kim, "Remote FPGA Reconfiguration Using MicroBlaze or PowerPC Processors," Application Note: XAPP441 (v1.1) ed., Xilinx.

A Hardware Solution for an "On the Fly" Encryption

Daniel Filipas

ABSTRACT

This paper presents an implementation of a secured transmission of binary data, using a hardware encryption based on multiple keys, stored in a small read-only memory. The advantages of such a solution are the increased speed of encryption (since a hardware implemenation is much faster than a software one) and an automatic process (since the user doesn't have to provide himself the keys for encryption/decryption). Also, the paper presents the results of simulation obtained using the Quartus II Web Edition 9.0 design software provided by Altera.

Keywords: encryption, hardware, memory

Introduction

Data encryption is a very important issue when important files are transmitted over a public channel (such as the Internet), so the algorithms and methods of protecting the information have to be considered as a priority.

Of course, there are lots of algorithms implemented and, as the time passes, they are more and more sophisticated, in order to prevent hackers' intrusions [1]. Every algorithm tries to operate on the data to be transmitted so that it might be protected against unauthorized "readers."

Almost every algorithm encrypts the plain message using a "key" (a sequence of binary digits supposed to be known only by the transmitter and the receiver) [2]. And every algorithm claims to offer security for the sent information, as long as the key is not available for others.

There are many software implementations of these algorithms (because the software doesn't need extra hardware devices, so it is a less expensive solution), yet they remain slower comparing to hardware solutions [3].

In the same time, many software solutions offered to the problem of data encryption require that the key for encryption and decryption to be provided by the user. That leaves the chance that someone unauthorized "listens" and "steals" the key, so the encryption becomes useless.

In this paper is provided a simple solution for an "on the fly" hardware encryption, using a read-only memory to store the keys.

A Simple Hardware Encryption

The Principle

The basic idea is the following: let's suppose that, instead of a single key, we use multiple keys (in this implementation there are 32 keys, each one having the length of 8 bits), a different key for each byte of data. All 32 keys are stored in a read-only memory. Every byte of data is simply added with a key. The key address in memory is provided by a counter, as shown in Fig. 1 (of course, it is possible to choose a different way to select the key, this solution was chosen only to illustrate the principle).

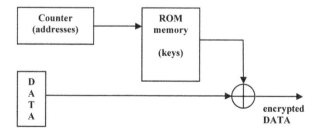

Figure 1

For every byte of data, the counter provides a different key address (one of the 32 available), so every byte is encrypted using the key stored in memory at that address. The transmission of the information is not delayed but for a clock cycle, so we can say that encryption is "on the fly."

At the receiver there is the same logic, except the adder (which is replaced by a substractor).

The only information sent through the public channel is the encrypted data. The keys are stored only in the ROM memories (one located at the transmission point, the other one at the receiver). At the receiver, the encrypted data is easily decrypted by substracting the key (if the receiver's memory stores the two's complement of the keys then it will be also a sum—this time with a negative number).

Examples

Let's take an example. Assuming that the plain, unencrypted data, is 00101001 and the current key is 01100111, the encrypted byte will be their sum:

$$00101001 + 01100111 = 10010000.$$

This is the only information sent by the transmitter.

At the receiver, one will have to substract the key (knowing that this is the same key that was used by the transmitter—because the two memories have the exact same lines):

$$10010000 - 01100111 = 00101001$$

As mentioned, if the receiver's ROM memory stores the two's complement of the keys, one can use the exact logic described earlier for encryption (involving the adder):

$$10010000 + 10011001 = 00101001$$

The carry-out bit was ignored (it has no importance in this case).

Considering the data and the keys as unsigned numbers, even if the sum between the data and the key is greater than 255, the encryption and the decryption will work properly.

Let's consider the following situation:

Data to be transmitted: 11010111 (binary representation for 215)

Encryption key: 11100101 (binary representation for 229)

In this case, the encrypted data will be:

$$11010111 + 11100101 = 10111100,$$

which is binary representation for 188, not the correct sum 444, because of the overflow. Yet, the decryption will provide the correct data:

$$10111100 - 11100101 = 11010111,$$

which is exactly the data we've encrypted.

This simple encryption (based only on a sum) provides an "on the fly" method which not only offers an increased speed of encryption, but also a good security for the keys (because they are invisible for the user).

Hardware Implementation

Fig. 2 presents an implementation of this method using Quartus II Web Edition 9.0 design software provided by Altera [4].

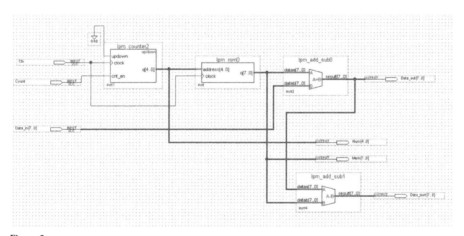

Figure 2

In order to offer an overview of the results for both the encryption and decryption, this implementation contains not only the adder used to encrypt data, but also the substractor, which would be a part of the receiver's logic. Here, it is used only to show how data is decrypted.

The read-only memory was initialized using hexadecimal values stored in a file. The content of the memory is shown in Fig. 3.

Addr	+0	+1	+2	+3	+4	+5	+6	+7
00	0E	17	38	22	19	17	15	7B
08	17	57	42	2C	16	0B	42	4D
10	2B	15	22	24	38	6D	63	58
18	4D	36	16	41	52	5D	20	0B

Figure 3

Of course, to improve system's security, a EPROM memory can be used, in order to have the possibility to periodically update the values of the keys. But this is beyond the scope of this paper.

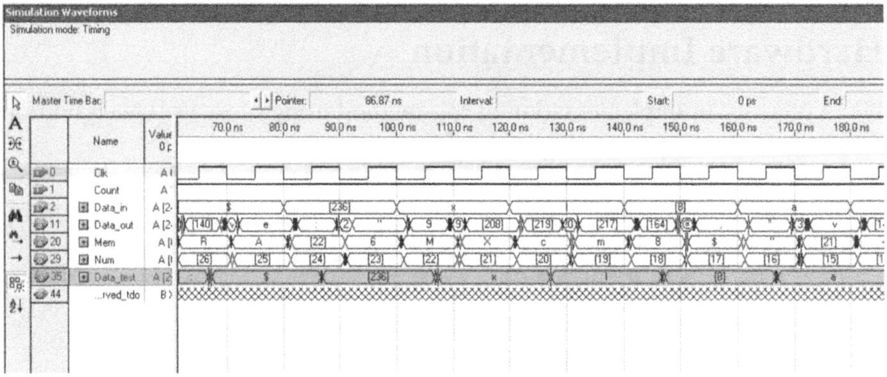

Figure 4

Simulation Results

Running the simulation for random values of Data_in byte, the result was the one shown in Fig. 4.

These waveforms show that the input bytes (Data_in values) and the decrypted bytes (Data_test values) are the same.

As we can see, the delay is just a clock cycle. This is probably the fastest solution for a secured transmission.

In Fig. 4 were also considered intermediary values (in order to observe the entire process):

-Mem—which shows the value of the key at every clock cycle,

-Num—which indicates the address of the key in the memory. In this simulation, the counting is up-down (it is very important that both counters—the transmitter's and the receiver's—to follow the same rule for counting, otherwise the decryption is impossible and data is lost).

-Data_out—which shows the encrypted information (Data_in + Mem).

In the waveforms above, every value of Data_in, Data_out and Data_test is represented by its corresponding character in ASCII code, for an easier reading.

In this case, the input waveforms were chosen to change every two clock cycles (of course, it is just an example, the input data may follow any other pattern—changes can occur every clock cycle or can be irregular).

However, the counter decrements its value every clock cycle, pointing to another address in memory (another key), so the key changes even if Data_in doesn't. For this reason, the output has about two different values for the same input.

This aspect illustrates another advantage of this implementation: even if someone unauthorized intercepts the encrypted information, he doesn't have any idea about the number of valid input data or about the number of the keys used for encryption, so the attacks against this method become more difficult.

As the simulation results show, for 6 valid input bytes, there are 12 output encrypted bytes (the noises—the unstable signals—are not considered).

Even if someone "listens" to the information being sent, he won't be able to find that there are two bytes encrypting the same value, because there are different keys they were encrypted with. And even if he finds it or guess it, he couldn't say which two bytes go together. When data frequency is not constant, this issue become almost impossible. So, the frequency of input data is, also, hidden.

And there is also another important thing to be noticed. Because of the key changing at every clock cycle, the same input byte will have a different encryption almost every time it appears. The chance of being added to the same key is very small. This chance decreases even more if the number of keys used is greater than the one considered here (32 keys).

And if we consider the frequent update of keys in memory (that would be possible only if a EPROM memory is available), the chance of "breaking" the system is about zero.

For the refresh of the keys, there are many methods that could be implemented:

-a right/left shift of the bits for every key (or only for some of the keys);

-an offset that could be added from time to time to every key;

-conditional change of the key, depending on the data bits etc.

Of course, the transmitter and the receiver have to use the same method.

We should focus only on the synchronization between the two counters, which is the most important issue here. If the counters are not synchronized, the decryption is impossible.

An idea for this would be to transmit blocks of data (not only bytes), so that the receiver could easily identify if the transmission was successful or not. At the beginning of every block of data, the transmitter would notify the receiver that there is something to be transmitted. If the block size is not always the same, then the transmitter has also to send a signal at the end of data block. A failure in transmission would generate a failure in decryption.

When the receiver has the entire block, the decryption can start.

Resource Usage

Fig. 5 presents the information offered by the resource usage report generated by Quartus II Web Edition.

Quartus II Version	9.0 Build 132 02/25/2009 SJ Web Edition
Revision Name	sch_mem
Top-level Entity Name	sch_mem
Family	Stratix II
Met timing requirements	Yes
Logic utilization	1 %
Combinational ALUTs	118 / 12,480 (< 1 %)
Dedicated logic registers	100 / 12,480 (< 1 %)
Total registers	100
Total pins	39 / 343 (11 %)
Total virtual pins	0
Total block memory bits	256 / 419,328 (< 1 %)
DSP block 9-bit elements	0 / 96 (0 %)
Total PLLs	0 / 6 (0 %)
Total DLLs	0 / 2 (0 %)
Device	EP2S15F484C3
Timing Models	Final

Figure 5

As Fig. 5 shows, this system uses less than 1% of the resources provided by the selected device (EP2S15F484C3). It means that such an encryption module could be very easily integrated, without consuming too much of the available memory blocks, dedicated logic registers and combinational ALUTs.

There is, indeed, a large number of pins (39—that is 11% of their total number), but most of them are only for testing purpose in this implementation.

Data_test, Mem and Num (a total of 21 pins) were insert only to give a better view of the process. They are not needed in a real system.

In fact, as a module of a transmission system, it would't use not even a single output pin, if we consider the Data_in and Data_out pins as a part of the transmitter's main architecture.

Conclusions

As the results of the simulation show, this hardware encryption offers a very fast encryption (the data to be transmitted is not delayed but for a clock cycle), a strong encryption (based on multiple keys) and an automatic process (since the user doesn't have to provide the keys).

The main disadvantage consists in the requirement of synchronizing the receiver's and the transmitter's key addressing mode. In this implementation, the synchronization implies the clock signal which enables the counting. But, as previously mentioned, if the information is sent in blocks of data, this issue is no longer important, because each one (the transmitter and the receiver) will have its own timing system, that will not affect the data.

The resources needed for implementation show that such a module would not increase too much the cost of the system.

The main advantage of this solution is the "on the fly" encryption.

The possibility of regularly updating the keys stored in memory by using an EPROM memory (so that the encryption may be even stronger) and a better way to address the memory could be future improvements of this encryption method.

References

1. http://www.truecrypt.org/docs/?s=encryption-algorithms

2. http://www.mycrypto.net/encryption/crypto_algorithms. html

3. http://www.encryptedusb.net/Software_vs_Hardware_Ba   sed_USB_encryption.html

4. Quartus II Web Edition is available at: https://www.altera.com/support/software/download/altera_d esign/quartus_we/dnl-quartus_we.jsp

SQL Generation for Natural Language Interface

László Kovács

ABSTRACT

A hot issue in the area of database management is to provide a high level interface for non-technical users. An important research direction is the application of natural language interface. The paper presents an interface module that converts user's query given in natural language into a corresponding SQL command. After clustering the input sentence, a push-down automaton is used to verify the syntax. The corresponding SQL code is generated by a semantic matcher module.

Keywords: NLP, NLI, SQL, formal grammar

Introduction

One area of research efforts in the query interfaces is focused on improving the usability. The main goal is to provide a high level interface that can be used by non-technical users without any requested DBMS oriented knowledge. An important area in this direction is the application of natural language interface for databases (NLIDB). The NLIDB means that a user can use some natural language to create query expressions and also the answer is presented in the same language. The history of NLIDB goes back as early as 1960's [2]. The era of peak research activity on NLIDB was in the 1980's. In that time, the development of a domain and language independent NLIDB module seemed as a realistic task. The proto-type projects showed that the building of a natural language interface is a much more complex task than it was expected.

Regarding the usability of NLIDB, there can be found some tests in the litera-ture that evaluates the efficiency of the NLI interfaces. In these tests the NLIDB is compared with traditional interfaces like SQL [1]. The results show that expert users can perform more efficiently the special command interface (SQL) than the NLI in-terface [6]. On the other hand, the un-experienced users could achieve better results with the NLI interface than with the imperative SQL interface. A similar result was experienced with the NLI interface for spreadsheet management [7] too.

In the years around the millennium the situation of NLIDB can be character-ized on one hand with the decreased interest on theory of general NLIDB (due to the disappointment in the research results to generate a general NLIDB), and on the other hand with the increased number of domain specific commercial prod-ucts and with the high activity on studying the natural language in general [3]. In the recent years, a lot of new related research areas has arisen and improved. The potential application area of domain specific NLIDB is unlimited. The research projects cover among others the scientific databases (chemistry, biology, geology, mathematics, physics,...), the libraries and the WEB queries.

Background

The late sixties and early seventies were an active period in database research. The first NLIDB research projects for databases used a domain specific engine like the LUNAR [2] system (1972) that contained data on chemical analysis of moon rocks. In the next decades the number of test systems increased and also the first general NLIDB applications appeared. The RENDEZVOUS (1977) [4] system was one of the first general purpose NLIDB modules. A key element of the de-velopments was to provide database independence (see LADDER [2]) and large flexibility in the grammar's usage (see ASK [2]).

Based on the success of Chomsky's transformational language model, the grammar oriented approaches have gained a great importance. Related to the viewpoint of generative linguistics, the most appropriate tools to process the sen-tences are the declarative logical programming languages. One of the first members of this group is the CHAT-80 [1] project. One of the commercial NLIDB products is the ELF [5] system. It provides an interface to the Access desktop database. The system understands plain-English queries and transforms it into SQL commands. A popular NLIDB interface is the English Query [5] from the Microsoft Its language repository is open, the mapping to the underlying database is generated manually by the developers. Its semantic modeling system stores the relationships between the database objects and the language elements. The natural language commands are translated into the corresponding SQL commands. Beside the mentioned systems, there are a lot of pilot NLIDB systems like INTELLECT, ASKjeeves or Ianywhere.

Our methodology is related to the current approaches of Giordani [12] and Tikk [13]. In the model of Giordani the sentences are represented by parsing trees. The training pool consists of pair of parsing trees: one tree (NLT) for the sentence in natural language, the other one (SQT) is for the sentence in SQL. There is a knowledge base to store the relationships between the nodes of NLT and SQT. For a new input NL sentence, a similar NLT is searched from the knowledge base. To measure the syntactic similarity between the pairs of trees tree kernel structures are used which computes the number of common substructures. The significance of work [13] is that it creates an efficient NL module for the Hungarian language. The system accepts only simple, well-formed interrogative sentences with a question word from a given list. The engine incorporates several sub-modules to perform a deeper analysis of the sentences. The morphological parser identifies the multi-word tokens of the input sentence and assigns part of speech labels to the tokens. The recognition of multi-word tokens is performed base don decreasing size of expression. The second part of the NL module groups related tokens in brackets. The context recognizer gets bracketed sentence alternatives as input. This module generates SQL like Context Language sentence alternatives. The main information elements during the context recognition are the attribute names, entity names type of entities, verbs used in the query and attribute values.

These approaches show the importance of two base components: first, a deep linguistic and morphologic analysis is required in the case of Hungarian language and second, the similarity based schema matching is an effective way to reduce the computational costs of the engine.

Grammar Model

The test language of the investigation is the Hungarian language which has a very complex grammar. The Hungarian language belongs to the family of agglomerative languages, where a stem word can be extended with several suffixes. During the joining of suffixes the chaining of tags may cause inflection of the root part. For example, the word

kutyáimmal

can be translated into the following expression:

with my dogs,

where

> *kutya*: stem(dog),
>
> *kutyá-im:* plural + genitive (my dogs),
>
> *kutyáim-mal:* preposition (with).

The second difficulty of the target language is the free word order, the ordering of the words within a sentence has only few constraints. The sentences:

> *Én olvasok egy könyvet a szobában,*
>
> *Olvasok egy könyvet a szobában,*
>
> *Egy könyvet olvasok a szobában,*
>
> *Könyvet olvasok a szobában,*
>
> *Egy könyvet olvasok én a szobában,*
>
> *A szobában olvasok egy könyvet,*
>
> *A szobában én olvasok egy könyvet,*
>
> *A szobában könyvet olvasok,*
>
> *A szobában egy könyvet olvasok*

are all grammatically correct and have only slight differences in the meaning (*I am reading a book in the room*).

Chomsky introduced four types of formal grammars in terms of their generative power known as Chomsky-hierarchy. A hotly contested issue over several decades has been the question where natural languages are located within this hierarchy. Chomsky showed [8] that NLs are not regular and he also presumed that NLs are not context-free. On the other hand, context sensitive languages are not adequate for practical use, as they can take up to exponential time to simulate on computers. Thus, the most approaches are based on grammar between context-free and context-sensitive levels. The traditional grammar formalism like TAG [9], HMM [10] are usually effective for languages with strict word ordering and with low set of acceptable words, but they are inefficient for larger size problems. The grammars like dependency grammar[10] or word grammar are strong on handling flexible structure but their implementation details are not well explored yet.

To cope with the complexity problem, the probabilistic context free grammar was selected. A context-free grammar G=(A,V,P) over an alphabet of terminals A is composed of a finite alphabet V of nonterminals and a finite set $P \subseteq V \notin V \times (V \cup A)^*$ of production rules. The production rules are given in the form $u \rightarrow v$ where u is nonterminal symbol and v is a sequence of terminal and nonterminal symbols. The context-free grammar can be represented with a push¬down automaton. The push-down automaton is based on the LIFO processing model and has the following formal description:

P(Q,S,G,P,q,F),

where

Q: set of states

S: the alphabet of the language

G: the alphabet of the automaton

P: set of transition rules

q: initial state

F: final states.

At each phase of the sentence processing, the state of the automaton is given with a triplet (w,q,s), where w: the input sequence to be processed, q: state of the automaton, s: content of the stack.

If for a given v terminal symbol several production rules exist, the model is called probabilistic CGF model (PCGF). The main benefits of PCFG model is that it can be learned from positive data alone and it provides a robust grammar. Although the averaged entropy related to the PCFG model is higher than of n-gram models, a combination of PCGF and HMM models should superior to the traditional models [11].

Conversion of NL into SQL

The NLIDB module has the task to convert a command given in natural language into SQL statements. This transformation is done usually in several distinct steps. The main components of the module are [3] shown in Fig 1.

The main goal of the engine is to convert the user's input given in natural language into an SQL command. The conversion usually based on four different base repositories:

• language dependent grammar base,

• domain specific semantic repository,

- database specific semantic repository,
- SQL specific grammar base.

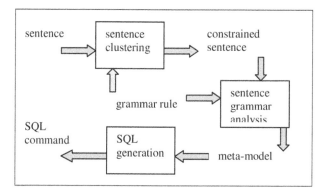

Figure 1. Engine schema

The conversion engine consists of four main modules to perform the conversion steps. The first module takes the user's input sentence and converts it into a sentence of the controlled language. The second module is for the checking the this generated sentence. The elements of the syntactically correct sentences are mapped into the concepts of the database domain in the third conversion module. The fourth module generates the SQL command from the semantic description.

The main module of the conversion engine performs a syntax checking of the incoming sentence. The syntax checking is based primary on the PCFG grammar. As the grammar tree of the full language is too complex, the full grammar can not be involved into the parser module. In order to cope with the complexity problem, the module involves only the grammar of a controlled Hungarian language. The restriction is based on the following elements:

- limited word pool,
- restricted ordering of words,
- limited inflection.

The PCFG grammar is stored in a normalized Chomsky format using the XML standard. The Chomsky normal form means that the right side of the production rule consists of only one or two symbols. The grammar is stored in a grammar tree where the parsing of sentence uses a top-down and left-to-right traversing of the tree. The stack stores the path to the current node under investigation. A rule node has a form

$$v \rightarrow w^*$$

where w* expression can contain some wildcard symbols to define

- type of inflection
- type of stem
- type of matching

For example, the rule

$$(1, "FBN", "FN[NOM] \ FNNM[NOM]", "2")$$

has the following meaning:

- FBN is terminal symbol
- It should match either to FN[NOM] or to FNNM[NOM]
- The internal checking routine with id #2 should be called for extra constraint validation
- FNNM[NOM] means that the stem is noun or pronoun and is in nominative case.

The PCFG parser module is based on the word stemmer module. The Humorph parser is used to determine the stem part and the different inflection components for a given input word. For example, for the input word 'fizetése'(his salary), the following output is generated:

$$fizetés[FN]+e[PSe3] + [NOM].$$

The list of stems and morphemes can be used to determine the semantic roles of a given word.

As the applied PCFG repository describes only a subpart of grammatically and semantically valid sentences, the incoming sentences should first converted into controlled format. The mapping is based on a clustering approach. The cluster centers are sentence schemas where each schema is a parameterized sentence. The rules have the general form:

$$s \rightarrow s'$$

where s is a normal parameterized input sentence and s' is the parameterized sentence of the controlled language. Let us take the following sample:

"hogyannevezik nevezzükDET#1#$E[ACC][PL]" → *"kérem a #$1tanárok# nevEt"*

In this sentence, the input sentence should consist of four words:

first word: fix word '*hogyan*',
second word: fix word '*nevezik*' or '*nevezzük*'
third word: determinant,

fourth word: *#1#E[ACC][PL]:* a parameter with id number 1, it should be of type E (entity name) and it is in a plural and accusative case.

The output sentence consists of four words, where the # separator symbol denotes the parameter substitution. The substation expression may contain some additional inflection rules and a default value too. Taking the input sentence:

Hogyan nevezik a tanárokat?

is converted into the output sentence

Kérem a tanárok nevét.

Having the sentence of the controlled language, the sentence elements will be mapped to the concepts of database domains. There are several tables for semantic level mapping:

- synonyms for the database concepts

- synonyms for the relationships

- relationship between the question words and database concepts

- relationship between basic question sentences and database concepts

The mapping for question words is given in the form

$$w \rightarrow (d,w')$$

where w is a question word, d is the domain of interpretation and w' is a list of substitution concepts. For example, in the rule

"mi","","TANTARGYAK","TARGYNEV"

the word 'tantargyak' denotes a table name (a domain) and the word 'targynev' is a fieldname (a concept name). The word 'mi' denotes a question word (what).

The SQL command generator application is developed in Java. The input of the program is the NL sentence, and there are output fields for the sentence of the controlled language and for the generated SQL command. The developed SQL generator program can be used for several purposes. First, it can be used as a module in a e-learning tool to train the SQL commands. The second application area is the intelligent database query interfaces for non-technical users. In domains like tourism, public transport ad-hoc and flexible queries should be supported.

In the current prototype system, the domain independent and domain specific repositories are all generated on manual way. This is a major restriction regarding the extension of the method to larger domains. In order to cope with this efficiency limits, the next phase of the project focuses on automated repository generation from external ontology databases.

Conclusion

In this paper, some results on development of an NLP engine for transforming natural language sentences into SQL commands were presented. The novelty of the approach relates to combination of the following characteristics: processing of the Hungarian language, multi-level stages of command generation and similarity based sentence processing. The generated system provides a flexible and efficient commend generation for a predefined application domain.

References

1. J. Melton and A. R. Simon,"SQL1999 Understanding Relational Language Components," Morgan Kaufmann, 2002.

2. Androutsopoulos, Ritchie and Thanish, "Natural language interfaces to databases-an introduction," Journal of Natural Language Engineering. v1 i1. pp. 29–81 1995.

3. L Kovács and D. Tikk, "Full-text Search Engines for Databases,"Encyclopedia of Artificial Intelligence, IGI Global Publisher, Hersey, 2008.

4. E. Codd: "Access to Relational Database for Causal Users (Rendezvous)," SIGART Newsletter, 1977, pp. 31–32.

5. Popescu, Etzioni and Kautz, "Towards a Theory of Natural Language Interfaces to Databases," ICIUI, 2003, pp. 149–157.

6. Odgen and Bernick, "Using Natural Language Interface," Handbook of Human-Computer Interaction, Elsevier, 1996.

7. A. Shankar and W. Yung, "gNarLI: A Practical Approach to Natural Language Interfaces to Databases," Term report, Harvard University, 2000.

8. N. Chomsky, "Syntactic Structures," Mouton De Gruyter, 1957.

9. A.Joshi,"Tree Adjunct Grammars," Journal of Computer Systems Science," Vol 10, 1975, pp. 136–163.

10. L. Kovács and E. Baksa-Varga, "A semantic model for knowledge base representation in a grammar induction system," CIMCI, 2008.

11. M. Johnson, "PCFG models of linguistic tree representations," Computational Linguistics, 1998, pp. 613–632.

12. Giordani, a.: Mapping Natural Language into SQL in a NLIDB, NLDB 2008, LNCS 5039, pp. 367–371.

13. Tikk, D., Kardkovacs Zs., Magyar G.,Babarczy A. and Szakadát I.: Natural Language Question Processing for Hungarian Deep Web Searcher, 2nd IEEE International Conference on Computational Cybernetics, edited by W. Elmenreich, W. Haidinger, T. Machado. ICCC , pages 303–309.

Web 2.0 Technologies with jQuery and Ajax

**Cornelia Györödi, Robert Györödi, George Pecherle,
Tamas Lorand and Rosu Alin**

ABSTRACT

The development of a web 2.0 portal using Ajax and jQuery techniques. This paper describes the development of a web portal using technologies like PHP, jQuery and Ajax. Regular web portals simply use PHP and MySQL, which is not enough to provide the interactivity the user needs from a web portal. jQuery technique is designed to change the way you write JavaScript, because it is very compact and easy to use and understand. jQuery is also very popular being used by Google, IBM, NBC, Amazon, Wordpress and many others. Ajax technique is used to increase responsiveness and interactivity of the web pages achieved by exchanging small amounts of data « behind the scenes » so that the entire web pages do not have to be reloaded each time there is a need to fetch data from the server.

Keywords: web portals, JavaScript, jQuery, Ajax, PHP, MySQL, HTML, CSS, DOM, XML

Introduction

Web 2.0 seems to be like Pink Floyd lyrics: "it can mean different things to different people, depending on your state of mind" [1]. So Web 2.0 for some people it means moving some of the thinking client side so making it more immediate, but the idea of the Web as interaction between people is really what the Web is. That was what it was designed to be as a collaborative space where people can interact [2]. In fact, it means using the standard which has been produced by all the people working on Web 1.0. It means using the document object model, it means for HTML and SVG and so on, it's using HTTP, so it's building stuff using the Web standards, plus Java script of course.

According to Tim O'Reilly, "Web 2.0 is the business revolution in the computer industry caused by the move to the internet as platform, and an attempt to understand the rules for success on that new platform" [3].

Some technology experts, notably Tim Berners-Lee, have questioned whether one can use the term in a meaningful way, since many of the technology components of "Web 2.0" have existed since the beginnings of the World Wide Web.

A web portal is a site that provides a single function via a web page or site. Web portals often function as a point of access to information on the World Wide Web [14]. The first attempt is to write the web portal in PHP and MySQL only, however the whole idea of the web portal is to be interactive and provide the accesibility that most users need.

This interactivity can be achieved in a very easy and fashionable way, by using a compact language such as jQuery. jQuery technology is a lightweight JavaScript library that emphasizes interaction between JavaScript and HTML. It was released in January 2006 at BarCamp NYC by John Resig. It is free and open source software [15].

jQuery works closely with Ajax, whose main characteristic is to load data on a web page without reloading the entire page. The advantages of Ajax include Bandwidth usage, and separation of data, format, style and function [6]. One downside is that for search engine optimization of web sites using Ajax, you have to provide public sitemaps.

Web 2.0 and the Related Technologies

Democracy and Ajax are the core elements of "Web 2.0" [4]. The shortest definition of it is: "Web 2.0 is made of people" [5]. The key aspects of web 2.0 are:

- The Web and all its connected devices as one global platform of reusable services and data

- Data consumption and remixing from all sources, particularly user generated data

- Continuous and seamless update of software and data, often very rapidly

- Rich and interactive user interfaces

- Architecture of participation that encourages user contribution [5].

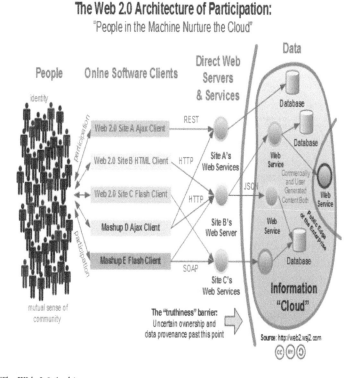

Figure 1. The Web 2.0 Architecture

Ajax, (AJAX—shorthand for "Asynchronous JavaScript and XML,") is a development technique for creating interactive web applications. The intent is to make web pages feel more responsive by exchanging small amounts of data with the server behind the scenes, so that the entire web page does not have to be reloaded each time the user requests a change. This is intended to increase the web page's interactivity, speed, and usability. More information about Ajax you can find in [6], [7] or [8]. The XHR (XMLHttpRequest) object is the core of the Ajax engine. It is the object that enables a page to get data from or post data to the server as a background request, which means that it does not refresh the browser during this process. In figure 2 we present how the classic and the AJAX web applications work (Fig.3).

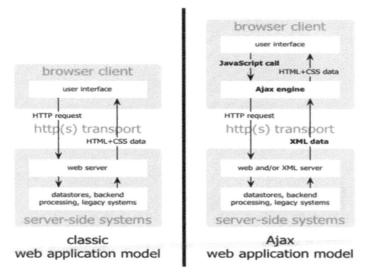

Figure 2. Comparison between classic and AJAX web applications

jQuery is actually an open source JavaScript library that simplifies the interaction between HTML and JavaScript. It is ideal for prototyping, it is completely unobtrusive, uses CSS to layer functionality and it has an easy to separate behavior.

Dave Methvin, Chief Technology Officer at PC Pitstop (a well known community where you can get computer help) says: "You start with 10 lines of jQuery that would have been 20 lines of tedious DOM JavaScript. By the time you are done it's down to two or three lines and it couldn't get any shorter unless it read your mind" [22].

The focus of jQuery can be resumed by "finding some elements" then "doing something with them" [19]. You can find below an example of how a block of text in HTML can be made to fade in with a "slow" effect (Fig. 3).

Applications that act on data are a fundamental of computer science. Historically, these applications have been written in wide variety of programming languages, with an equally wide variety of storage mechanisms for the data. Over time, programming languages evolved to use an essentially hierarchical model (part of the suite of advancements encompassed by object-oriented development). In comparison, the most popular form of reasonably scalable data storage is the relational database tables, columns, and rows model. Developers wind up developing systems to bridge two worlds the hierarchical world of a modern programming language and the tabular world of relational databases.

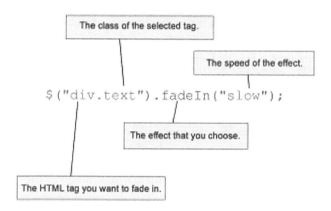

Figure 3. The simplicity of jQuery

MySQL is a database management system distributed, and supported by MySQL AB. MySQL AB is a Swedish commercial company, founded by the MySQL developers, now a subsidiary of Sun Microsystems. MySQL is a relational database management system. MySQL software is Open Source. MySQL has many attractive features to offer: speed, ease of use, query language support, capability, connectivity and security, portability, small size, availability and cost, open distribution and source code.

Client-side scripts are embedded in web pages and executed by the JavaScript interpreter built into browser.

They add extra functionality to an otherwise static HTML page.

JavaScript was developed from a language called LiveScript, which was developed by Netscape for use in its early browsers. JavaScript source code is embedded within the HTML code of web pages and interpreted and executed by the browser when the page is displayed.

HTML (Hypertext Markup Language) it is a markup language that is used to present the data to users through web browsers [11]. Hypertext is ordinary text that has been dressed up with extra features, such as formatting, images, multimedia, and links to other documents. Markup is the process of taking ordinary text and adding extra symbols. These symbols are called tags. "These tags can describe the appearance or layout of the text, but the majority simply describe the content (this is a main heading) and leave many of the appearance and layout decisions to the browser" [10].

CSS (Cascading Style Sheets) is a language that is used to define the way a document's content is presented to the user [10]. Although CSS is mostly used with HTML and XHTML, it can be applied to any kind of XML document, including SVG (Scalable Vector Graphics) and XUL (XML User Interface Language). The presentation is specified with styles that are placed directly into HTML elements, the head of the HTML document, or separate style sheets. Style sheets are constructed from style rules, each rule specifying the way one ore many HTML elements are displayed to the user.

Styling rules can be included directly on HTML's element who's appearance we want to change. This is done by using the style attribute of the element. Also CSS rules can be defined inside the "style" element which is usually used embedded in the head of the document. The third way we can include CSS in a document is by using separate files which are included using the "link" element.

Practical Part

The developed application is a portal for the internal use of a dentistry medical centre for managing the medical activity and the database needed for it.

The principal idea of this application is:

- rich application
- less traffic between client and server
- intuitive interface
- the interface behaviours are more responsive
- the client interacts with the server asynchronously, in this way the data is moved (transferred) between the client and the server without making the user to wait

The Application's Architecture

The Application's Interaction Structure

The current web application is designed for a dentistry medical centre. It can be fragmented in two areas: the first one for the visitors of the web page, and another one for the medical sphere.

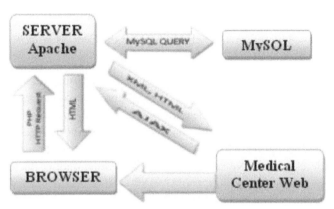

Figure 4. Application architecture & interaction

The Technologies we used

Technologies:

- DOM—Document Object Model—a platform and language independent standard object model
- jQuery & AJAX
- PHP & MySQL—we generated the pages with PHP, loading only the specific part of the HTML code

Languages:

- HTML—markup language
- CSS—stylesheet language
- XML—markup language
- JavaScript & JQuery
- SQL—query language

Prototype is used for Ajax calls, cross-browser calls, easy setting of the sent parameters and the sending options (request method, contentType, encoding, headers), multitude of events for which callback functions can be attached.

Files Used

- index.html is the only html file used. It loads the main page when it is accessed. It contains separate div tags for the two kind of menus (visitors, and medics).

The visitor's menu div contains the links grouped in a table that access the specific pages, and target them to the "mainFrame" frame. These links are:

- "Home Page"—accesses the main page (mainpage.html)
- "Services"—gives information about the Medical Centre's services and the services price list in a dynamic slide (services.html)
- "Schedule"—by selecting a doctor from the list, the visitor can schedule an appointment to the Dentistry Centre. The appointments can be set starting from the next day. The visitor can select the time interval from a dynamically created table. A time interval selected by another visitor cannot be used (that time intervals are highlighted with red, and the free ones with light green). After the registration, an e-mail message is sent to the corresponding doctor to inform him/her. (programming.php)
- "Advices"—the visitor can read advices on how to maintain his/her teeth. This page (advices.html) contains a separate internal frame which contain the bookmarked advices (iframe.html).
- "Contact"—contact information. (contact.php)

The other div tag initially displays the log in form, and dynamically changes the appropriate div tag (dentist's menu, radiologist's menu, administrator's menu, etc.) by AJAX.

The username and password are sent to Login.php that searches for the user then saves the user's ID and "specialization" for managing the access level of the pages. Without this information the user has no access to the medical pages.

When another page is loaded, or when exiting the browser, the user is logged out using AJAX, by calling the login.php, like during log in, or natural log out.

The medical part is more complex. A username and a password are required to log in. Based on the user type, a specific menu becomes accessible. There are three types of menus: for the dentist, for the radiologist and for the administrator. The dentist and the radiologist have a lot of functions to manage the patients. The administrator has the privileges to modify the information saved about the medics, to make changes in the entire medical centre's timetable and to manipulate the online schedule for medics. The administrator can view the medical activity (by using the logs), and can manage IP restrictions, too

There are three types of menus for the medics:

- The doctor's menu (the menu for the dentist and the radiologist that are a little different. The radiologist has no access to the registered users information, so that link was hidden):
- "Schedules"—(Schedules.PHP): the medic can add, view, modify or delete the scheduled patients. When accessed, the PHP script looks for the user ID in the "Timetable" table, to show the current user timeline then look for the ID

in "Schedule" table to dynamically update the scheduled tasks. The light green background of the cell means that the doctor is working, so those cells are activated and they can be selected; the red ones mean the doctor has a scheduled task, the gray ones mean the medic is not in the Centre. When a green cell is clicked, the system dynamically saves the patient information and the timestamp into the "Schedule" table. The mouse-over event on the red table shows who was registered to that timestamp, and the onclick event can delete the scheduled task.

• "Patient Administration" dynamically shows a small menu for patient administration. Here the dentist can view and add patients to the registry. Only the dentist can manage the registered patients, and make the monthly report. When accessing the "Registry" menu, the "Registry.PHP" is loaded into the "main-Frame," and displays his registry, looking for id in the "Registry" table where all the registry inputs of all the doctors are saved. The numbering for patient entry is separate for all doctors. On the registry.php file, there is the list of the doctor's registry, and an input tag, where we can make a search by the name of a patient. On the keypress event of the tag, an AJAX function is called, for searching suggestions. By selecting a user from the suggestions, the table is filtered, and only that user is displayed.

When accessing the "Add to registry" menu, the "Addreg.php" file is accessed, and opened in a small popup window. Here you will see a set of fields for the patient information. The first input tag, designed for the name has suggestion options, too. When a user from the suggestion list is selected, all his data is automatically entered in the form and the doctor must only fill in the treatment fields.

The "Price" field is filled automatically depending on the "Treatment code" field. If the patient is under 18 and wasn't registered, a prompt appears to confirm if you want to add to the registered patients list. If the question is answered positively, the cost is replaced from the pricelist for registered users, and the patient is added to the registry. Then a new popup window appears to enter the information needed to register the patient. This popup window has two div tags, one for the necessary information to register, and another for more information about the patient teeth. The doctor can enter more such information for the patient. When this popup window is active another one isn't accessible.

The "Records" menu accesses the "Records.PHP" and displays a list of the registered patients. This page contains an input tag with suggestion options, too. When a patient from the list below is clicked, a little popup appears with other necessary information of the patient. On this popup you can modify information about the patient, and in the top right corner, there is a little icon to delete the patient.

The "Monthly Report" menu shows a list of the treatments for all registered patients during a specified month. (Report.PHP)

"Timetable Edit"—to modify the timing for the current doctor. (Edit_timetable.php)

The administrator's menu:

- "Medics"—can manage (add, modify, delete) medic's information, and view their status (online/offline). By selecting this menu, the Administration.PHP file is accessed, with a parameter to show this content. All of the medics are listed, with their personal information. By clicking on a medic, their information is loaded into the above input tags for editing. Each row has a delete button to delete the selected doctor.

- "Schedules"—can manage the schedules of all the doctors. The Adminstration.PHP is accessed by another specific parameter then by selecting a doctor from the drop-down list, an internal frame appears for the selected doctor. All the operations that can be done by the medic can also be done by the administrator.

- "Center Timetable"—can modify the entire Centre's timetable. The Administration.PHP file is used with another parameter to read the schedules saved by the medics. This information is saved in input tags for editing.

- "Frauds"—can view and delete the restricted IP addresses saved in the "Denied" table.

- "Log events"—on log in, log out, or unauthorised access the log.db file is updated. This file is displayed here.

- jQuery.JS, jQuery.form.JS—the jQuery language and one of its plugin used for the login form [16].

- Disablestatus.JS—to hide the status window content

- Testinput.JS—Used in Addreg.PHP, Addpac.PHP to validate the forms before zending them.

- Suggest.JS—To show suggestions when the user is searching for a patient.

Some of the possible operations are:

- View—the data is fetched from the server into a JSON array, a FilteringTable is being created with the corresponding data. First of all, the column names are brought and then the data for each row in the FilteringTable that correspond to a record from a table in the database. The primary key from the database table is used to uniquely identify each row in the FilteringTable.

- Add—a FilteringTable is loaded with existing data from the target table. For adding, comboboxes or textboxes are used as follows: if the target table does not have foreign keys, the components used are textboxes otherwise the connections between two tables are made by a previous loading of the comboboxes with the value and the id.

- Delete—data from the server is loaded in a FilteringTable and below it an empty one is build. The rows wanted to be deleted, respectively the corresponding records are dragged in the bottom table making usage of the drag and drop feature of another JavaScript library named Dojo. If the administrator changes his mind and doesn't want anymore to delete a record he can drag the corresponding row back to the original table. After all desired rows to be deleted were dragged, the delete button can be used and after the delete confirmation the records are deleted from the database.

- Edit—when the administrator selects a row from the initial loaded FilteringTable, data from that row is populating the comboboxes respectively the textboxes, and then he can edit the text in the textboxes or can chose another option in the comboboxes, after all this he can save the changes made.

Conclusion

This portal gives us a very good example of the advantages of using Ajax. We could have built the web page in a classical way without using web 2.0. In the classical way is reloaded on almost every action of the client, which results in a higher traffic between the client and the server and an unpleasant experience for the user. This portal gives us a very good example of the advantages of using Ajax and jQuery. It is meant to be a practical guide for those looking to make quality web portals quickly and without having to write a lot of code. The technologies and the model presented in this article are an example and a starting point for those who need to develop such a system, using new, easy-to-use and advanced web programming techniques and languages.

References

1. Kevin Maney, Technologie—"Tech people appear hyped about their industry again," on http://www.usatoday.com/tech/columnist/kevinmaney/2005-10-11-tech-industry_x.htm

2. Tim Berners-Lee, Wendy Hall, James Hendler, Nigel Shadbolt, Daniel J. Weitzner—"Creating a Science of the Web". Science 313, 11 August 2006.

3. John Musser with Tim O'Reilly–"Web 2.0 Principles and Best Practices" An O'Reilly Radar Report, November 2006, ISBN 0-596-52769-1.

4. Paul Graham—"Web 2.0," on http://www.paulgraham.com/web20.html

5. Dion Hinchcliffe's Web 2.0 Blog—"The State of Web 2.0," 2 April 2006.

6. http://en.wikipedia.org/wiki/AJAX

7. http://www.w3schools.com/ajax/default.asp

8. Kris Hadlock—"Sams Ajax for Web Application Developers," Sams Publisher, 2006.

9. http://tomcat.apache.org

10. CSS—http://en.wikipedia.org/wiki/CSS

11. HTML—http://en.wikipedia.org/wiki/Html

12. Marty Hall, Larry Brown—"Core Web Programming" (Second Edition), The Sun Microsystems Press, 2001.

13. Russ Weakley—"Sams Teach Yourself CSS in 10 Minutes," Sams Publishing, 2005.

14. Web portal—http://en.wikipedia.org/wiki/Web_portal

15. jQuery—http://en.wikipedia.org/wiki/Jquery

16. Use jQuery Javascript library to make easy effects for your website—http://www.nowcss.com/articles/use-jquery-javascript-library-to-make-easy-effects-for-your-website

17. Bear Bibeault, Yehuda Katz—"jQuery in Action", February 2008, Manning Publications, ISBN: 1933988355.

18. Karl Swedberg, Jonathan Chaffer—"Learning jQuery : Better Interaction Design and Web Development with Simple JavaScript Techniques", July 2007, ISBN 1847192505.

19. John Resig—"Building Interactive Prototypes with jQuery" http://ejohn.org/files/jquery-atmedia.pdf

20. PHP—http://en.wikipedia.org/wiki/PHP

21. MySQL—http://en.wikipedia.org/wiki/MySQL

22. jQuery official website—http://jquery.com/

Reconfigurable Computing – A New Paradigm

Erica Mang, Ioan Mang and Popescu-Rotoiu Constantin

ABSTRACT

Computational science applications and advanced scientific computing have made tremendous gains in the past decade. Researchers are regularly employing the power of large computing systems and parallel processing to tackle larger and more complex problems in all of the physical sciences. For the past decade or so, most of this growth in computing power has been "free" with increased efficiency more-or-less governed by Moore's Law. However, increases in performance are becoming harder to achieve due to the complexity of the parallel computing platforms and the software required for these systems. Reconfigurable computing, or heterogeneous computing, is offering some hope to the scientific computing community as a means to continued growth in computing capability.

Keywords: morphware, flowware, configware, recon-figurable computing, FPGA

Introduction

The von Neumann architecture (vN) is a design model for a stored-program digital computer that uses a processing unit and a single separate storage structure to hold both instructions and data. The general structure of a vN machine consists of: 1) a memory for storing program and data. Harvard architectures contain two parallel accessible memories for storing program and data separately; 2) a control unit (also called control path) featuring a program counter that holds the address of the next instruction to be executed; 3) an arithmetic and logic unit (also called data path) in which instructions are executed. The main advantage of the vN computing paradigm is its flexibility, because it can be used to program almost all existing algorithms. However, each algorithm can be implemented on a vN computer only if it is coded according to the vN rules. With the fact that all algorithms must be sequentially programmed to run on a vN computer, many algorithms cannot be executed with their potential best perfor-mance. Algorithms that usually perform the same set of inherent parallel operations on a huge set of data are not good candidates for implementation on a vN machine. The von Neumann (figure 1) basic common model [11] lost its dominance decades ago [3], also having been criticized for being overhead-based. In industry it has been replaced by a cooperation of vN CPU and non-vN accelerators. Today, the micro-processor has become the tail wagging the dog and the basic accelerator model is data-stream-based—not instruction-stream-based. Also, since 2006, RC is also a hot spot in supercomputing, mostly FPGA-based.

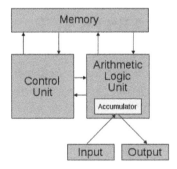

Figure 1. von Neumann architecture

The separation between the CPU and memory leads to the Von Neumann bottleneck, the limited throughput (data transfer rate) between the CPU and memory compared to the amount of memory. In most modern computers, throughput is much smaller than the rate at which the CPU can work. This seriously limits the effective processing speed when the CPU is required to perform minimal processing on large amounts of data. The CPU is continuously forced to wait for needed data to be transferred to or from memory. Since CPU speed and memory size have increased much faster than the throughput between them, the bottleneck has become more of a problem.

The traditional hardware/software distinguishes software running on programmable computing engines (microprocessors) driven by instruction streams scanned from RAM, and application-specific fixed hardware like accelerators which are not programmable after fabrication. The operations of accelerators are primarily driven by data streams and are needed because of the microprocessor's performance limits caused by the sequential nature of its operation.

The contemporary common model of computing systems is the cooperation of microprocessor and its accelerators including an interface between both (figure 2) [8]. This model holds not only for embedded systems, but also for the PC needing accelerators not only for running its own display. The accelerators are a kind of slaves. Operating system and other software is running on the microprocessor, which is the host and master of the accelerators. The host may send parameters (like for mode select, start, stop, reset etc.) and receive interrupts and some result data. Such accelerator design is affected by the 2nd design crisis. Compared to microprocessor design the SoC (System on Chip) design productivity in terms of gates per day is slower by a factor of about 10-4 [7]. Another symptom of increasing design implementation problems and the silicon technology crisis is the drastically decreasing number of wafer starts for newer technology fabrication and the still decreasing low number of ASIC design starts. Another major cost factor of the application-specific silicon needed for accelerators is increasing mask cost, driven by growing wafer size and the growing number of masks needed. ASIC (application-specific IC) stands for mask-configurable gate arrays and similar methodologies.

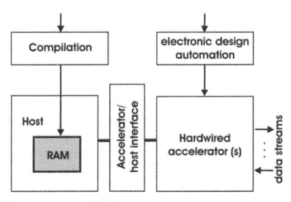

Figure 2. Embedded microprocessor model.[8]

The gap between vN type procedural compute engines and application-specific hardware is morph-ware, the fastest growing segment of the semiconductor market. Morphware is the new computing paradigm, the alternative RAM-based general purpose computing platform model. Morphware is a term used for reconfigurable hardware, for instance a FPGA or a Reconfigurable datapath array. A morphware unit can be structurally programmed from configware sources compiled into configware code to be downloaded into the hidden RAM of the morphware unit. Compared to application-specific hardwired hardware, morphware provides flexibility and avoids the need for expensive application-specific silicon. So we need two kinds of input sources: traditional software for programming instruction streams, and, configware (Configuration Ware) for structural reconfiguration of morphware. So, configware is the program source for morphware, i. e. for reconfigurable platforms like FPGAs (field-programmable gate arrays), or, to coarse-grained reconfigurable platforms like reconfigurable datapath arrays (rDPAs). Software is the counterpart to configware. In contrast to software which is instruction-stream-based and deserves procedural programming for instruction scheduling onto von-Neumann-like machine resources, configware deserves structural programming like e. g. for placement and routing before the application run time [8].

By introducing morphware we obtain a new general model of embedded computers the accelerator has become reconfigurable. With a morphware accelerator the host may also use the host/accelerator interface to organize the reconfiguration process. Also mixed-type accelerators are possible: hardware and morphware.

There are two classes of morphware: fine grain reconfigurable morphware, and, coarse grain reconfigurable morphware. Reconfigurability of fine granularity means, that the functional blocks have a datapath width of about one bit what means, that programming at low abstraction level is logic design. All products on the market are FPGAs (field-programmable gate arrays, called FRGAs or rGAs: ((field-) reconfigurable gate arrays). Modern FRGAs support mapping entire systems onto the chip by offering on board all components needed. In contrast to fine grain morphware using CLBs of smallest datapath width, coarse grain morphware uses reconfigurable Data Path Units (rDPUs) with wide data paths (for instance, 32 bit path width). Instead of FRGAs we have rDPAs (reconfigurable DPU Arrays).

Reconfigurable computing is a new computing paradigm that bridges the gap between software and hardware, combining the high performance of hardware with the flexibility of software. Reconfigurable computing technologies offer the promise of substantial performance gains over traditional architectures via the customizing, even at run-time, the topology of the underlying architecture to match the specific needs of a given application. This type of computing is based upon Field Programmable Gate Arrays (FPGAs). These devices contain an array of computational elements whose functionality is determined through multiple SRAM configuration bits. These elements, also known as logic blocks, are connected using a set of routing resources that are also programmable. In this way, custom circuits can be mapped to the FPGA by computing the logic functions of the circuit within the logic blocks, and using the configurable routing to connect the blocks together to form the necessary circuit.

Morphware in Computing Sciences

The growth rate of algorithmic complexity, whereas the growth rate of microprocessor integration density and the improvement o computational efficiency has slowed down and goes toward a saturation. The performance requirements for wireless communication is jumping up by huge steps from device generation to device generation. Also in a number of other application areas, like multimedia, or, scientific computing for instance, suffer from similar growth of requirements. Conventional systems for high-performance computing (HPC) have grown into mammoth structures with concomitant requirements for power and cooling, where reliability is a challenge due to the massive number of components involved. A highly promising alternative is the microprocessor interfaced to a suitable coarse grain array, maybe for converting a PC into a PS (personal supercomputer). But such a PS will be accepted by the market only, when it comes along with a good co-compiler, the feasibility of which has been demonstrated.

The future of the microprocessor is no more very promising: only marginal improvements can be expected for performance area efficiency. Power dissipation is going worse, generation by generation. Pipelined execution units within vN machines yield only marginal benefit for the price of sophisticated speculative scheduling strategies. Multi-threading needs substantial overhead required for any kind of multiplexing [4]. All these bad messages add to old limitations like the vN bottleneck [4]. Because of the increasing weakness of the microprocessor we need a new computing paradigm as an auxiliary resource to cooperate with the microprocessor. Morphware came just in time. Future acceptance of stand-alone operation of morphware is not very likely. Adding a rDPA and a good co-compiler to a microprocessor enables the PC to become a PS (personal supercomputer).

About Reconfigurable Computer Architectures

Reconfigurable computing is defined as the study of computation using reconfigurable devices. For a given application, at a given time, the spatial structure of the device will be modified such as to use the best computing approach to speed up that application. If a new application has to be computed, the device structure will be modified again to match the new application. Contrary to the vN computers, which are programmed by a set of instructions to be executed sequentially, the structure of reconfigurable devices are changed by modifying all or part of the hardware at compile-time or at run-time, usually by downloading a socalled bitstream into the device.

Configuration respectively reconfiguration is the process of changing the structure of a reconfigurable device at star-up-time respectively at run-time. Progress in reconfiguration has been amazing in the last two decades. This is mostly due to the wide acceptance of the Field Programmable Gate Array (FPGAs) that are now established as the most widely used reconfigurable devices.

Todman et al. [7] provided a 5-class classification of RC architectures as shown in Figure 3 (a) to (e). The first four classes are characterized by the physical presence of a single controlling processor. They differ in the way that the processor communicates with the reconfigurable fabric (RF) of the system. The structure in figure a because of this simplicity, it is by far the most common RC architecture found in commercial systems. Here, reconfigurable fabrics are connected to the processor through its system I/O bus. Although it provides the least data bandwidth between the processor and the RF, it is easiest to implement. Figure b and c depict systems that incorporate RF into two different locations within the processor's memory subsystem.

Data bandwidth between the processor and the RF is usually the performance bottleneck of a system. Figure d shows a system that integrates RF directly into the data path of the controlling processor as functional units. It allows the RF to have access to all local information about the running processor, such as the register file. Such tight integration ensures maximum integration between software and hardware. Figure e represents a new class of RC that is made only possible with advances in reconfigurable hardware technologies. Instead of connecting reconfigurable fabrics to a processor system, these machines embed processors within reconfigurable fabrics. These embedded processors can either be implemented physically or as soft processors. Soft processors are processors that are built as needed by an application using reconfigurable hardware. This class of RC system has the benefit of allowing a user to determine the type and number of processors needed in the system, especially by using soft processor, thereby increasing system performance and efficiency. Most importantly, this class of system breaks away from the processor-centric compute model in the previous 4 classes of systems. Figure 3 illustrates the sixth class of system that consists of two or more machines in the previous 5 classes connected through a direct network [2]. On a system level, these systems share similar properties such as system topology and routing strategies with conventional multi-processor systems. However, because of the proximity of computational fabric to the network, RC systems provide much higher potential performance benefit over multi-processor systems. For example, sending a word of data from a hardware application on one FPGA to another directly connected FPGA takes only a few clock cycles for synchronization. If the system is fully synchronized, latency can potentially be further reduced to zero cycle, virtually doubling the size of the FPGA. By shifting away from the sequential compute model of the controlling processor, this class of system has much higher performance potential than the previous four.

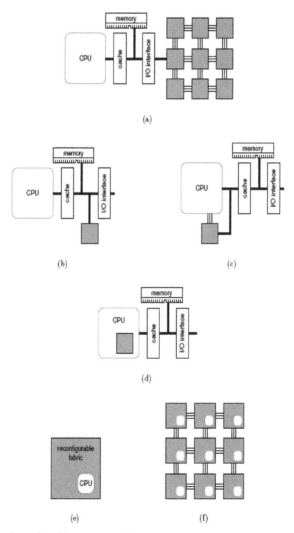

Figure 3. 6 classes of reconfigurable computer architectures.

One of the most important structures that differen-tiate a reconfigurable computer from a conventional processor-based system is its reconfigurable fabric [9]. Many different types of reconfigurable fabrics have been proposed in the literature but most widely used fabric is the field programmable gate array (FPGA).

The configuration granularity of a reconfigurable hardware fabric affects its flexibility in implementing different logic functions. There is always a trade-off between flexibility and efficiency of the fabric. Fine grain reconfigurable fabrics are very flexible. They can be used to implement any sequential and combinational Boolean logic function, but are slower and physically bigger in general. On the other hand, coarse grain reconfigurable fabrics are faster, occupy smaller areas, but are limited to implementing only one of the predefined functions. Some reconfigurable fabrics, such as modern FPGAs, contain a mix of both fine grain and coarse grain reconfigurable units. For example, Xilinx Virtex-4 FPGAs [13] contain dedicated blocks. This block can be programmed by the user to perform a combination of multiplication, addition or subtraction. Although the same functions could have been implemented using general fine-grain programmable fabrics on the FPGA, having such dedicated blocks result in designs that are smaller, faster, and consume less energy. The correct mix of coarse grain and fine grain reconfigurable units is highly application specific. As a reconfigurable computing platform, designers must adjust the mix according to the area, power and performance requirements for the target application domain.

Field Programmable Gate Array (FPGA) is one of the most readily available commercial programmable logic devices. Starting as ASIC replacements similar to other PLDs, FPGAs have slowly evolved into complex embedded system platforms that are flexible and are able to deliver performances comparable to ASICs. Reconfigurable devices can be used in a wide number of fields, and reconfiguration can be of great interest for: rapid prototyping, In-System Customization, Multi-modal Computation, Adaptive Computing Systems.

Reconfigurable computers are sometimes difficult to be classified because their machines can be reconfigured to compute in many different modes. This is particularly true for fine-grain reconfigurable hardware such as FPGAs. For instance, one design may choose to configure an FPGA into a shared memory multi-processor system using soft processors, while another design requires the same FPGA to be configured as a fully synchronous data flow machine.

Cryptography on FPGAs

Most cryptographic algorithms function more efficiently when implemented in hardware than in software. Here are some potential advantages of recon-figurable hardware (RCHW) in cryptographic applications:

Algorithm Agility—refers to the switching of cryptographic algorithms during operation of the targeted application. Advantages of algorithm independent protocols are: ability to delete broken algorithms, choose algorithms according to certain preferences, ability to add new algorithms. Whereas algorithm agility is costly with traditional hardware, FPGAs can be reprogrammed on-the-fly.

Algorithm Upload—fielded devices are upgraded with a new encryption algorithm e.g. the product has to be compatible to new applications. From a cryptographical point of view, algorithm upload can be necessary because a current algorithm was broken, a new standard was created or that the list of ciphers in an algorithm independent protocol was extended.

Architecture Efficiency—the more specific an algorithm is implemented the more efficient it can become. FPGAs allow design and optimization with specific parameter set. Due to the nature of FPGAs, the application can be changed totally or partially.

Resource Efficiency—The majority of security protocols are hybrid protocols. It means, that a public-key algorithm is used to transmit the session key. After the key was established a private-key algorithm is needed for data encryption. Since the algorithms are not used simultaneously, the same FPGA device can be used for both through run-time reconfiguration.

Algorithm Modification—There are applications which require modification of standardized cryptographic algorithms or to customize block cipher such as DES or AES with proprietary S-boxes for certain applications.

Throughput—Modular arithmetic operations include for example exponentiation and multiplication, squaring, inversion, and addition for elliptic curve cryptosystems. FPGA implementations have the potential of running substantially faster than software implementations.

Cost Efficiency—There are two cost factors, that have to be taken into consideration, when analyzing the cost efficiency of FPGAs: cost of development and unit prices. The costs to develop an FPGA implementation of a given algorithm are much lower than for an ASIC implementation, because one is actually able to use the given structure of the FPGA (e.g. look-up table) and one can test the reconfigured chip endless times without any further costs. This results in a shorter time-to-market period, which is nowadays an important cost factor. The unit prices are not so significant when comparing them with the development costs. However, for high-volume applications, ASIC solutions usually become the more cost-efficient choice.

In [10] we presented a hardware implementation of RC6 algorithm using VHDL (VHSIC Hardware Description Language). For this implementation we use Xilinx Foundation Software and VIRTEX XCV1000 board family. Figure 4 presents the encryption module.

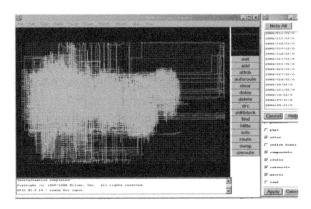

Figure 4. The encryption module of RC6.

Adaptive Cryptographic Systems

Applications like e-commerce, e-government, virtual private network, on-line banking must provide a high degree of security. A large variety of standards, have been developed to provide high security. With this large variety of standards and the customized implementation possibilities for each standard, cryptography can be seen as one of the most versatile application domains of computer science. Depending on criteria such as speed, degree of flexibility and degree of security, single implementations of cryptography application were developed either as software or as intellectual property component.

Flexibility and performance offered by reconfigurable hardware is important in cryptography. Flexibility offers the possibility to use the same hardware to switch from one algorithm to the next one at run-time, according to factors such as the degree of security, the computational speed, the power consumption. Also, according to some parameters, a given algorithm can be tuned. Moreover, algorithms that has been broken and where the security is no more insured can be changed by means of reconfiguration. The system can easily be upgraded to include new standards, developed while the system was already deployed. The corresponding algorithm can therefore be compiled and included in the library of bitstreams for the device configuration. On the other hand, performance can be used to efficiently implement the components, by using the inherent parallelism and building efficient operators for computing Boolean operation on a very large amount of data. This results on a large throughput and a cost efficiency.

The general architecture of an adaptive cryptographic engine proposed by Prasanna and Dandalis [6] [12] basically consists of a database to hold the different configuration that can be downloaded at run-time onto the device, like an FPGA for instance, to perform the computation and a configuration controller to perform the reconfiguration, i.e. downloading the corresponding bitstream form the database into the FPGA. Each bitstream represents a given algorithm implementing a given standard and tuned with some parameters according to the current user's need.

With the recent development in FPGA, it is possible to have a complete system on programmable chip (processor, peripherals, custom hardware components, interconnection) implemented on an FPGA. The configuration controller therefore must no more resides off chip. It can be implemented as custom onchip hardware module or as software running on an embedded processor. Also the possibility to reconfigure only part of the chip opens new possibilities. In the architecture presented in [6] [12], the whole device must be reset on reconfiguration, thus increasing the power consumption because of the amount of the data that must be downloaded on a chip. Power consumption is usually a big problem in mobile environments, and the implementation must consider such issues. Besides this power saving, partial reconfiguration also provides the possibility of keeping a skeleton structure into the device and perform only few modifications at run-time on the basic structure to move from one algorithm to the next one. In [4], a cryptographic application is implemented as exchangeable module of a partial reconfigurable platform. The system, which is based on the AES algorithm consumes only 954 Virtex slices and 3 block RAMS. The cryptographic algorithm is used in this case just as a block to test the partial reconfigurable platform, instead of using the partial reconfiguration to enhance the flexibility of the cryptographic algorithm.

Figure 5 presents a possible architecture of an adaptive cryptography system, using the previous mentioned advantages of partial reconfigurable devices.

The main difference with the architecture presented in [6] is the use of partial reconfiguration, which allows for an integration of all components on a single chip. Also, in contrast to the adaptive architecture for a control system, the loader module resides into the device. Depending on the implementation chosen, the loader can reside inside or outside the device. However, if the configuration happens through the normal SelectMap port, then we need an external loader module for collecting configuration data from the database and copy them on the configuration port.

In figure 5, the architecture is logically divided into two main blocks. A fix one, which remains continuously on the chip. It consist of the parts, which are common to all the cryptographic algorithms in general or common to the algorithms in a given class only. On the figure, we show only one reconfigurable slot; however, it can be implemented as set of configurable blocks, each of which can be changed by means of reconfiguration to realize a given customized standard.

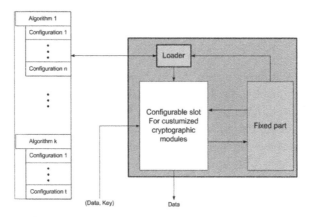

Figure 5. Architecture of an adaptive cryptographic system

The last point concerns the development of building blocks that will be compiled in bitstreams to be downloaded into the device at run-time. A designer is no more required to focus on the hardware implementation of the cryptographic algorithm. A lot of work was done in this direction, and the results are available. We need mostly to focus on the architecture of the overall system and find out how a viable partitioning can be done, according to the reconfiguration scheme. Most of the work have focussed in various implementations of a given approach or the implementations mostly parameterizable and based on the Elliptic Curve approach. Generators for producing a customized description in a hardware description language have been developed for example in [5]. This can be used to generate various configurations that will be used at run-time to move from one implementation to the next one.

Conclusions

The HPC community is currently facing a capability gap that is only going to get worse. There are numerous hardware and software development challenges that lie ahead as we attempt to construct larger computer systems to focus on computational science applications requirements. Reconfigurable computing holds the promise of a solution, but it will take substantial effort to reach maturity.

Morphware has become an essential and indispensable ingredient in SoC (System on a Chip) design and beyond. Already HDLs like VHDL, Verilog, or others, are languages at higher abstraction levels, and should be taught also to CS students. We should not hesitate to reform CS and CSE curricula for avoiding a disqualification for the job market of the near future. Introductory undergraduate programming lab courses should not support the development of a procedural-only mind set. Such courses should rather be a guide to the world of embedded systems requiring the algorithmic cleverness for partitioning an application problem into cooperating software, flowware, and configware blocks.

References

1. T. Todman, G. Constantinides, S. Wilton, O. Mencer, W. Luk, and P. Cheung, "Reconfigurable computing: architectures and design methods," in IEE Proceedings: Computer & Digital Techniques, vol. 152, no. 2, March 2005, pp. 193–208.

2. C. Bobda, Introduction to Reconfigurable Computing, Springer-Verlag, Ed., 2007.

3. A. Burks, H. Goldstein, J. von Neumann: Preliminary discussion of the logical design of an electronic computing instrument; US Army Ordnance Department Report 1946.

4. J. Castillo, P. Huerta, V. López, and J. I. Martínez, "A secure self-reconfiguring architecture based on open-source hardware," reconfig, vol. 0, p. 10, 2005.

5. R. C. C. Cheung, N. J. Telle, W. Luk, and P. Y. K. Cheung, "Customizable elliptic curve cryptosystems." IEEE Trans. VLSI Syst., vol. 13, no. 9, pp. 1048–1059, 2005.

6. A. Dandalis and V. K. Prasanna, "An adaptive cryptographic engine for internet protocol security architectures," ACM Trans. Des. Autom. Electron. Syst., vol. 9, no. 3, pp. 333–353, 2004.

7. P. Gillick: "State of the art FPGA development tools; Reconfigurable Computing Workshop," Orsay, France, Sept. 2003.

8. R. Hartenstein, Morphware and Configware, A. Y. Zomaya, Ed. New York: Springer-Verlag, 2006.

9. Hayden Kwok-Hay So, BORPH: An Operating System for FPGA-Based Reconfigurable Computers," A dissertation for the degree of Doctor of Philosophy, 2007

10. I. Mang, E. Mang, "Hardware Implementation with Off-Line Test Capabilities of the RC6 Block Cipher," 2002 Military Comunications Conference, Anaheim, USA, IEEE Catalog Number: 02CH37397C.

11. http://morphware.net/.

12. V. K. Prasanna and A. Dandalis, "Fpga-based cryptography for internet security." [Online]. Available: halcyon.usc.edu/~pk/prasannawebsite/papers/dandalisOSEE00.pdf.

13. Xilinx, XtremeDSP for Virtex-4 FPGAs User Guide. http://direct.xilinx.com/bvdocs/userguides/ug073.pdf.

In-Network Adaptation of Video Streams Using Network Processors

Mohammad Shorfuzzaman, Rasit Eskicioglu and Peter Graham

ABSTRACT

The increasing variety of networks and end systems, especially wireless devices, pose new challenges in communication support for, particularly, multicast-based collaborative applications. In traditional multicasting, the sender transmits video at the same rate and resolution to all receivers independent of their network characteristics, end system equipment, and users' preferences about video quality and significance. Such an approach results in resources being wasted and may also result in some receivers having their quality expectations unsatisfied. This problem can be addressed, near the network edge, by applying dynamic, in-network adaptation (e.g., transcoding) of video streams to meet available connection bandwidth, machine characteristics, and client preferences. In this paper, we extrapolate from earlier work of Shorfuzzaman et al. 2006 in which we implemented and assessed an MPEG-1 transcoding system on the Intel IXP1200 network processor to consider the feasibility of in-network transcoding for other video formats and network processor architectures. The use of "on-the-fly" video adaptation near the edge of the network offers the promise of simpler support for a wide range of end devices with different display, and so forth, characteristics that can be used in different types of environments.

Introduction

The rapid growth of distributed computing and the Internet has led to demand for collaboration over wide area networks. This demand has been only partially met by existing multimedia and collaborative applications such as video-on-demand, teleconferencing, and telemedicine, which use the Internet for communication. For many such applications, group communication is a core component and the timely transfer of various types of media streams is a requirement.

Multicasting [1] is one of the building blocks of many collaborative applications and provides efficient communication between a single sender and multiple receivers. Messages originating from the sender are duplicated in the network as they are routed to the receivers that constitute the multicast group. Messages are forwarded through the use of a tree of routers called a "multicast tree" that is rooted from the sender, or possibly another predetermined point in the network, and which contains all multicast destinations (i.e., receivers) as leaves.

Initial efforts at implementing multimedia and collaborative applications for well-connected, high-end devices have proven to be successful (ivs [2], nv [3], vat [4], and vic [5] are widely used video and audio conferencing tools deployed over the Internet and the multicast backbone (MBONE) [6]). However, the usability of these new applications has been limited by a number of problems. One problem is how to deal with heterogeneity in the Internet. This heterogeneity, resulting from an increasing variety of networks and end systems, poses new challenges in communication support for collaborative applications. For example, consider a scenario where receivers have end systems ranging from simple, low-power Personal Digital Assistants (PDAs) to high performance workstations. Due to limited processing capabilities or slow network links, low-end receivers may not be capable of handling the same video streams as high-end receivers. Thus, different users in a group may have different requirements with respect to Quality of Service (QoS).

Multicasting performs one-to-many transmission so video is normally transmitted at the same rate to all receivers independent of their network attachment and end systems equipment. This means the source can only generate data at a rate that meets the capability of the most constrained receiver, although receivers having high bandwidth links would be capable of receiving correspondingly higher quality video streams. Additionally, not all the video streams possess equal value to all recipients since receivers may have different levels of interest in the incoming video streams. Unfortunately, most existing collaborative applications are not capable of capturing and exploiting user interest and thus must transmit the same, full quality, video streams to all participants. This approach results in resource wastage. Further, ignoring receivers' interests may also result in some receivers' quality expectations being unsatisfied since bandwidth may be wasted on unimportant streams.

Video adaptation (or transcoding) is a viable solution to these problems. Video streams originating from the source can be transcoded (i.e., modified) dynamically in the network according to the requirements of heterogeneous receivers and the capacity of their access links "downstream" in the multicast tree. Figure 1 illustrates in-network transcoding. Three high performance and one low performance receivers are connected to the video-quality adjustment nodes (i.e., routers) through high and low bandwidth links. The adjustment nodes dynamically adapt the rate of an incoming stream to meet the requirements of the receivers and network links they deliver to.

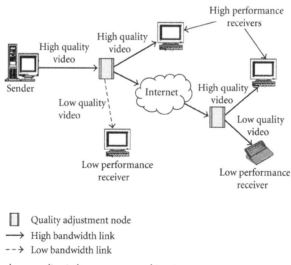

Figure 1. In-network transcoding in heterogeneous multicasting.

Work on active networks [7] has identified a number of issues that suggest that an active network-based approach to dynamic adaptation of video streams could be beneficial. Active networks allow users to inject customized programs into the network nodes and also support individual packets being programmed to perform specific actions as they traverse through the network. In the active networks paradigm, these packets are called "capsules" and they carry not only data but also references to the routines to be invoked at the nodes through which a capsule will pass. In this network model, programmability migrates from the application layer to the network layer and the network and application layers are, essentially, bridged together. Active network services running at the network layer can also exploit such information as knowledge of network topology and load conditions to achieve greater efficiency while application-level schemes can only use indirect metrics like data loss rate to speculate on network conditions.

In this paper, we seek to support the use of a wide range of end devices, varying connection characteristics and different user interests through the use of in-network video transcoding techniques implemented near the network edge in a fashion similar, but not limited, to that of active networks. The edge of the network being the boundary between the core network infrastructure and access network equipment provides an ideal location for doing video adaptation. In our system, video adaptation is done using a video adaptation node. The architecture of our prototype video adaptation node conforms to the node architecture provided by the active networks "reference model" [8].

The recent development of network processors has been motivated by the desire to support high data processing speed and greater programmability (for flexibility) in the network. Such devices offer an ideal environment for deploying the proposed system and this research contributes by helping to determine whether or not they are sufficiently powerful to support in-network video transcoding. Our current implementation uses the IXP1200 network processor for implementing the nodes that transcode MPEG-1 (MPEG-1 was chosen due to the limited instruction store and processing capability of the IXP1200.) video data to a desired bit rate. The functionalities provided by the active video adaptation node are arranged according to an active network architecture [8]. We implement our video adaptation process as an Active Application (AA), one of the major components of an active node. Capsules are not used.

We use requantization and selective frame dropping as transcoding techniques to adapt the video streams. Requantization is the process of dequantizing the Discrete Cosine Transform (DCT) coefficients of the video stream and then "requantizing" them with a new quantization step size to reduce the bit rate. In frame-dropping, frames that are not referenced by any other frames in the video sequence are dropped to keep the generated bit rate of a video stream from exceeding the allocated channel bandwidth and to reduce the frame rate. We evaluate our transcoding techniques in terms of transcoding latency, throughput, and accuracy. Finally, we provide some simple extrapolation of our results for

MPEG-1 using the IXP1200 to different encoding schemes and more powerful network processors.

The remainder of this paper is organized as follows. Section 2 provides related work, Section 3 overviews videocoding techniques, and Section 4 reviews video adaptation algorithms. Sections 5 and 6 discuss a simple low-pass filter and frame resizing, respectively. Section 7 presents a brief discussion of the use of network processors for video transcoding, which is followed by Section 8, which reviews and compares current network processor architectures. Sections 9 and 10 present the implementation details and experimental results for our system, respectively. Finally, the paper concludes in Section 11 and discusses some directions for future work.

Related Work

A number of approaches to dynamically adaptive video multicast have been proposed in recent years aiming to address various issues and challenges including network heterogeneity in the Internet. The approaches can generally be divided into two categories. The first category adopts layered video [9–12] at the source (where video is composed of multiple layers with a base layer providing the lowest quality video signal, and each additional layer enhancing the quality of the base layer). Layered video is transmitted over multiple multicast sessions where each session corresponds to one layer. A receiver may subscribe to as many sessions as can be effectively supported by its processing capacity and link bandwidth. The second category uses video filtering/transformation [13–16] inside the network to produce a video stream of the desired quality "on the fly."

These existing adaptation approaches have a number of drawbacks and are subject to network heterogeneity problems. First, the video stream used in layered multicast schemes has to be layer encoded which makes such schemes restrictive and incompatible with most existing video applications. Second, the use of receiver-driven resource reservation in some approaches [15] leads to suboptimal use of network resources due to the lack of receivers' knowledge about the current network load and the varying nature of the network load over time. For example, if the receiver makes its reservation during a busy period, the network can only provide limited resources leaving the receiver with poor video quality even if the load is mitigated later. Third, the packet discarding technique used in some approaches [10] to handle network congestion is regarded as flawed [17] as it does not provide the best overall performance in terms of bandwidth utilization and end-to-end QoS. Instead of dropping a packet or sending it over a congested link by dropping high-frequency coefficients of video streams [14], the packet could be forwarded through a suboptimal route to attain better overall performance and efficient use of bandwidth. Fourth, many approaches focus only on single specific aspects of the problem. For example, Akamine et al. [13] describe a technique for the construction of multicast trees to be used in video transmission that satisfy different QoS requirements, but their work focuses only on which nodes should do video filtering. How the filtering mechanisms are implemented is not discussed. Finally, most work focuses only on congestion and bandwidth issues while the varying preferences of clients and the heterogenous characteristics of clients' devices also make group communication with multicast difficult.

Yamada et al. [16] present an active network-based video-quality adjustment method for heterogenous video multicast using the IXP1200 network processor. This was the first effort to use network processors in adaptive video multicasting. They only implemented a low-pass filter as a quality adjustment technique for real-time multicasting of MPEG-2 video. Their system, as described, cannot perform the required video adjustment at an acceptable rate.

Addressing these problems in collaborative applications requires an efficient mechanism for in-network adaptation of video streams, which influences user perceived quality and resource requirements both for the end-systems and the network. As described, though several application level schemes have already employed dynamic adaptation, none of them provides a complete solution to the problems faced by collaborative applications. Responding to this issue, the problem addressed in this paper is "how can network performance in collaborative applications be improved by detecting and managing preferences from the receivers for use in dynamic, in-network adaptation of data streams?" To this end, we discuss a framework that not only addresses network heterogeneity by considering clients' network connections and device characteristics but also supports delivering activity-based user interest hints into the network and using those hints at routers to adapt to changing user requirements through the dynamic modification of data streams.

Different Video Coding Standards

This section reviews video coding standards with a focus on the major video compression techniques. The characteristics of these standards play a key role in building practical video adaptation systems. Understanding the differences between MPEG-1 and the other standards provides a basis for extrapolating from our MPEG-1 results to other formats.

MPEG-1 Video Coding

In MPEG-1, video is represented as a sequence of individual still images consisting of a two-dimensional array of picture elements (pels). MPEG-1 video compression employs two basic coding techniques: intraframe coding and interframe coding.

In intraframe coding, spatial redundancy in the same video frame is reduced by DCT-based frequency transformation. In interframe coding, similarity between pels in adjacent frames, temporal redundancy, is reduced by motion compensation (MC). MPEG-1 divides the frames in a sequence into three types: intracoded frames (I-frames), forward predicted frames (P-frames), and bidirectional predicted frames (B-frames). An I-frame is encoded by intraframe coding without any reference to past or future frames. P and B frames are encoded using interframe coding. P-frames are coded with respect to the temporally closest preceding I-frame or P-frame. B-frames are encoded with respect to immediately adjacent I or P-frames past, future, or both.

An MPEG-1 video bitstream is divided into six layers: the video sequence, group of pictures, picture, slice, macroblock, and block layers [18]. The video sequence layer contains one or more groups of pictures (GOPs). A GOP contains a sequence of pictures/frames beginning with an I picture followed by several P and B pictures. A picture corresponds to a single frame in the video sequence consisting of one or more 16-pixel high stripes called slices. A slice contains a contiguous sequence of raster ordered macroblocks. Each macroblock contains a group of six 8×8 DCT blocks, four luminance blocks and two chrominance blocks. Each block corresponds to the basic coding unit on which the DCT is applied and consists of 64 pels arranged in an 8×8 array.

MPEG-2 Video Coding

The MPEG-2 coding standard [19] supports a wide range of bit rates, resolutions (both spatial and temporal), quality levels, and services for applications such as digital storage, High-Definition TV (HDTV), and so forth.

Unlike MPEG-1, MPEG-2 supports interlaced video input images which are scanned as even and odd fields to form frames. Thus, there are two new picture types. "Frame pictures" are obtained by interleaving the lines of an odd field and its corresponding even field while "field pictures" are formed from a field of pixels alone. All picture types can be I, P, or B frames. A coded I-frame consists of an I-frame picture, a pair of I-field pictures or an I-field picture followed by a P-field picture. A coded P-frame consists of a P-frame picture or a pair of P field pictures. A coded B-frame consists of a B-frame picture or a pair of B-field pictures.

MPEG-2 maintains MPEG-1 syntax, but uses extensions to add flexibility and functions. "Scalable" extensions support video data streams with multiple resolutions and the ability to partition the data stream into two pieces, one part containing all of the key headers, motion vectors, and low-frequency DCT coefficients and the second part transmitting less critical information such as high-frequency DCT coefficients. Other extensions offer temporal flexibility so not all frames have to be reconstructed.

MPEG-4 Video Coding

MPEG-4 was originally targeted to support low bit rates and error prone channels (e.g., for wireless devices) but also includes support for object-based user interactivity. MPEG-4 allows video objects to be placed anywhere in the coordinate system and transformations can be used to change the geometrical appearance of the objects. Streamed data can be applied to video objects to modify their attributes and the user's viewing point can be changed.

The basis of MPEG-4 video coding [20] is a block-based predictive differential video coding scheme as in MPEG-1 and MPEG-2. MPEG-4 video also specifies the coded representation of visual objects that can be synthetic (as in interactive graphics) or natural (as in digital TV). These visual objects can be combined to form compound objects. MPEG-4 multiplexes and synchronizes the visual objects before transmission to provide QoS and allows interaction with the scene generated at the receiver's end.

MPEG-4 video provides methods for compressing textures, for texture mapping of 2D and 3D meshes, compression of implicit 2D meshes, and compression of time-varying geometry streams that animate meshes. MPEG-4 also supports coding of video objects with spatial and temporal scalability. Scalability allows decoding a part of a stream and constructing images with reduced quality, reduced spatial resolution, reduced temporal resolution, or with equal temporal and spatial resolution but reduced quality.

H.261 Video Coding

H.261 [21] has many elements in common with MPEG-1. Both intraframe and interframe coding techniques are used for compression. Like MPEG-1, H.261 uses DCT-based frequency transformation and motion compensation (MC). The video is also organized in layers. However, there are some differences between these two coding standards. In H.261, the quantization is a single variable instead of a matrix of 64 terms and the syntax is simpler with only four layers. To minimize delay, only the previous picture is used for motion compensation. So, there are no B frames.

H.263 Video Coding

H.263 [22] is an evolutionary improvement to H.261, building on ideas from MPEG-1 and MPEG-2. H.263 is intended for low bitrate communication and it supports additional video frames. H.263 has MPEG-like blocks and macroblocks with prediction and motion compensation. The zigzagged quantized coefficients are coded using the MPEG run-level methods although with different tables. The video has four layers as in H.261.

Four optional modes enhance the functionality of H.263. The "unrestricted motion vector" mode allows motion vectors to point outside a picture. The "syntax-based arithmetic coding" mode supports arithmetic instead of huffman coding giving the same picture quality with fewer coded bits. The "advanced prediction" mode uses overlapped block motion compensation with four 8×8 block vectors instead of a single 16×16 macroblock motion vector. The "PB-frames" mode allows a P-frame and a B-frame to be coded together as a single PB-frame.

H.264 Video Coding

H.264 [23], MPEG-4 Part 10, or Advanced Video Coding (AVC) achieves very high-data compression. The goal of H.264/AVC was to provide good quality at substantially lower bit rates. An additional goal was to do this in a flexible way that would allow the standard to be applied to a wide variety of applications and to work well in a variety of networks and systems.

The basic functional elements (prediction, transform, quantization, and entropy encoding) are similar to previous standards. H.264 provides a number of new features that allow it to compress video much more effectively. These include what follows. (i) Multipicture motion compensation using up to 32 previously-encoded pictures as references. This usually allows modest improvements in bit rate and quality in most scenes. (ii) Variable block-size motion compensation (VBSMC) with block sizes as large as 16×16 and as small as 4×4, enabling very precise segmentation of moving regions. (iii) Quarter-pixel precision for motion compensation, enabling very precise description of the displacements of moving areas. (iv) A 4×4 integer block transform is used as opposed to the 8×8 DCT blocks. (v) Context-adaptive binary arithmetic coding (CABAC) is used to losslessly compress syntax elements in the video stream knowing the probabilities of syntax elements in a given context. (vi) Context-adaptive variable-length coding (CAVLC) a lower-complexity alternative to CABAC, is used for the coding of quantized transform coefficient values.

Video Adaptation Algorithms

To support the transmission of pre-encoded video over heterogeneous networks, the video streams need to be dynamically adapted based on the channel bandwidth and receivers' requirements. The device or system that performs this process is called a video transcoder. One salient function provided by video transcoding is bit rate conversion, which accepts a pre-encoded video stream as input and produces an output stream having a different bit rate. Other functionalities that may be provided by a transcoding process include conversion of the frame rate, spatial resolution, or compression standard (coding syntax). Figure 2 illustrates the transcoding process.

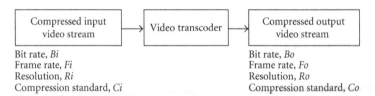

Figure 2. Video format conversion using a transcoder.

Different transcoding operations entail different levels of processing complexity. This complexity is determined by how much a compressed video stream must be decompressed before a transcoding operation is applied. Thus, a transcoding operation can be optimized by performing it in the appropriate stage of the compression/decompression process. Figure 3 shows different regions where various transcoding operations can be performed on a compressed discrete cosine transform and motion compensated video bit-stream. Region 1 represents uncompressed source image data where operations such as frame resizing (i.e., conversion of spatial resolution) and frame dropping (by reestimating motion vectors) can be performed relatively simply although a large amount of data has to be processed due to its uncompressed nature. Region 2 contains the same amount of data as region 1, but transcoding operations at this region can be performed without using the computationally intensive functions of Forward-DCT and Inverse-DCT transforms. Requantization (i.e., bit rate conversion) can be performed at this point by applying the new quantization factor on the dequantized DCT coefficients. In region 3, the data size is considerably smaller due to the absence of zero coefficients in DCT blocks that are quantized and run length encoded. Operations such as frequency filtering (i.e., bit rate conversion) and color to monochrome conversion are feasible at this region. Finally, region 4 contains fully compressed data and allows standard-specific and relatively simple operations such as intelligent frame dropping (i.e., frame rate conversion).

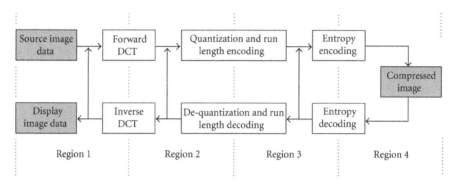

Figure 3. Different levels of compression/decompression process on a generic discrete cosine transform and motion compensation-based video.

Adaptive Requantization

Requantization is an efficient transcoding technique for converting MPEG and H.261/263 video at a high bit rate to a lower bit rate. The requantization process involves several steps.

Figure 4 shows a requantization transcoder with bit rate control. First, the original video stream is decoded through variable length decoding (VLD) [24] to obtain the quantized DCT coefficients with coding information such as quantizer scale (also called quantizer step size), macroblock type, and motion vectors. A near-optimal decoding technique based on Huffman decoding is used to generate the quantized DCT values from the variable length codes in the compressed stream. An inverse quantizer then dequantizes these decoded coefficients using the quantization step size and produces the actual DCT coefficients. These coefficients are requantized with a larger quantization step size to reduce the bit rate. The quantized coefficients are then coded again with other coding information including the new quantization step and modified macroblock information through variable length coding (VLC) to get the resulting transcoded stream.

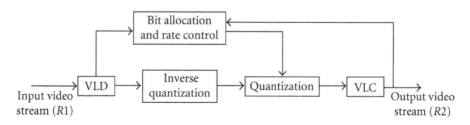

Figure 4. Transcoding using requantization.

Quantization

The quantization process entails the division of the integer DCT coefficients by integer quantizing values. Intra- and interframe coding conform to different quantization rules. The quantized DCT coefficient (QDCT) in intracoding is calculated from the unquantized coefficient (DCT) by the following formulae [18]:

$$QDCT = \frac{(16 \times DCT) + (Sign(DCT) \times quantizer\_scale \times Q)}{2 \times quantizer\_scale \times Q}, \tag{1}$$

where Q is the quantization table value for the coefficient and the function Sign() in the rounding term produces the following values:

$$Sign(DCT) = \begin{cases} +1, & when\ DCT > 0, \\ 0, & when\ DCT = 0, \\ -1, & when\ DCT < 0. \end{cases} \tag{2}$$

For intercoding, a similar equation is used for the quantization with the exception that the rounding is always to the smaller integer value. Hence, the equation does not hold any rounding term:

$$QDCT = \frac{(16 \times DCT)}{2 \times quantizer\_scale \times Q}. \tag{3}$$

Dequantization

Dequantization of the quantized DCT coefficients is performed by the inverse of the quantization procedure. For intra coding [18]

$$DCT = \frac{(2 \times QDCT) \times quantizer\_scale \times Q}{16}, \tag{4}$$

and for inter coding

$$DCT = \frac{((2 \times QDCT) + Sign(QDCT)) \times quantizer\_scale \times Q}{16}. \tag{5}$$

Rate Control

Rate control in requantization is used to determine quantization parameters, and is responsible for preserving consistent video quality while satisfying both bandwidth and delay constraints. The relationship between quantizer step size and bit rate for a video stream can be used to determine the quantizer step size and bit allocation during requantization on a frame, slice, or macroblock basis. We used slice level rate control. The rate controller needs to know the target bit rate that is to be transmitted. At the slice level, the actual bit count in the original video stream can be scaled to obtain the target bit count. The scaling factor is the ratio between the transcoder's desired output (e.g., R2) and input bit rates (e.g., R1). This maintains the proportion of bits allocated among different frame types in the transcoded video sequence. The actual bit count from the original stream and corresponding target bit count for the i th slice in a frame are calculated as follows:

$$B_{target}(i) = B_{actual}(i) \times \frac{R2}{R1}, \tag{6}$$

$$B_{actual}(i) = B_{stream}(i) + \Delta,$$

where Δ is defined as

$$\Delta = \begin{cases} 0, & \text{for the first slice of the} \\ & \text{first frame of any type,} \\ B_{actual}(i-1) - B_{target}(i-1), & \text{otherwise.} \end{cases} \tag{7}$$

To meet the target bit rate, the quantizer step size is adjusted based on feedback to the rate controller (as shown in Figure 4). The rate controller updates the quantizer step size for the next slice on the basis of the difference between the target and actual bit count for the previous slice (i.e., the value of Δ). The new quantizer step size for the i th slice in a frame is calculated as follows:

$$Q(i) = Q_{base}(i) + offset, \tag{8}$$

where $Q_{base}(i)$ is the original quantizer step size for that slice and offset is determined by the value of Δ for the previous slice. For the first slice of each frame, offset is initialized to the mean value used for the previous frame of the same type.

As quantization is the only operation in the DCT-based video compression algorithm that introduces quality loss, requantization can produce some noticeable edge effects on the transcoded video stream. However, as each DCT coefficient is requantized to a smaller value, the bit rate reduction achieved by the mechanism is significant.

Frame Dropping in Compressed Domain

Frame dropping can be used to keep the generated bit rate of a video stream from exceeding the allocated channel bandwidth and to reduce the frame rate. Thus, a frame dropping mechanism is used to reduce the data rate of a video stream in a sensible way by discarding a number of frames according to importance and transmitting the remaining frames at a lower rate. Usually, in a transcoding process, the video transcoder reuses the decoded motion vectors to speed up the re-encoding process [25]. In this case, the frames cannot be discarded because the motion vectors of each frame are estimated from their immediate predecessor frames. However, if frame dropping is allowed in a transcoding process, those motion vectors cannot be reused because the motion vectors of the current frame are no longer estimated from the immediate past frame. If frame dropping needs to be used, the current frame must be decompressed completely and the motion vectors have to be estimated again before recompression. This method introduces heavy computational overhead, which is undesirable in real-time transcoding. However, frames that are not referenced by other frames in the video sequence can be discarded in a specific interval to reduce the data rate thus avoiding the computation for recomputing motion vectors.

In an MPEG-1 video sequence, for example, I and P frames in a GOP are referenced by subsequent P and B frames in the group. Hence, I and P frames in the video sequence cannot be dropped without going through the process of re-estimation of motion vectors (done in region 1 of video compression/decompression processing shown in Figure 3) and thus requires complete decompression and recompression of the video sequence. On the other hand, B frames are not referenced by any other frames in the sequence. Therefore, a number of B frames in a specific interval can be discarded to control the bit rate while maintaining acceptable image quality. In this case, the transcoding operation is performed completely in the compressed domain (region 4 in Figure 3). By dropping a specific number of B frames, it is possible to produce a video stream with a desired rate, however, due to the small size of B frames in the video sequence, this approach has limited impact. A sample frame dropping scenario is illustrated in Figure 5.

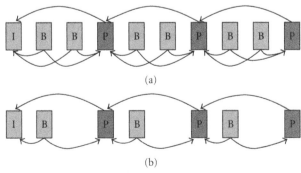

(a)

(b)

Figure 5. (a) A sample precoded MPEG-1 video sequence. (b) The transcoded sequence with alternate B frames dropped.

Frame Dropping in Pixel Domain

To achieve increased data reduction, a pixel domain frame dropping technique could be used. In this case, the frame must be decompressed completely and motion estimation must be done again. To reduce the computational overhead of motion vector re-estimation, a bilinear interpolation method has been developed [26] to estimate the motion vectors for the current frame relative to the previous nondropped frame.

If the motion vectors between adjacent frames are known, the problem of tracing the motion from frame four to frame one as shown in Figure 6 could be partly solved using the repeated applications of bilinear interpolation. A shifted macroblock as shown in Figure 7 is located in the middle of four neighbor macroblocks. The bilinear interpolation is then defined as

$$MV_{int} = (1-\alpha)(1-\beta)MV_1 + (\alpha)(1-\beta)MV_2$$
$$+ (1-\alpha)(\beta)MV_3 + (\alpha)(\beta)MV_4. \tag{9}$$

Here, $MV_1, \ldots, MV_4$ are the motion vectors of the four neighboring macroblocks. α and β are determined by the pixel distance to MV_1. The weighting factor of each neighboring macroblock is inversely proportional to the pixel distance. By repeating the motion tracing, it is possible to create an extended motion vector for each macroblock in the current frame relative to its previously nondropped frame.

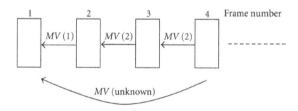

Figure 6. A motion tracing example.

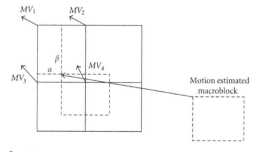

Figure 7. Interpolation of motion vectors.

Bilinear interpolation only partially solves the motion vector reuse problem. Hence, further adjustment of the re-estimated motion vectors has to be performed by using a smaller search range. For each macroblock, the new position located by the interpolated and composed motion vectors is used as the search center for the final motion re-estimation stage.

The frame rate is controlled by dynamically determining the length of dropped frames. The goal is to make the motion of the decoded sequence smoother. A threshold is set beforehand and if the accumulated magnitude of motion vectors after a nondropped frame exceeds this threshold, this frame is encoded. The threshold is determined by using the number of frames to divide the accumulated magnitude of motion vectors in a buffer. The threshold is recursively updated after transcoding each frame because the number of encoded frames should be dynamically adjusted according to the variation of the generated bits when the last nondropped frame is transcoded.

Low-Pass Filter

A low-pass filter provides rate reduction by progressively eliminating high-frequency components of the video signal [16]. In essence, the low-pass filter eliminates an appropriately determined number of DCT coefficients from the high-frequency ones that comprise a luminance or chrominance block. The low-pass parameter is related to the number of DCT coefficients left in each block after quality adjustment. At the beginning of each GOP, initial low-pass parameter values are set independently for I, P, and B pictures based on the compression ratio for the current GOP. The compression ratio for a GOP is calculated from the predicted size (in bits) of the GOP, the predictor for the total bits used by header data in the GOP, and the number of bits allowed for the current GOP, which in turn is calculated from a specified target rate, the number of pictures in the GOP, and the frame rate.

This technique implies that the rate averaged over a GOP-time is regulated by the target rate. However, the result of per-packet adjustment does not necessarily match the target rate. To make up the balance, an adjustment value is introduced. After the initial low-pass parameter value is set, it is changed dynamically for each of the following macroblocks in the GOP based on the size difference between the previous original and filter macroblock. Using this technique the low-pass parameter value for each macroblock is appropriately determined. By eliminating the specified number of DCT coefficients, it is possible to produce a video stream that has the desired rate.

Frame Resizing

One common solution to reduce bit rate is to generate a new compressed video with a lower spatial resolution from the original precoded video bit stream. This method requires downsizing of the original video and estimation of new motion vectors for each intercoded macroblock in the downsized video.

The algorithm proposed in [27] can achieve arbitrary image/video downsizing. This algorithm takes advantage of compressed domain processing techniques and is processed completely in DCT domains without introducing further computation. When combined with the transcoding method described in [28], which can estimate the motion vectors from the input bit stream for arbitrary downscaled video, the proposed method can efficiently process video stream downsizing.

In a spatial domain, for an arbitrary downsizing ratio R, defined as the ratio of original resolution to the desired resolution, more than one pixel in the original frame may contribute to one single pixel in the downsized frame [27]. For example, one 8×8 output block in the downsized frame can come from as many as M × N related blocks, which the supporting area in size of 8Rx×8Ry (where Rx and Ry are the horizontal and vertical downsizing ratio, resp.) may cover in the original frame. For arbitrary downsizing, these supporting areas may not align to the block border. This approach realizes downsizing in two steps: (1) extracting the supporting area from the original frame, and (2) downsizing it into an 8×8 output block.

Due to the noninteger downsizing ratio, some related blocks in the original frame might partially contribute to certain output blocks in the downsized frame. These related blocks can be totally covered or partially covered by the supporting area. The spatial information (DCT) of the supporting area is extracted by partially decoding the related blocks. The size of the extracted DCT block depends on the covered pixels of each related block. Then the supporting area can be represented by combining the extracted pixels from all the related blocks in DCT domain.

In a natural image, most of the signal energy is concentrated in the lower frequency part in the DCT domain. A reasonable downsizing scheme, as proposed in [29], is to retain only the lower frequency components and discard the high-frequency components of the block. Thus, most of the energy of the original block is preserved. As the supporting area of size 8Rx×8Ry may contribute to one 8×8 output block, it is necessary to discard the high-frequency component and extract only the low-frequency part of size 8×8 to downsize the block to 8×8 in the DCT domain.

The motion vector estimation approach proposed in [28] extends the existing video downsizing methods by considering an arbitrary downsizing scheme operating on several macroblocks. Since different numbers of pixels from the precoded macroblocks are used to form the new macroblock in the downsized video, existing methods using the spatial activity as a weighting factor for motion vector re-estimation are not well suited for the case of video downsizing by an arbitrary scale factor. The reason is that motion vectors are usually obtained by finding a matched macroblock within a search window of a reference frame by minimizing the sum of absolute differences (SAD) between the two macroblocks under comparison. To minimize the SAD, the new motion vector should be skewed toward the motion vector of the precoded macroblock that has more pixels involved in forming the new macroblock. For this reason, we consider another weighting factor, which is obtained by multiplying the number of horizontal pixels by the number of vertical pixels engaged from a precoded macroblock. Then the motion vector for each macroblock in the downsized video can be computed from the motion vectors and spatial activity (i.e., number of nonzero AC coefficients) of the related macroblocks of the precoded video, the weighting factor, and the downsizing factors.

Network Processors for Video Transcoding

To deliver enhanced next generation services such as converged voice and data, streaming video, and differentiated Quality of Service (QoS), an efficient in-network processing architecture needs to be developed. Such an architecture must be fast enough to process network data, flexible enough to allow for application specific functions and future upgrades, and reliable enough to provide QoS guarantees.

Network processors (NPs), specialized programmable CPUs optimized to perform packet processing at wire speed, can be used for this purpose. Network processors can perform many functions such as packet classification and possibly modification of packet contents at wire-speed near the edge of the network. The feasibility of network processor-based video transcoding is an area of research that has not yet been fully addressed.

Overview of Network Processors

Network processors have evolved over time to introduce greater processing and storage capability and, in some cases, additional functionality. These are critical issues in determining the feasibility of video transcoding using network processors.

Intel IXP1200

The IXP1200 contains one StrongARM processor core, six programmable multithreaded co-processors (microengines), SRAM, SDRAM, and PCI and IX bus interface units.

The StrongARM 32-bit RISC microprocessor core running at 232 MHz is used for processing control packets, and doing tasks such as managing forwarding tables and other network state information. The microengines are minimal 32-bit RISC processor cores that are typically used to receive, process, and transmit packets independently. Each microengine supports four hardware threads so up to 24 threads can be executed "in parallel." The instruction store of each microengine has space for 1024, 32-bit instructions that each execute in one clock cycle.

The IX bus unit provides the on-chip scratchpad memory, receive and transmit queues (FIFOs), and a hash generation unit. The 64-bit IX bus connects the processor to Media Access Control (MAC) devices and is responsible for moving data to and from the receive and transmit FIFOs.

Intel IXP2400

The Intel IXP2400 [30] offers a wire-speed OC-48 data plane as well as control plane capability on a single chip. Each IXP2400 contains eight multithreaded packet-processing microengines, a low-power general-purpose Intel XScale core, network media and switch fabric interfaces, memory and PCI controllers, and interfaces to flash PROM and peripheral devices.

The eight 32-bit microengines run at 400/600 MHz and support multithreading up to eight threads each. These microengines provide a variety of network processing functions in hardware. Each of the microengines has space for 4096, 40-bit instructions. The IXP2400 also offers Intel's Hyper Task chaining technology which allows a single stream packet/cell processing problem to be decomposed into multiple, sequential tasks that can be easily linked together. The hardware design uses fast and flexible sharing of data and event signals among threads and microengines to manage data-dependent operations among multiple parallel processing stages.

The integrated 32-bit XScale core offers high-performance processing of routing table maintenance and system management functions. The memory controllers facilitate efficient access to 32-bit SRAM and 64-bit DRAM, which hold the routing table, networking data, and so on. In addition, a programmable hash engine (48, 64, and 128 bit) is provided.

Intel IXP2800

The Intel IXP2800 [31] offers increased processing to support deep packet inspection and filtering, traffic management, and forwarding at up to OC-192 (10 Gbps) wire speed on a single chip. Its store-and-forward architecture combines a high-performance Intel XScale core with sixteen 32-bit independent multi-threaded microengines that cumulatively provide up to 25 Giga-operations per second.

The 32-bit Intel XScale core operates at up to 750 MHz. The sixteen 32-bit microengines running at up to 1.5 GHz, support multi-threading with up to eight threads each, and provide space for 8192, 32-bit instructions.

IBM PowerNP

The IBM PowerNP [32] supports multiple network interfaces including Gigabit Ethernet at 2.5 Gbps and OC-3 to OC-48 packet-over-SONET (POS). The core of the PowerNP contains 16 programmable protocol processing engines and seven coprocessors. Additional custom logic supports management of data movement at the physical and MAC layers.

The protocol processors are grouped into pairs which share a co-processor to accelerate packet processing. Each protocol processor supports two threads and includes a 3-stage pipeline (fetch, decode, and execute), general-purpose registers, eight instruction caches, and a dedicated ALU. The instruction memory (128 KB) consists of eight embedded RAMs and is initialized with picocode for packet processing and system management.

EZChip (NP-1c)

The NP-1c [33] provides a scalable and programmable network processor architecture providing 10 Gbps wire speed. EZchip uses Task Optimized Processing Core (TOP core) technology. TOPs employ a super-pipelined and superscalar architecture for increased processing power. There are four types of TOPs, each having a customized instruction set and data path: (i) TOPparse identifies and extracts various packet headers and fields to classify packets; (ii) TOPsearch performs various table lookups required for layer 2 switching, layer 3 routing, layer 4 session switching, and layer 5–7 context switching and policy enforcement; (iii) TOPresolve allocates packets to an appropriate output port and queue; (iv) TOPmodify modifies packet contents.

Data plane packet processing in the TOPcore is pipelined; packets are passed from TOPparse to TOPmodify. A set of software commands from the system's host processor control the operations performed by the TOP processors. The programmability of the NP-1c makes it possible to adapt to new applications through simple changes in software without necessitating hardware changes.

Agere (PayloadPlus)

The Agere PayloadPlus [34] network processor exploits pattern matching optimization technology to achieve high performance. Two main components are provided: the Fast Pattern Processor (FPP) and the Routing Switch Processor (RSP). The FPP is a pipelined, multi-threaded processor, that receives packets through the physical interface and carries out protocol recognition and classification at layers 2 through 7. The FPP reassembles traffic into protocol data units (PDUs) and sends them to the RSP which does queuing, packet modification, traffic shaping, and traffic management.

Motorola (C-5e)

Motorola's C-5e [35] is capable of layer 2–7 processing at 5 Gbps. The C-5e contains 16 Channel Processors (CPs) for packet forwarding which each contain a transmit and receive Serial Data Processor (SDP) used for processing bit streams. The programmability of the SDPs supports diversity in media access control (MAC) interfaces, as well as parsing requirements, and can support different protocol implementations on a port-by-port basis. Each CP also contains a RISC core that is used for application-specific processing.

The Executive Processor (XP) integrated in the C-5e is responsible for supervisory tasks and management of the host processor. An on-chip Table Lookup Unit (TLU) offers a high-speed flexible classification engine that supports over 46 million IPv4 lookups per second. The TLU is connected to a 64-bit 128 MB SRAM. The C-5e also contains 128 MB SDRAM for payload storage. By connecting multiple C-5e NPs through their fabric interfaces to a fabric switch, it is possible to achieve Terabits per second of aggregate bandwidth. The C-5e NP's highly configurable Fabric Processor (FP) enables implementation of per-flow congestion control, segmentation and re-assembly, and integrated scheduling of up to 128 queues.

Implementation of the Active Video Adaptation Node

We used the Intel IXP1200 network processor to implement our active video adaptation node [36]. More powerful, second generation, NPs suggest that still better results than those we report are now achievable. The architecture of our active video adaptation node conforms to the node architecture provided by the active networks "reference model" [8]. An active node runs a Node Operating System (NodeOS) and one or more Execution Environments (EEs) and provides services to users through Active Applications (AAs). The functionality of an active network node is divided among these three major components.

Active Node Components

Figure 8 illustrates the architecture of an active network node. Underlying each active network node is a Node Operating System that manages the resources of the active node such as processors, channels, and memory. The channels implemented by the NodeOS carry packets to and from underlying communication substrates and also perform protocol processing. An Execution Environment provides a virtual machine programming interface for executing programs on the active node. Thus, an EE is analogous to a shell program in a general purpose computing system exporting, in this case, an interface through which end-to-end network services can be implemented. Multiple EEs can be present on a single active node at the same time. EEs are isolated from the details of resource management by the NodeOS. An EE can accept active packets that initiate the execution of packet specific programs, also called Active Applications. AAs program the virtual machine provided by an EE to implement an end-to-end service. The code constituting the AA may be contained in a packet itself or, more likely, preloaded at the node. An EE can invoke multiple AAs to provide multiple services simultaneously and manages the initiation, execution, and termination of these AAs. All of the EE and AA functionalities are programs running on the microengines and the NodeOS functionalities are provided by the operating system running on the StrongARM.

We have implemented our video adaptation algorithm as an AA. The video adaptation AA is notified of a target output rate for the input video stream by the EE that initiates it. For the adaptation of multiple independent video streams belonging to different multicast groups, multiple AAs may be initiated by the same or different EEs. The same is also true for the adaptation of a single video stream into streams having different data rates. Figure 9 illustrates these two scenarios.

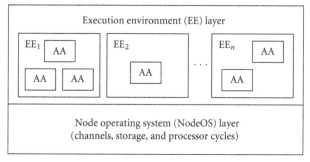

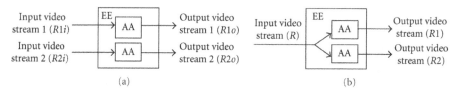

AA-active application

Figure 8. Schematic representation of the active node architecture.

Figure 9. (a) Two video streams with rates R 1i and R 2i are adapted to streams with rate R 1o and R 2o , (b) A single stream with rate R is adapted to two different streams with rate R 1 and R2.

Flow of Video Packets through the Active Node

Figure 10 shows a general flow of video packets through the active node. Once video packets are received on an input port they are classified based on information contained in the packet headers such as protocol number, port numbers in UDP headers, and/or Type ID in an ANEP [37] header. Incoming packets may have to wait in one or more queues before classification. The classification of packets determines the input channel to the appropriate EE to which packets are directed. Afterwards, the input channel processing packets are passed on to the corresponding EE. Upon receiving a packet, the EE sends it to the appropriate AA and receives the result packet from the AA after adaptation of the packet in accordance with the specified target rate. Video adaptation AAs used by the EE are chosen based on a set of identifiers consisting of a source IP address and port number, a multicast group address for sending the video packet, and a destination port number. On the output side, the EE sends the adapted video packets to the scheduler through output channels. Packets are then transmitted through appropriate output ports. Before transmission, the packets may have to wait in output queues. Besides active video packets having an ANEP header, the node can also process legacy traffic (conventional IP packets) by setting up the appropriate channels that simply forward the packets without applying any video adaptation.

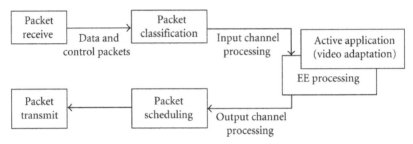

Figure 10. Video packet flow through the active node.

Mapping the Algorithms to the IXP1200

Reception and classification of packets, transcoding, and scheduling and transmitting adapted packets are all implemented on the microengines to provide wire-speed packet processing. The processing done by each microengine differs and is determined prior to run time.

Receiving Packets

We allocate microengine zero for receiving packets. All four hardware threads are used for this task. Incoming packets received by microengine zero are queued to avoid packet loss during packet processing by other microengines. Each thread on the receiving microengine queues packets to be used by the microengines that classify, transcode, and finally retransmit them. We have implemented array-based circular queues in SRAM where each entry in the queue contains a packet descriptor consisting of the packet buffer handle (in SRAM) and the packet size. We experimented with two different queue configurations: single input and multiple input.

Single Input-Queue Configuration

In this configuration, one 100 Mbps port is mapped to a single packet queue to be served by all four threads of the classification microengine. Each of the four threads in the receiving microengine is dedicated to receiving packets from the single port and to queuing them. The single queue implementation can be used for the adaptation of a single input video stream into single or multiple output streams having different data rates. Figure 11 shows the single input-queue configuration.

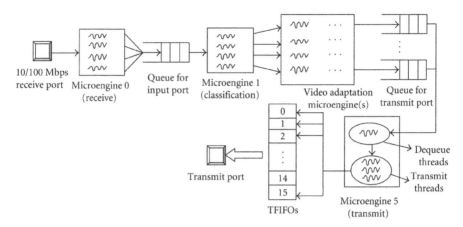

Figure 11. Single queue configuration for the video transcoding node.

Multiple Input-Queue Configuration

In this configuration a queue is created for each of the four threads in the receiving microengine. The assignment of these receiving threads to input ports can be done in different ways. Each thread can be assigned to a single port or to a different port (specified in advance). Thus, the receiving microengine can receive packets from up to four ports. The multiple-queue implementation can be used for transcoding single or multiple video streams. In single stream transcoding, packets received by the four threads are put in the queues sequentially. In multiple-stream transcoding, each queue contains packets belonging to a separate video stream that is handled by a thread assigned to that queue. The multiple-queue configuration is illustrated in Figure 12.

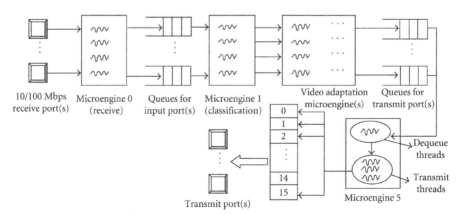

Figure 12. Multiple queue configuration for the video transcoding node.

Classification of Packets

We allocate microengine one for dequeuing packets from the input queues and classifying them. Packet classification separates convention IP data packets from the video packets to be transcoded. Both dequeuing and classification of a given packet are performed by a single thread. Packets are also analyzed to extract MPEG-1 video start codes. In the single queue configuration, each thread waits for its turn to retrieve a packet from the queue. In the multiple-queue configuration, threads wait for new entries in their respective queues.

Video Transcoding

We allocate three microengines (2, 3, and 4) for transcoding video packets from the classification microengine. All three microengines are used by the requantization technique while one microengine is sufficient for implementing the frame dropping technique. Video transcoding for a packet is done by a single thread in each of these video processing microengines, as shown in Figures 11 and 12.

Requantization

Processing DCT coefficients during requantization requires a simple but frequent operation due to the large portion of MPEG-1 video data coming from the block layer consisting of these coefficients. Implementing the entire requantization process in one microengine is not possible since each microengine has a limited instruction store capable of holding only 1024 instructions. Hence, we allocate microengine 2 for processing up to the macroblock layer and microengines 3 and 4 for processing the block layer.

Packet data are fed into the input buffer from the SDRAM. Microengine 2 processes the data from the sequence layer to the macroblock layer and moves the necessary coding information to the shared SRAM and SDRAM for processing the block layer on microengines 3 and 4. The picture and slice layers are parsed to extract the frame type (I, P, or B) and quantization scale, respectively. The frame type determines the macroblock coding type (i.e., intra- or intercoding) which defines the dequantization approach required (i.e., intraframe or interframe). The quantization scale is used to dequantize the original DCT coefficients. The coding information includes the macroblock type and quantization scale for processing the DCT coefficients. Microengine 2 also processes the macroblock layer based on the macroblock type to obtain the macroblock pattern, motion vectors, and macroblock quantization scale. The macroblock pattern and quantization scale (if it is different from the slice layer quantization scale) are also included in the coding information. The macroblock pattern provides a coded block pattern that describes which blocks within the macroblock are coded.

The block layer processing is divided into two parts. The DC components of the block are processed by microengine 3 and the AC components are processed by microengine 4. The microengine threads obtain the coding information from the SRAM and SDRAM and additional information such as the quantization table (intra or inter), the VLC tables, and a new quantization scale (chosen according to the rate control mechanism described in the previous section) from the IXP 1200's scratchpad memory. The microengines decode the quantized DCT coefficients and dequantize them to get the actual DCT coefficients. The coefficients are then requantized with the new quantization step and are encoded using VLC to get the transcoded DCT coefficients. The microengines store the processed DCT coefficients in the output buffer and write them back to the SDRAM. Figure 13 illustrates the data processing through the input and output buffers during requantization. Once the whole packet has been processed, the thread puts it in the correct output queue (one for each of the four threads in microengine 4). The transmit microengine dequeues the packets from the output queues in round robin fashion and transmits them through one or more output ports.

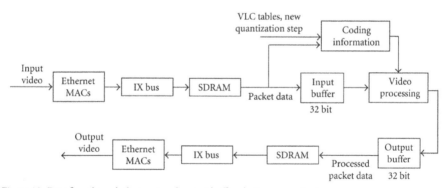

Figure 13. Data flow through the input and output buffers during requantization.

Frame Dropping

Frame dropping refers to a compressed domain transcoding technique which is relatively simple and entails less video computation. We allocate one microengine (number 2) for transcoding the video stream through frame dropping. As the transcoding technique selectively drops a number of B frames to produce an output video stream with the desired rate, the microengine processes the video data from the sequence layer to the picture layer to recognize the frame type. The picture rate in the sequence layer is updated based on the new frame transmission rate. The microengine achieves the new transmission rate by discarding a specific number of B frames. The microengine threads put the packets that belong to a nondropped frame into the output queues. A single queue is created for each thread in the microengine. Like requantization, packets are dequeued from the output queues in a circular manner and are transmitted through appropriate output port(s).

Transmitting Packets

We allocate microengine 5 for dequeuing packets from the output queues and transmitting them. One thread is assigned to dequeue the packets and the remaining threads are used to schedule and send the packets out on the wire as illustrated in Figures 11 and 12. Once a packet is received from the output queue, new checksums are calculated for the IP and UDP headers based on the new packet size and contents. Packets are then transmitted out of the IXP1200.

Hashing

The IXP1200 provides a hardware hash unit located within the IX bus unit and the hash unit implements a hash function that produces values with a uniform statistical distribution regardless of the input. Packet processing that requires one or more table lookups is greatly eased by the hardware assisted hashing functionality provided by the IXP1200. This hashing unit is only accessible to microengines and is capable of performing either 48 bit or 64 bit hashes.

In our framework, we have used a hash table to store, retrieve, and update hints from the receivers at the active node. These hints describe user preferences such as interest levels in particular video streams and the capability of the end devices such as processing power, screen size, and so on. Receivers transmit the hints upstream (through the active node) to the sender in capsule form. Video packets originating from the source pass through the active node that adapts the packets based on the hints from the intended receivers and network connections.

Implementation Complexity and Portability

The active video adaptation node entails greater implementation complexity than a conventional router to provide support for video adaptation. This complexity and the associated overhead is not insignificant. Fortunately, the "cost" of designing the adaptation node is incurred only once and may be amortized over the number of network processors it runs on. Further, the programmability of NPs will allow for relatively easy extension of adaptation node functionality. Despite the high-level similarity of NP architectures, there is currently no readily accepted standard programming model for network processors. Thus, our code is largely IXP specific.

The different phases of the video adaptation algorithm executed by each microengine are predetermined prior to execution. This makes the allocation of work simpler than assigning it to the microengines dynamically. The concept of "microblock" in packet receiving is used to balance the code performance and modularity. A microblock is a sequence of microengine code that operates on a single packet that is currently being processed. One or more microblocks can be combined together in a loop, called a "dispatch" loop that calls these microblocks in a particular order to perform specific functions. We have used a while loop as the dispatch loop that calls the packet receiving microblock and a packet queuing microblock to receive packets from the input ports and to queue them for use by the other microengines. As the packet length is unknown during the reception of the start of the packet, a fixed size buffer (large enough to hold the maximum size packet) is allocated for each packet. Hardware supported SRAM LIFO stacks are used for such buffer allocation without any overhead for writing code to create stacks. This approach is largely generalizable to most current NP architectures.

Another challenge was to determine the granularity of segmentation for an MPEG-1 video stream at the server. We decided to segment the video stream into a sequence of independent packets on a per slice basis since the slice in a frame represents the smallest independent coding unit in an MPEG-1 video sequence. This suited the comparatively low power of the IXP1200 but could still be used with more powerful NPs. The granularity of segmentation does not significantly affect coding complexity.

We used a nonpreemptive thread arbiter and shared variables to implement intra-microengine thread communication and mutual exclusion. The nonpreemptive thread arbiter allows one thread to run until the thread itself explicitly releases control of the microengine by waiting for a signal, swapping out on a memory read, or voluntarily releasing control. Shared variables are implemented in the hardware with absolute registers providing extremely fast interthread communication and mutual exclusion. Synchronization was a key performance issue in our IXP 1200 implementation and will likely continue to be regardless of network processor architecture.

Most of the computation overhead and complexity comes from implementing different levels of decompression and compression tasks during the actual transcoding of the video packets. However, multiple microengines capable of wire-speed packet processing made the transcoding task fast enough to provide a realistic video transfer rate (24–30 frames per second for MPEG-1) despite the limitations of the IXP1200. Processing requiring table lookups was simplified and expedited by the hardware assisted hashing functionality provided by the IXP1200.

Implementing our video adaptation algorithm on other network processors would require a modified strategy for allocating various tasks such as reception and classification of packets, transcoding, and scheduling and transmitting adapted packets based on the hardware resources provided by the particular network processor. Similarly, other architecture specific coding patterns would have to be revised. Not surprisingly, porting NP code is similar to porting low-level parallel code.

Protoype Evaluation

We now present the results obtained from our evaluation of our IXP1200-based video transcoder. The metrics used to measure transcoder performance included transcoding latency, throughput, and accuracy. These criteria capture the effectiveness of transcoding MPEG-1 streams using the IXP1200. Transcoding latency determines how fast video transformation takes place. Low transcoding latency is preferred. The goodness of transcoding latency is determined by how close the transcoded video transfer rate is to the actual video transfer rate (i.e., for MPEG-1, 24–30 frames per second). Transcoding throughput determines the number of streams that can be processed simultaneously. Finally, the amount of "blockiness," "blurriness," and "noise" in the transcoded video determines the accuracy of transcoding which is assessed by comparing the quality of the transcoded streams with that of the original streams.

A test environment was set up to verify the practicality and applicability of the video transcoding mechanism. The experimental system consisted of a video server (sender), an IXP1200-based transcoding node, and several clients connected to the trancoding node. A number of experiments were conducted to transcode MPEG-1 video streams according to the various requirements of the clients and their link bandwidths.

For our experiments, we used a selection of MPEG-1 video streams whose properties are summarized in Table 1. The frame size represents the width and height of each frame in pixels. The average size of I, P, and B frames are given in bytes. The frame pattern represents the order in which frames in a GOP are displayed. Each of the video streams is viewed at a rate of 30 fps.

Table 1. Properties of the test MPEG-1 video sequences.

Clip Name	Frame Size	I	P	B	Frame Pattern
ski.mpeg	192 × 144	2877	1631	1012	IBBPBBPBBP
danger.mpeg	240 × 176	3586	1959		IPIIPI
canyon.mpeg	144 × 112	2265	1881	445	IBBPBBIBBP
vessel.mpeg	256 × 256	4567	4844	4345	IBBPBBIBBP
blazer.mpeg	128 × 96	2431	1419	567	IBBPBBPBBP
rotate.mpeg	160 × 112	2670			I

Transcoding Latency

We experimented using various numbers of microengine threads to get an idea of the capabilities of the IXP1200. The test video streams were transmitted from the video server to the video transcoding node at a rate of 300 Kbps. We set the output target rate of the active node to 200 Kbps. We then conducted experiments for each video sequence to observe any packet loss. The system was found to be capable of processing the video streams at that input rate.

Requantization

Figure 14 and Table 2 show the transcoding latency per frame for each test video stream using requantization. The transcoding latency for requantization includes the time required for decoding the frame through VLD, further processing related to dequantization and quantization of DCT coefficients, and encoding using VLC.

Table 2. Transcoding latency per frame using requantization.

Clip Name	Transcoding Latency (ms)			
	1 Thread	2 Threads	3 Threads	4 Threads
ski.mpeg	12.21	7.44	4.96	4.51
danger.mpeg	45.00	27.41	18.22	16.61
canyon.mpeg	9.52	6.41	4.36	4.06
vessel.mpeg	54.00	32.90	21.67	19.90
blazer.mpeg	9.88	6.52	4.56	4.19
rotate.mpeg	42.95	26.18	17.45	15.87

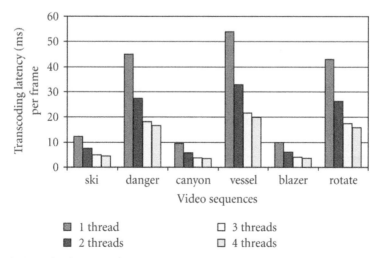

Figure 14. Transcoding latency per frame using requantization.

To take advantage of the IXP1200's multithreading architecture and to improve transcoding performance, multiple threads in each microengine can be used. The latencies (approximate values in milliseconds) are shown in Table 2 and Figure 14 for different numbers of threads running on the transcoding microengines. Employing two threads leads to lower transcoding latency and the same is true for higher numbers of threads. However, employing more than three threads provides little benefit. The reason for this is the increasing level of intramicroengine mutual exclusion that is required.

The transcoding latencies shown in Table 2 indicate that the test video sequences can be transcoded at 24–30 frames or more per second while using two or more threads in each video transcoding microengine. This meets the minimum display frame rate for MPEG-1 video. Note that a single thread implementation cannot meet this transcoding rate for all the test video sequences. (e.g., "danger.mpeg," "vessel.mpeg," and "rotate.mpeg" are transcoded at rates of around 22.22, 18.51, and 23.28 fps which are at least close to the minimum display rate, 24 fps.) The salient point to note from Table 2 (with reference to Table 1) is the relationship between frame size and transcoding latency. The smaller frame sizes or coding bit rates imply sparser blocks in the frame resulting in greater speedup during requantization. The opposite is true for larger frames.

In our next experiment, we evaluated the transcoding latency for the transcoding of two video streams (e.g., intended for different multicast groups). (No actual multicast implementation was done. For assessing performance of transcoding multiple streams, however, this was not required.) Two threads (dedicated) in each video transcoding microengine were responsible for transcoding one video stream. The transcoding latency obtained for each video stream was slightly higher than (previous experiment) when they are separately transcoded with two threads in each microengine. For the streams "canyon.mpeg" and "rotate.mpeg," the latencies obtained per frame were 7.80 and 30.64 milliseconds, respectively, which are slightly higher than in the case of the single stream transcoding (6.41 and 26.18 milliseconds from Table 2). This is due to intra-microengine mutual exclusion.

Frame Dropping

Table 3 and Figure 15 show the transcoding latency (approximate values in microseconds) per frame for several test video streams that contain B frames in the sequence. The major component of the transcoding latency using frame dropping includes the time required to process the video data from the sequence to the picture layer and the slice headers of a frame.

Table 3. Transcoding latency per frame using frame dropping.

Clip Name	Slices	Transcoding Latency (μs)			
		1 Thread	2 Threads	3 Threads	4 Threads
ski.mpeg	11	450	335	290	281
canyon.mpeg	7	345	248	219	214
vessel.mpeg	15	590	403	341	338
blazer.mpeg	8	388	268	237	231

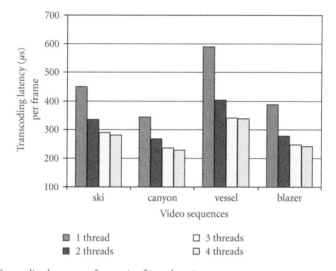

Figure 15. Transcoding latency per frame using frame dropping.

As in requantization, employing two threads leads to lower transcoding latency than using one thread and the same is true for higher number of threads. However, as shown in Table 3 and Figure 15, employing more than two threads contributes little to the performance. This is due to the greater amount of intra-microengine mutual exclusion that is performed by the video adaptation code.

Transcoding latencies obtained for frame dropping indicate the real-time performance of this compressed domain transcoding technique. Compared to requantization, transcoding speed is much higher in this case. This is due to the amount of video data that must be processed by the frame dropping code. Approximately 4.83% of video data coded at 333 Kbps, as an example, come from the sequence to the picture layer and the slice headers of a frame.

Since the frame dropping technique does not process macroblock and block layer data, the transcoding latency for a frame depends on the number of slices in the frame. As each frame is processed per slice, more slices result in more packets that require increased processing time. The opposite is true for a smaller number of slices per frame. This is reflected in Table 3.

In this case also, we evaluated the latency for the transcoding of two video streams intended for different multicast groups. Two threads in each video transcoding microengine were responsible for transcoding one video stream. The transcoding latency obtained for each video stream was slightly higher than (previous experiment) when they are separately transcoded with two threads in each microengine. For the streams "ski.mpeg" and "vessel.mpeg," the latencies obtained per frame were 346 and 418 microseconds, respectively, which are a little higher than the values obtained in the case of the single stream transcoding (335 and 403 microseconds from Table 3).

Throughput

Next, we measured and compared the throughput attained by the active video adaptation node for the requantization and frame dropping techniques.

Requantization

For our throughput experiments, we set a target of 30% reduction in data rate for the output streams. The input rate of the test video streams from the video server to the transcoding node was then gradually increased until the node experienced packet loss. Thus, the throughput for each video stream was measured using the highest possible injection rate at which the node could perform the transcoding without losing packets.

Throughputs affored (approximate values in Kbps) are shown in Table 4 and Figure 16 for different numbers of threads running on the video transcoding microengines. Using two threads leads to higher throughput than using one thread and the same is true for higher numbers of threads. However, employing more than three threads has decreasing significance. The reason is, again, the amount of intra-microengine mutual exclusion. Overall, requantization produces a significant reduction in data rate while maintaining reasonable image quality (as discussed later), but at the expense of incurred delay. The results from Table 4 show that requantizing streams with high transcoding latency results in decreased throughput.

Table 4. Throughput of video transcoding for MPEG-1 sequences.

Clip Name	Throughput (Kbps)			
	1 Thread	2 Threads	3 Threads	4 Threads
ski.mpeg	962	1277	1409	1450
danger.mpeg	880	1335	1565	1620
canyon.mpeg	1044	1366	1596	1634
vessel.mpeg	859	1208	1423	1470
blazer.mpeg	973	1185	1333	1402
rotate.mpeg	870	1279	1591	1650

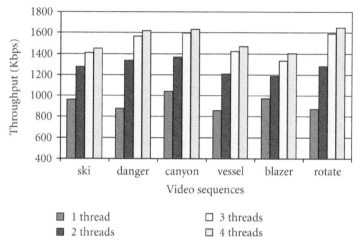

Figure 16. Throughput using requantization.

We also evaluated throughput when transcoding two video streams targeted for different multicast groups. The total throughput attained for these two streams was somewhat lower than the overall throughput attained when they were separately transcoded using two threads in each microengine. For example, the throughput obtained from this experiment for the video streams "ski.mpeg" and "vessel.mpeg," 2214 Kbps, was a little lower than the aggregate throughput obtained in the case of the single stream implementation (1277+1208=2485 Kbps from Table 4).

Frame Dropping

As in requantization, the input rate of the test video streams from the video server to the active node was gradually increased until the node experienced packet loss. Since the test video sequences were coded at 30 frames per second, we decided to drop six B frames from every 30 consecutive frames to meet the minimum requirement of MPEG-1 picture rate (24 frames per second). Table 5 and Figure 17 show the throughput attained for the test video streams that contain B frames.

Table 5. Throughput of video adaptation for different test MPEG-1 sequences using frame dropping.

Clip Name	Throughput (Kbps)			
	1 Thread	2 Threads	3 Threads	4 Threads
ski.mpeg	1194	1477	1576	1590
canyon.mpeg	1313	1624	1700	1713
vessel.mpeg	1002	1389	1490	1506
blazer.mpeg	1257	1521	1652	1669

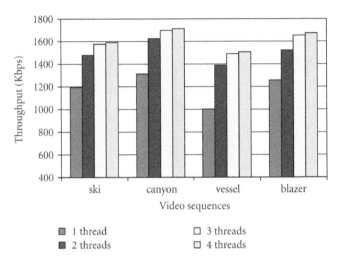

Figure 17. Throughput using frame dropping.

The throughputs (approximate values in Kbps) are shown for changing numbers of threads running on the video adaptation microengines. The trend in the change of throughput for frame dropping based on the change in the number of microengine threads is similar to that for requantization. As in our compressed domain frame dropping, B frames are selectively dropped, the reduction in output data rate depends on the number and size of the B frames in the video sequence. A video stream having high average size of B frames produces less post frame dropping throughput. This is illustrated in Table 5 for the sequence "vessel.mpeg."

We also evaluated throughput when transcoding two video streams targeted for different multicast groups. The total throughput attained for these two streams was, again, a little lower than the overall throughput attained when they were separately transcoded using two threads in each microengine. For example, the throughput obtained from this experiment for video streams "blazer.mpeg" and "vessel.mpeg," 2657 Kbps, was slightly lower than the total throughput obtained in the case of the single stream implementation (1389+1521=2910 Kbps from Table 5).

Compared to requantization, frame dropping produces less reduction in data rate. Moreover, the reduction in data rate achieved by the frame dropping technique is limited by the number and size of B frames in the video sequence. For this reason, this compression domain frame dropping technique may not always be able to meet the data rate desired by the receiver. However, this transcoding technique is well suited to be used for ensuring that a receiver receives frames at a rate appropriate to its processing capabilities. On the other hand, requantization produces larger reduction in data rate though it involves more processing and thus takes longer than the other technique. Unlike the frame dropping technique, requantization reduces the data rate without affecting the frame rate, but of course at the cost image quality.

Accuracy of Video Adaptation

We also measured the quality of the transcoded video streams by comparing them with the original streams. In evaluating the transcoded video quality, we made use of peak signal-to-noise ratio (PSNR) and percentage error (PE) introduced, as our error metrics. The PSNR measures are estimates of the quality of a transcoded image compared to the corresponding original image. PSNR in decibels (dB) is computed as

$$PSNR = 20 \log_{10} \left(\frac{255}{RMSE} \right) \tag{10}$$

for an 8-bit (pixel values of 0 to 255) image where RMSE represents the root-mean-squared error of the transcoded image. For an original image Fo(i,j) of N by N pixels and the corresponding transcoded image Ft(i,j) of the same size, RMSE is computed as

$$RMSE = \frac{\sqrt{\sum_{i=1}^{N} \sum_{j=1}^{N} [F_t(i,j) - F_0(i,j)]^2}}{N}. \tag{11}$$

Next, the PE introduced in a transcoded image is calculated from the relative error (RE) as follows:

$$RE = \frac{\sum_{i=1}^{N} \sum_{j=1}^{N} \left(|F_t(i,j) - F_0(i,j)| \right)}{\sum_{i=1}^{N} \sum_{j=1}^{N} F_0(i,j)}, \tag{12}$$

$$PE + RE \times 100\%$$

In computing RMSE and RE, the RGB values for each pixel in a frame were considered.

Typical PSNR values range from 20 to 40. Transcoded images with higher PSNR and lower PE values are judged to be better. Table 6 summarizes the average PSNRs and PEs for the I, P, and B frames, respectively, of several requantized test video sequences given a 30% reduction in output data rate. The values obtained for each frame type indicate the degree of quantization that was achieved by the transcoder in reducing the bit rate (lower PSNR and higher PE values specify coarser quantization and vice versa).

Table 6. Quality of various test MPEG-1 video sequences-PSNR and PE.

Clip Name	I frame		P frame		B frame	
	PSNR	PE	PSNR	PE	PSNR	PE
ski.mpeg	40.92	0.51	33.26	0.72	33.88	0.70
canyon.mpeg	28.57	6.56	28.64	6.53	28.27	6.90
danger.mpeg	26.60	7.34	22.98	11.38		
vessel.mpeg	24.83	2.32	23.99	2.50	26.57	1.96
blazer.mpeg	29.02	2.06	28.57	2.07	28.30	1.97
rotate.mpeg	22.90	6.52				

It is important to note that these error metrics do not always correlate well with perceived image quality though they do provide a good measure of relative quality. A higher PSNR does not necessarily always imply a reconstructed image of better quality. For this reason, actual transcoded images from several streams are provided below to allow the visual effects of quantization to be seen. As the requantization achieves rate reduction by making the DCT values smaller (and some are rounded to zero), the transcoded video loses sharpness. Figure 18 shows the quality variation in several images comparing the original and corresponding transcoded streams.

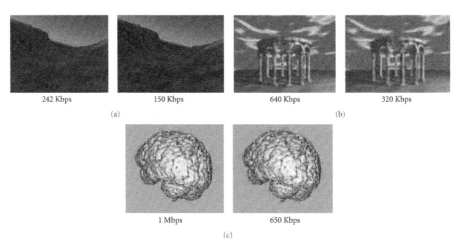

242 Kbps	150 Kbps	640 Kbps	320 Kbps
	(a)		(b)

1 Mbps	650 Kbps
	(c)

Figure 18. Video quality variation in original and transcoded image (a) canyon.mpeg, (b) rotate.mpeg, and (c) vessel.mpeg.

Another useful technique for demonstrating errors is to construct an error image that shows pixel by pixel errors. Error images are created by taking the difference between the transcoded and original pixels. These error images are difficult to visualize as the difference values are often small and some are zeros which commonly represent black. To make the errors more visible, the difference values are multiplied by a constant and the entire image is translated to a gray level by adding an offset. Figure 19 shows error images for three selected test sequences.

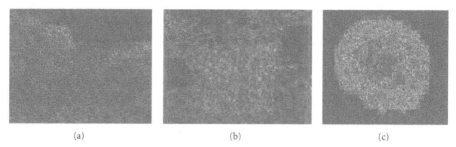

        (a)   (b)   (c)

Figure 19. Error images for selected video streams.

The quality of the transcoded video stream using frame dropping was evaluated by quantifying the smoothness of the motion in the decoded sequence. If the frame (picture) rate is less than 12 fps it is easily detectable by the human eye. As we maintain the minimum frame rate (24 fps) required by the MPEG-1 standard in the frame dropping technique, the transcoded streams exhibit sufficient smoothness of motion in the decoded sequences.

Conclusions

In this paper, we discussed the design and implementation of a network processor-based transcoder for in-network adaptation of video streams to support collaborative applications. Our transcoder uses the IXP1200 network processor to transcode MPEG-1 streams.

Transcoding was done by requantizing the DCT coefficients with larger quantization values to reduce the bit rate. To verify the practicality of the video adaptation scheme, we conducted experiments and presented results in terms of transcoding latency, throughput, and accuracy of video adaptation. Our video transcoding node implementation can dynamically adapt the test video streams on a packet-by-packet basis at an acceptable rate for use near the network edge (where only a small number of concurrent streams are likely).

Transcoding latencies obtained for test video sequences confirm the real-time performance of the video transcoding. As expected, the speed depends on the bit rate of the compressed video stream; a high bit rate stream incurs higher transcoding latency. We also evaluated the quality of the transcoded video by measuring the average PSNR and percentage error (PE) and through the use of error images.

The current implementation of the transcoder uses the microengines provided by the IXP1200. Involving the StrongARM processor is worth considering for future work as is implementation using more powerful network processors. Our results were not compared to any other system as currently no similar adaptation scheme exists. We did compare the performance of our prototype to an earlier system exploiting only the basic capabilities of the IXP1200 (one thread in each video adaptation microengine) as a baseline.

The prototype adaptation node could be re-implemented relatively easily on more recent IXP series network processors. The use of the IXP2400 or, particularly, the IXP2800 would result in reduced transcoding latency and higher throughput given the increased number and speed of the microengines and due to the larger number of threads supported per microengine. Coding of the adaptation routines would also be simplified on such machines owing to their larger instruction memory capacities. This would improve readability and portability of the code and, possibly, efficiency as well. More aggressive transcoding might also be attempted. Further, the increased capabilities of these newer network processors would be far more effective in supporting the concurrent transcoding of multiple streams (for different multicast transmissions) and/or higher resolution streams corresponding to new encoding standards (e.g., MPEG-2 and H.263). Finally, the significant control processor capabilities of network processors such as the PowerNP and C-5e can be effectively exploited in practical deployments.

Acknowledgement

This work was supported, in part, by a University of Manitoba Graduate Fellowship.

References

1. L. Chen and G. Singh, "Enhancing multicast communication to support protocol design," in Proceedings of the 11th International Conference on Computer Communications and Networks (ICCCN '02), pp. 328–333, Miami, Fla, USA, October 2002.

2. T. Turletti, "INRIA Videoconferencing system (IVS)," ConneXions-The Interoperability Report Journal, vol. 8, no. 10, pp. 20–24, 1994.

3. R. Frederick, "Experiences with real-time software video compression," in Proceedings of the 6th International Workshop on Packet Video, pp. F1.1–F1.4, September 1994.

4. S. McCanne and V. Jacobson, "Visual audio tool," Lawrence Berkeley Laboratory, ftp://ftp.ee.lbl.gov/conferencing/vat.

5. S. McCanne and V. Jacobson, "vic: a flexible framework for packet video," in Proceedings of the 3rd ACM International Conference on Multimedia, pp. 511–522, San Franscisco, Calif, USA, November 1995.

6. H. Eriksson, "MBONE: the multicast backbone," Communications of the ACM, vol. 37, no. 8, pp. 54–60, 1994.

7. D. L. Tennenhouse and D. J. Wetherall, "Towards an active network architecture," Computer Communication Review, vol. 26, no. 2, pp. 5–17, 1996.

8. K. L. Calvert, "Architectural framework for active networks," RFC Draft, version 1.0, July 1999.

9. P. S. Goncalves, J. F. Rezende, O. M. Duarte, and G. Pujolle, "Improving layered video multicast using active networks," Pierre and Marie Curie University, Paris, France, March 2001.

10. R. Ramanujan and K. Thurber, "An active network based design of a QoS adaptive video multicast service," in Proceedings of the World Conference on Systems, Cybernetics and Informatics, pp. 643–650, July 1998.

11. H.-F. Hsiao and J.-N. Hwang, "Layered FGS video over active network with selective drop and adaptive rate control," in Proceedings of IEEE International Conference on Acoustics, Speech and Signal Processing (ICASSP '03), vol. 5, pp. 752–755, Hong Kong, April 2003.

12. L. Cheng and M. R. Ito, "Layered multicast with TCP-friendly congestion control using active networks," in Proceedings of the 10th International Conference on Telecommunications, pp. 806–811, March 2003.

13. H. Akamine, N. Wakamiya, M. Murata, and H. Miyahara, "On the construction of heterogeneous multicast distribution trees using filtering in an active network," in Proceedings of the 1st International Workshop on Quality of Future Internet Services (QoFIS '00), pp. 272–284, Berlin, Germany, September 2000.

14. R. Keller, S. Choi, M. Dasen, D. Decasper, G. Fankhauser, and B. Plattner, "An active router architecture for multicast video distribution," in Proceedings of the 19th Annual Joint Conference of the IEEE Computer and Communications Societies (INFOCOM '00), vol. 3, pp. 1137–1146, Tel-Aviv, Israel, March 2000.

15. R. Wittmann, K. Krasnodembski, and M. Zitterbart, "Heterogeneous multicasting based on RSVP and QoS filters," in Broadband European Networks and Multimedia Services, vol. 3408 of Proceedings of SPIE, pp. 357–365, Zurich, Switzerland, May 1998.

16. T. Yamada, N. Wakamiya, M. Murata, and H. Miyahara, "Implementation and evaluation of video-quality adjustment for heterogeneous video multicast," in Proceedings of the 8th Asia-Pacific Conference on Communications (APCC '02), pp. 454–457, September 2002.

17. Y. Jia, I. Nikolaidis, and P. Gburzynski, "Buffer space trade-offs in multihop networks," in Proceedings of the Conference on Communication Networks and Services Research (CNSR '03), pp. 74–79, May 2003.

18. J. L. Mitchell, W. B. Pennebaker, C. E. Fogg, and D. J. LeGall, MPEG Video Compression Standard, Chapman & Hall, Boca Raton, Fla, USA, 1996.

19. "Information Technology—Generic Coding of Moving Pictures and Associated Audio Information—Part 2 (Video)," ISO/IEC 13818-2, 1998.

20. "Visual: a compression codec for visual data—part 2," ISO/IEC 14496-2, 1998.

21. H.261, "Video codec for audiovisual services at px64 kbits," International Telecommunications Union Telecommunications Standardisation Sector, ITU-T Recommendation H.261, 1993.

22. D. H.263, "Video coding for low bitrate communication," International Telecommunications Union Telecommunications Standardisation Sector, ITU-T Recommendation H.263, 1996.

23. T. Wiegand, G. J. Sullivan, G. Bjøntegaard, and A. Luthra, "Overview of the H.264/AVC video coding standard," IEEE Transactions on Circuits and Systems for Video Technology, vol. 13, no. 7, pp. 560–576, 2003.

24. "Information Technology—Coding of Moving Pictures and Associated Audio for Digital Storage Media at up to about 1.5 Mbit/s—Part 2 (Video)," ISO/IEC 11172-2, 1993.

25. G. Keeman, R. Hellinghuizen, F. Hoeksema, and G. Heideman, "Transcoding of MPEG-2 bitstreams," Signal Processing: Image Communication, vol. 8, pp. 481–500, 1996.

26. J. Hwang, T. Wu, and C. Lin, "Dynamic frame-skipping in video transcoding," in Proceedings of the 2nd IEEE Workshop on Multimedia Signal Processing (MMSP '98), pp. 616–621, Redondo Beach, Calif, USA, December 1998.

27. H. Shu and L.-P. Chau, "An efficient arbitrary downsizing algorithm for video transcoding," IEEE Transactions on Circuits and Systems for Video Technology, vol. 14, no. 6, pp. 887–891, 2004.

28. Y. Liang, L.-P. Chau, and Y.-P. Tan, "Arbitrary downsizing video transcoding using fast motion vector reestimatlon," IEEE Signal Processing Letters, vol. 9, no. 11, pp. 352–355, 2002.

29. R. Dugad and N. Ahuja, "A fast scheme for image size change in the compressed domain," IEEE Transactions on Circuits and Systems for Video Technology, vol. 11, no. 4, pp. 461–474, 2001.

30. "Intel IXP2400 Network Processor—Product Brief," Intel Corp., 2003.

31. "Intel IXP2805 Network Processor—Product Brief," Intel Corp., 2005.

32. J. R. Allen, Jr., B. M. Bass, C. Basso, et al., "IBM PowerNP network processor: hardware, software, and applications," IBM Journal of Research and Development, vol. 47, no. 2-3, pp. 177–193, 2003.

33. "NP1c Network Processor—Product Brief," EZchip Technology, 2002.

34. Agere Systems Proprietary, "The challenge for next generation network processors," white paper, April 2001.

35. "C-5e Network Processor—Product Brief," Motorola, Plantation, Fla, USA, 2003.

36. M. Shorfuzzaman, R. Eskicioglu, and P. Graham, "Video transcoding using network processors to support dynamically adaptive video multicast," in Proceedings of the 20th IEEE International Conference on Advanced Information Networking and Applications (AINA '06), vol. 1, pp. 471–476, Vienna, Austria, April 2006.

37. D. S. Alexander, B. Braden, C. A. Gunter, et al., "Active network encapsulation protocol (ANEP)," RFC Draft, July 1997.

A Survey of Visual Sensor Networks

Stanislava Soro and Wendi Heinzelman

ABSTRACT

Visual sensor networks have emerged as an important class of sensor-based distributed intelligent systems, with unique performance, complexity, and quality of service challenges. Consisting of a large number of low-power camera nodes, visual sensor networks support a great number of novel vision-based applications. The camera nodes provide information from a monitored site, performing distributed and collaborative processing of their collected data. Using multiple cameras in the network provides different views of the scene, which enhances the reliability of the captured events. However, the large amount of image data produced by the cameras combined with the network's resource constraints require exploring new means for data processing, communication, and sensor management. Meeting these challenges of visual sensor networks requires interdisciplinary approaches, utilizing vision processing, communications and networking, and embedded processing. In this paper, we provide an overview of the current state-of-the-art in the field of visual sensor networks, by exploring several relevant research directions. Our goal is to provide a better understanding of current research problems in the different research fields of visual sensor networks, and to show how these different research fields should interact to solve the many challenges of visual sensor networks.

Introduction

Camera-based networks have been used for security monitoring and surveillance for a very long time. In these networks, surveillance cameras act as independent peers that continuously send video streams to a central processing server, where the video is analyzed by a human operator.

With the advances in image sensor technology, low-power image sensors have appeared in a number of products, such as cell phones, toys, computers, and robots. Furthermore, recent developments in sensor networking and distributed processing have encouraged the use of image sensors in these networks, which has resulted in a new ubiquitous paradigm—visual sensor networks. Visual sensor networks (VSNs) consist of tiny visual sensor nodes called camera nodes, which integrate the image sensor, embedded processor, and wireless transceiver. Following the trends in low-power processing, wireless networking, and distributed sensing, visual sensor networks have developed as a new technology with a number of potential applications, ranging from security to monitoring to telepresence.

In a visual sensor network a large number of camera nodes form a distributed system, where the camera nodes are able to process image data locally and to extract relevant information, to collaborate with other cameras on the application-specific task, and to provide the system's user with information-rich descriptions of captured events. With current trends moving toward development of distributed processing systems and with an increasing number of devices with built-in image sensors, a question of how these devices can be used together appears [1]. There are several specific questions that have intrigued the research community. How can the knowledge gained from wireless sensor networks be used in the development of visual sensor networks? What kind of data processing algorithms can be supported by these networks? What is the best way to manage a large number of cameras in an efficient and scalable manner? What are the most efficient camera node architectures? Inspired by the tremendous potential of visual sensor networks as well as by the current progress in this research field, we provide in this paper an overview of the current research directions, challenges, and potential applications for visual sensor networks.

Several survey papers on multimedia sensor networks and visual processing can be found in the current literature. In [2], Misra et al. provide a survey of proposed solutions for different layers of the network protocol stack used for multimedia transmission over the wireless medium. Charfi et al. [3] provide a survey on several challenging issues in the design of visual sensor networks design, including coverage requirements, network architectures, and energy-aware data communication and processing. Here, we go one step further, by discussing these and other aspects of visual sensor networks in more detail and taking a multidisciplinary look at these topics. An extensive survey of wireless multimedia sensor networks is provided in [4], where Akyildiz et al. discuss various open research problems in this research area, including networking architectures, single layer and crosslayer communication protocol stack design, and multimedia sensor hardware. Here, we discuss similar problems, but considering visual sensor networks as distributed systems of embedded devices, highly constrained in terms of available energy, bandwidth resources and with limiting processing capabilities. Thus, we are focusing on the low power and low complexity aspects of visual sensor networks. Considering that many aspects of visual sensor networks, such as those related to the design of the networking protocol stack or data encoding techniques in the application layer have already been thoroughly discussed in [2, 4], we focus here on other aspects of data communication, by emphasizing the need for collaborative data communication and sensor management in visual sensor networks. Thus, this paper complements these other survey papers and can be a valuable source of information regarding the state-of-the-art in several research directions that are vital to the success of visual sensor networks.

Characteristics of Visual Sensor Networks

One of the main differences between visual sensor networks and other types of sensor networks lies in the nature of how the image sensors perceive information from the environment. Most sensors provide measurements as 1D data signals. However, image sensors are composed of a large number of photosensitive cells. One measurement of the image sensor provides a 2D set of data points, which we see as an image. The additional dimensionality of the data set results in richer information content as well as in a higher complexity of data processing and analysis.

In addition, a camera's sensing model is inherently different from the sensing model of any other type of sensor. Typically, a sensor collects data from its vicinity, as determined by its sensing range. Cameras, on the other hand, are characterized by a directional sensing model—cameras capture images of distant objects/ scenes from a certain direction. The 2D sensing range of traditional sensor nodes is, in the case of cameras, replaced by a 3D viewing volume (called field of view, or FoV).

Visual sensor networks are in many ways unique and more challenging compared to other types of wireless sensor networks. These unique characteristics of visual sensor networks are described next.

Resource Requirements

The lifetime of battery-operated camera nodes is limited by their energy consumption, which is proportional to the energy required for sensing, processing, and transmitting the data. Given the large amount of data generated by the camera nodes, both processing and transmitting image data are quite costly in terms of energy, much more so than for other types of sensor networks. Furthermore, visual sensor networks require large bandwidth for transmitting image data. Thus both energy and bandwidth are even more constrained than in other types of wireless sensor networks.

Local Processing

Local (on-board) processing of the image data reduces the total amount of data that needs to be communicated through the network. Local processing can involve simple image processing algorithms (such as background substraction for motion/object detection, and edge detection) as well as more complex image/vision processing algorithms (such as feature extraction, object classification, scene reasoning). Thus, depending on the application, the camera nodes may provide different levels of intelligence, as determined by the complexity of the processing algorithms they use [5]. For example, low-level processing algorithms (such as frame differencing for motion detection or edge detection algorithms) can provide a camera node with the basic information about the environment, and help it decide whether it is necessary to transmit the captured image or whether it should continue processing the image at a higher level. More complex vision algorithms (such as object feature extraction, object classification, etc.) enable cameras to reason about the captured phenomena, such as to provide basic classification of the captured object. Furthermore, the cameras can collaborate by exchanging the detected object features, enabling further processing to collectively reason about the object's appearance or behavior. At this point the visual sensor network becomes a user-independent, intelligent system of distributed cameras that provides only relevant information about the monitored phenomena. Therefore, the increased complexity of vision processing algorithms results in highly intelligent camera systems that are oftentimes called smart camera networks [6].

In order to extract necessary information from different images, a camera node must employ different image processing algorithms. One specific image processing algorithm cannot achieve the same performance for different types of images—for example, an algorithm for face extraction significantly differs from algorithm for vehicle detection. However, oftentimes it is impossible to keep all the necessary image processing algorithms in the constrained memory of a camera node. One solution to this problem is to use mobile agents—a specific piece of software dispatched by the sink node to the region of interest [7]. Mobile agents collect and aggregate the data using a specific image algorithm and send the processed data back to the sink. Furthermore, the mobile agents can migrate between the nodes in order to perform the specific task, thereby performing distributed information processing [8]. In this way, the amount of data sent by the node, as well as the number of data flows in the network, can be significantly reduced.

Real-Time Performance

Most applications of visual sensor networks require real-time data from the camera nodes, which imposes strict boundaries on maximum allowable delays of data from the sources (cameras) to the user (sink). The real-time performance of a visual sensor network is affected by the time required for image data processing and for the transmission of the processed data throughout the network. Constrained by limited energy resources and by the processing speed of embedded processors, most camera nodes have processors that support only lightweight processing algorithms. On the network side, the real-time performance of a visual sensor network is constrained by the wireless channel limitations (available bandwidth, modulation, data rate), employed wireless standard, and by the current network condition. For example, upon detection of an event, the camera nodes can suddenly inject large amounts of data in the network, which can cause data congestion and increase data delays.

Different error protection schemes can affect the real-time transmission of image data through the network as well. Commonly used error protection schemes, such as automated-repeat-request (ARQ) and forward-error-correction (FEC) have been investigated in order to increase the reliability of wireless data transmissions [9]. However, due to the tight delay constraints, methods such as ARQ are not suitable to be used in visual sensor networks. On the other hand, FEC schemes usually require long blocks in order to perform well, which again can jeopardize delay constraints.

Finally, multihop routing is the preferred routing method in wireless sensor networks due to its energy-efficiency. However, multihop routing may result in increased delays, due to queueing and data processing at the intermediate nodes.

Thus, the total delay from the data source (camera node) to the sink increases with the number of hops on the routing path. Additionally, bandwidth becomes a scarce resource in multihop networks consisting of traditional wireless sensor nodes. In order to support the transmission of real-time data, different wireless modules that provide larger bandwidths (such as those based on IEEE 802.11 b,g,n) can be considered.

Precise Location and Orientation Information

In visual sensor networks, most of the image processing algorithms require information about the locations of the camera nodes as well as information about the cameras' orientations. This information can be obtained through a camera calibration process, which retrieves information on the cameras' intrinsic and extrinsic parameters (explained in the Section 5.1). Estimation of calibration parameters usually requires knowledge of a set of feature point correspondences among the images of the cameras. When this is not provided, the cameras can be calibrated up to a similarity transformation [10], meaning that only relative coordinates and orientations of the cameras with respect to each other can be determined.

Time Synchronization

The information content of an image may become meaningless without proper information about the time at which this image was captured. Many processing tasks that involve multiple cameras (such as object localization) depend on highly synchronized cameras' snapshots. Time synchronization protocols developed for wireless sensor networks [11] can be successfully used for synchronization of visual sensor networks as well.

Data Storage

The cameras generate large amounts of data over time, which in some cases should be stored for later analysis. An example is monitoring of remote areas by a group of camera nodes, where the frequent transmission of captured image data to a remote sink would quickly exhaust the cameras' energy resources. Thus, in these cases the camera nodes should be equipped with memories of larger capacity in order to store the data. To minimize the amount of data that requires storage, the camera node should classify the data according to its importance by using spatiotemporal analysis of image frames, and decide which data should have priority to be stored. For example, if an application is interested in information about some particular object, then the background can be highly compressed and stored, or even completely discarded [12].

The stored image data usually becomes less important over time, so it can be substituted with newly acquired data. In addition, reducing the redundancy in the data collected by cameras with overlapped views can be achieved via local communication and processing. This enables the cameras to reduce their needs for storage space by keeping only data of unique image regions. Finally, by increasing the available memory, more complex processing tasks can be supported on-board, which in return can reduce data transmissions and reduce the space needed for storing processed data.

Autonomous Camera Collaboration

Visual sensor networks are envisioned as distributed and autonomous systems, where cameras collaborate and, based on exchanged information, reason autonomously about the captured event and decide how to proceed. Through collaboration, the cameras relate the events captured in the images, and they enhance their understanding of the environment. Similar to wireless sensor networks, visual sensor networks should be data-centric, where captured events are described by their names and attributes. Communication between cameras should be based on some uniform ontology for the description of the event and interpretation of the scene dynamics [13].

Table 1. Applications of visual sensor networks.

General application	Specific application
Surveillance	Public places
	Traffic
	Parking lots
	Remote areas
Environmental monitoring	Hazardous areas
	Animal habitats
	Building monitoring
Smart homes	Elderly care
	Kindergarten
Smart meeting rooms	Teleconferencing
	Virtual studios
Virtual reality	Telepresence systems
	Telereality systems

Applications of Visual Sensor Networks

With the rapid development of visual sensor networks, numerous applications for these networks have been envisioned, as illustrated in the Table 1. Here, we mention some of these applications.

(i) Surveillance: Surveillance has been the primary application of camera-based networks for a long time, where the monitoring of large public areas (such as airports, subways, etc.) is performed by hundreds or even thousands of security cameras. Since cameras usually provide raw video streams, acquiring important information from collected image data requires a huge amount of processing and human resources, making it time-consuming and prone to error. Current efforts in visual sensor networking are concentrated toward advancing the existing surveillance technology by utilizing intelligent methods for extracting information from image data locally on the camera node, thereby reducing the amount of data traffic. At the same time, visual sensor networks integrate resource-aware camera management policies and wireless networking aspects with surveillance-specific tasks. Thus, visual sensor networks can be seen as a next generation of surveillance systems that are not limited by the absence of infrastructure, nor do they require large processing resources at one central server. These networks are adaptable to the environment dynamics, autonomous, and able to respond timely to a user's requests by providing an immediate view from any desired viewpoint or by analyzing and providing information from specific, user determined areas.

(ii) Environmental monitoring: Visual sensor networks can be used for monitoring remote and inaccessible areas over a long period of time. In these applications, energy-efficient operations are particularly important in order to prolong monitoring over an extended period of time. Oftentimes the cameras are combined with other types of sensors into a heterogeneous network, such that the cameras are triggered only when an event is detected by other sensors used in the network [14].

(iii) Smart homes: There are situations (such as patients in hospitals or people with disabilities), where a person must be under the constant care of others. Visual sensor networks can provide continuous monitoring of people, and using smart algorithms the network can provide information about the person needing care, such as information about any unusual behavior or an emergency situation.

(iv) Smart meeting rooms: Remote participants in a meeting can enjoy a dynamic visual experience using visual and audio sensor network technology.

(v) Telepresence systems: Telepresence systems enable a remote user to "visit" some location that is monitored by a collection of cameras. For example, museums, galleries or exhibition rooms can be covered by a network of camera nodes that provide live video streams to a user who wishes to access the place remotely (e.g., over the Internet). The system is able to provide the user with any current view from any viewing point, and thus it provides the sense of being physically present at a remote location through interaction with the system's interface [15]. Telereality aims to synthesize realistic novel views from images acquired from multiple cameras [16].

Research Directions in Visual Sensor Networks

Visual sensor networks are based on several diverse research fields, including image/vision processing, communication and networking, and distributed and embedded system processing. Thus, the design complexity involves finding the best tradeoff between performance and different aspects of these networks. According to Hengstler and Aghajan [17] the design of a camera-based network involves mapping application requirements to a set of network operation parameters that are generally related to several diverse research fields, including network topology, sensing, processing, communication, and resource utilization.

Due to its interdisciplinary nature, the research directions in visual sensor networks are numerous and diverse. In the following sections we present an overview of the ongoing research in several areas vital to visual sensor networks: vision processing, wireless networking, camera node hardware architectures, sensor management, and middleware, as illustrated in Figure 1. The survey begins by addressing problems in vision processing related to camera calibration. Then, research related to object detection, tracking, and high-level vision processing is discussed. The survey next provides an overview of different networking problems, such as those related to real-time data communication, camera collaboration and route selection. Next, various sensor management policies, which aim to provide balance between vision and networking tasks, are discussed. Since both vision processing and communication tasks are limited by the camera node hardware, an overview of the latest camera node's prototype solutions are provided, along with a description of network architectures for several visual sensor network testbeds. Finally, an overview of visual sensor networks middleware that bridges the gap between the application and the low level network structure is provided. In the last part of this paper, we provide an overview of some of the many open research problems that lie in the intersections of these different research areas.

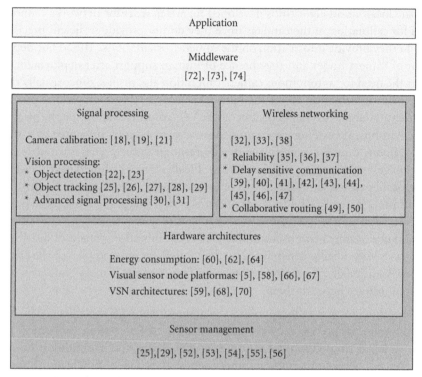

Figure 1. Several research areas that contribute to the development of visual sensor networks.

Signal Processing Algorithms

Camera Calibration

Obtaining precise information about the cameras' locations and orientations is crucial for many vision processing algorithms in visual sensor networks. The information on a camera's location and orientation is obtained through the calibration process, where this information (presented as the camera's orientation matrix R and translation vector T) is found from the set of feature points that the camera sees.

Calibration of cameras can be done at one processing center, which collects image feature points from all cameras in the system and, based on that, it estimates the calibration parameters for the entire system. However, such a calibration method is expensive in terms of energy and is not scalable, and thus it is not suitable for energy-constrained visual sensor networks. Therefore, visual sensor networks require distributed energy-efficient algorithms for multicamera calibration.

The localization algorithms developed for wireless sensor networks cannot be used for calibration of the cameras since they do not provide sufficient precision, nor do they provide information on the cameras' orientations. The ad hoc deployment of camera nodes and the absence of human support after deployment imposes the need for autonomous camera calibration algorithms. Since usually there is no prior information about the network's vision graph (a graph that provides information about overlapped cameras' FoVs), communication graph, or about the environment, finding correspondences across cameras (presented as a set of points in one camera's image plane that correspond to the points in another camera's image) is challenging and error prone. Ideally, cameras should have the ability to self-calibrate based on their observations from the environment. The first step in this process involves finding sets of cameras that image the same scene points. Finding correspondences among these cameras may require excessive, energy expensive inter-camera communication. Thus, the calibration process of distributed cameras is additionally constrained by the limited energy resources of the camera nodes. Additionally, the finite transmission ranges of the camera nodes can limit communication between them.

Therefore, camera calibration in a visual sensor network is challenged by finding the cameras' precise extrinsic parameters based on existing calibration procedures taken from computer vision, but considering the communication constraints and energy limitations of camera nodes. These calibration methods should cope successfully with changes in the communication graph (caused by variable channel conditions) and changes in the visual graph (due to the loss of cameras or a change in the cameras' positions and orientations).

Calibration based on a known object is a common calibration method from computer vision, that is, widely adopted in visual sensor networks [18, 19]. In [18] Barton-Sweeney et al. present a light-wight protocol for camera calibration based on such an approach, where the network contains a fraction of wireless nodes equipped with CMOS camera modules, while the rest of the nodes use unique modulated LED emissions in order to uniquely identify themselves to the cameras. This calibration method requires distance information among the cameras, which is obtained through finding epipoles (illustrated in Figure 2) among the pairs of cameras. The authors distinguish two cases for estimation of the distances between two cameras, the case when cameras, in addition of observing the common target (node), can see each other, and the case when they cannot see each other. In the first case the distances between the cameras and the node can be determined up to a scale factor [20]. In the second case, the epipoles estimation is based on estimation of fundamental matrix (based on a minimum of 8 points in the common view), which results in noisy data.

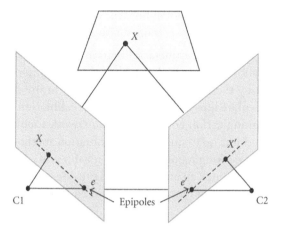

Figure 2. Epipoles of a pair of cameras—the points where the line that connects the centers of the cameras intersects the cameras' image planes [10, 18].

Thus, in [18] the authors do not provide fully automatic camera calibration methods, but instead they point out the difficulty of finding appropriate network configurations that can ease the calibration process.

Funiak et al. [19] provide a distributed method for camera calibration based on collaborative tracking of a moving target by multiple cameras. Here, the simultaneous localization and tracking (SLAT) problem is analyzed, which refers to estimation of both the trajectory of the object and the poses of the cameras. The proposed solution to the SLAT problem is based on an approximation of a Kalman filter. The restrictions imposed by the communication network are not considered in the proposed method.

Devarajan et al. [21] add the underlying communication network model into their proposed camera calibration algorithm, thereby analyzing its performances with respect to the calibration accuracy as well as communication overhead. Their calibration procedure is based on the bundle adjustment method that minimizes a nonlinear cost of the camera parameters and a collection of unknown 3D scene points projected on matched image correspondences. The distributed calibration is performed by clusters of cameras that share the same scene points. The simulation results prove the advantage of using distributed over centralized calibration. The average error in the estimated parameters is similar in both cases, but the distributed calibration method requires less time since it performs optimization over a smaller number of estimating parameters. Additionally, the communication burden is smaller and more evenly distributed across the camera nodes in the case of distributed calibration compared to the centralized approach. However, this method includes finding accurate multiimage correspondences, requiring excessive resources and computational burden, which makes this calibration pro-tocol less attractive for resource constrained visual sensor networks.

Most of the algorithms for camera calibration in visual sensor networks are based on existing calibration methods established in computer vision, and rarely are they influenced by the underlying network. Thus, future camera calibration algorithms should explore how the outcome of these calibration algorithms can be affected by the communication constraints and network topology. In particular, it is necessary to find out how multicamera calibration methods can be affected by the underlying networking requirements for reliable and energy efficient inter-camera communication. Such an analysis would provide an insight into the trade-offs between the desired calibration precision and cost for achieving it.

Also, the calibration methods should be robust to the network's dynamics; for example, considering how the addition of new cameras or the loss of existing cameras affect the calibration process. Above all, the calibration algorithms should be light-weight, meaning that they should not be based on extensive process-ing operations. Instead, they should be easily implementable on the hardware platforms of existing camera nodes. Due to the ad hoc nature of visual sensor networks, future research is required to develop camera calibration algorithms that determine precise calibration parameters using a fully automatic approach that requires minimal or no a priori knowledge of network distances, network geometry or corresponding feature points.

Vision-Based Signal Processing

The appearance of small CMOS image sensors and the development of distrib-uted wireless sensor networks opens the door to a new era in embedded vision processing. The challenge is how to adapt existing vision processing algorithms to be used in resource-constrained distributed networks of mostly low-resolution cameras. The main constraint comes from the amount of data that can be trans-mitted through the network. Additionally, most vision processing algorithms are developed without regard to any processing limitations. Furthermore, timing constraints of existing algorithms need to be carefully reconsidered, as the data may travel over multiple hops. Finally, many vision processing algorithms are developed for single camera systems, so these algorithms now need to be adapted for multicamera distributed systems.

The limited processing capabilities of camera nodes dictate a need for light-weight vision processing algorithms in visual sensor networks. However, distrib-uted processing of image data and data fusion from multiple image sources re-quires more intelligent embedded vision algorithms. As the processing algorithms start to become more demanding (such as those that rely on extraction of feature points and feature matching across multiple cameras' views) the processing capabilities can become a bottleneck. Considering the hierarchical model for vision processing provided in [17], here we describe the main vision processing tasks for visual sensor networks.

Object Detection and Occupancy Reasoning

The initial phase of visual data processing usually involves object detection. Object detection may trigger a camera's processing activity and data communication. Object detection is mostly based on light-weight background substraction algorithms and presents the first step toward collective reasoning by the camera nodes about the objects that occupy the monitored space.

Many applications of visual sensor networks require reasoning about the presence of objects in the scene. In occupancy reasoning, the visual sensor network is not interested in extracting an individual object's features, but instead extracting the state of the scene (such as information about the presence and quantity of objects in the monitored scene) based on light-weight image processing algorithms. An example of such occupancy reasoning in visual sensor networks is the estimation of the number of people in a crowded scene, as discussed in [22]. Here the estimates are obtained using a planar projection of the scene's visual hull, as illustrated in Figure 3. Since the objects may be occluded, the exact number of objects cannot be determined, but instead lower and upper bounds on the number of objects in each polygon are tracked. The estimated bounds on the number of objects are updated over time using a history tree, so that the lower and upper bounds converge toward the exact number of objects in each polygon.

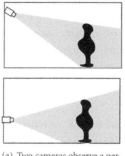
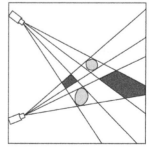

(a) Two cameras observe a person from different positions. The cameras' cones are swept around the person's silhouette

(b) Polygons obtained as the intersection of planar projections of cones in the case of two objects. Visual hull presents the largest volume in which an object can reside. The dark-colored polygons do not contain any objects

Figure 3. Finding the polygons that contain people based on a projection of the person' silhouettes on the planar scene [22].

Determining good camera-network deployments and the number of camera nodes to use is also addressed in recent work on occupancy estimation problems. For example, in [23] Yang et al. study a model for managing (tasking) a set of cameras that collectively reason about the occupancy of the monitored area. Their goal is to provide an upper bound on the number of cameras needed to reason about the occupancy for a given accuracy. This task is performed by minimizing the area potentially occupied by the moving objects. Using the Monte Carlo method, the authors in [23] find the number of cameras necessary to provide a visual hull area for one object. However, in the case of multiple objects in the scene, the visual hull area does not converge to the actual area covered by the objects, due to occlusions. Thus, the authors compare several heuristic approaches (uniform, greedy, clustering, and optimal) for finding a subset of the cameras that minimize the visual hull area for the scenario with multiple objects in the scene.

Since detection of objects on the scene is usually the first step in image analysis, it is important to minimize the chances of objects` fault detection. Thus, reliability and light-weight operations will continue to be the main concerns of image processing algorithms for object detection and occupancy reasoning.

Object Tracking

Object tracking is a common task for many applications of visual sensor networks. Object tracking is a challenging task since it is computationally intensive and it requires real-time data processing. The basic methods for target tracking include temporal differencing and template correlation matching [24]. Temporal differencing requires finding the regions in frames separated in time that have been changed, and thus it fails if the object stops moving or if it gets occluded. On the other hand, template correlation matching aims to find the region of an image that best correlates to an image template. This method is not robust to changes in the object's appearance, such as object size, orientation, or even light conditions. Sophisticated tracking algorithms, which rely on motion parameter estimation and probability estimates (such as tracking algorithms based on Kalman filtering [25] or particle filtering [26]) are suitable for smart camera networks with advanced processing capabilities.

The availability of multiple views in visual sensor networks improves tracking reliability, but with the price of an increased communication overhead among the cameras. Therefore, in resource-constrained visual sensor networks it is important to use lightweight processing algorithms and to minimize the data load that has to be communicated among the cameras. Lau et al. [27] provide an example of a simple algorithm for tracking multiple targets based on hue histograms. After background substraction and segmentation, the histogram of detected blobs in the scene is found and then compared with the histograms found for previous frames in order to track the objects.

Ko and Berry [28] investigate a distributed scheme for target tracking in a multicamera environment. Their collaborative strategy is based on establishing information links between the cameras that detect the target (initiators) and their neighboring cameras that can share information about the tracked target. The cameras extract several target features (edge histogram, UV color histogram, and local position of target) which are correlated across the nodes in order to decide whether information links should be established between the nodes. Such an approach improves the accuracy of the target detection and significantly reduces the communication load.

The success of the proposed tracking algorithms can be jeopardized in the case when the tracked objects are occluded. Object occlusion, which happens when a camera looses sight of an object due to obstruction by another object, is an unavoidable problem in visual sensor networks. Although in most cases the positions of moving occluders cannot be predicted, still it is expected that a multicamera system can handle the occlusion problem more easily due to providing multiple object views. This problem is discussed in [29], where the authors examine the dependance of single object tracking on prior information about the movement of the tracked object and about static occluders. The real challenge in visual sensor networks however, is to avoid losing the tracked object due to occlusions in the situation when not all cameras are available for tracking at the same time. Thus, future research should be directed toward examining the best sensor management policies for selecting camera nodes that will enable multiple target views, thereby reducing the chances of occlusion while using the minimum number of cameras.

Advanced Signal Processing in VSNs

Many novel applications of visual sensor networks are based on advanced vision processing that provides a thorough analysis of the objects' appearances and behaviors, thereby providing a better understanding of the relationships among the objects and situation awareness to the user. In these applications the objective is to provide the automated image understanding by developing efficient computational methods based on principled fundamental issues in automated image understanding. These issues include providing and understanding the performance of methods for object recognition, classification, activity recognition, context understanding, background modeling, and scene analysis.

In such an application a visual sensor network can be used to track human movements but also to interpret these movements in order to recognize semantically meaningful gestures. Human gesture analysis and behavior recognition have gained increasing interest in the research community and are used in a number of applications such as surveillance, video conferencing, smart homes, and assisted living. Behavior analysis applications require collaboration among the cameras, which exchange preprocessed, high level descriptions of the observed scene, rather than the raw image information. In order to reduce the amount of information exchanged between the cameras, research is directed toward finding an effective way of describing the scene and providing the semantic meaning of the extracted data (features). An example of such research is provided in [45], where Teixeira et al. describe a camera-based network that uses symbolic information in order to summarize the motion activity of people. The extracted basic functions of human activity are analyzed using a sensing grammar, which provides the probability likelihood of each outcome. The sequences of basic features of human activity are fed into a inference model, that is, used to reason about the macroscopic behaviors of people—the behavior in some area over a long period of time.

Human behavior interpretation and gesture analysis often use explicit shape models that provide a priori knowledge of the human body in 3D. Oftentimes, these models assume a certain type of body movement, which eases the gesture interpretation problem in the case of body self-occlusion. Recent work of Aghajan and Wu [46] provides a framework for human behavior interpretation based on a 3D human model for estimation of a user's posture from multiple cameras' views. This model is reconstructed from previous model instances and current multiple camera views, and it contains information on geometric body configuration, color/texture of body parts, and motion information. After fitting ellipses to corresponding body parts (segments), human posture is estimated by minimizing the distance between the posture and the ellipses.

Another approach in designing context-aware visual based networks involves using multimodal information for the analysis and interpretation of the objects' dynamics. In addition to low-power camera nodes, such systems may contain other types of sensors such as audio, vibration, thermal, and PIR. By fusing multimodal information from various nodes, such a network can provide better models for understanding an object's behavior and group interactions.

The aforementioned vision processing tasks require extracting features about an event, which in the case of energy and memory constrained camera nodes can be hard or even impossible to achieve, especially in real-time. Thus, although it is desirable to have high-resolution data features, costly feature extractions actually should be limited. This implies the need for finding optimal ways to determine when feature extraction tasks can be performed and when they should be skipped or left to other active cameras, without degrading overall performance. Also, most of the current work still use a centralized approach for data acquisition and fusion. Thus, future research should be directed toward migrating the process of decision making to the sensors, and toward dynamically finding the best camera node that can serve as a fusion center to combine extracted information from all active camera nodes.

Communication Protocols

Communication protocols for the "traditional" wireless sensor networks are mostly focused on supporting requirements for energy-efficiency in the low data rate communications. On the other hand, in addition to energy-efficiency, visual sensor networks are constrained with much tighter quality of service (QoS) requirements compared to "traditional" wireless sensor networks. Some of the most important QoS requirements of visual sensor networks, such as requirements for low data delay and data reliability, are not the primary concerns in the design of communication protocols for "traditional" wireless sensor networks. Additionally, the sensing characteristics of image sensors can also affect the design of communication protocols for visual sensor networks. For example, in [30], we found that the performance of a coverage-aware routing protocol that was initially developed for wireless sensor networks can change when such a protocol is applied to a visual sensor network. This change in protocol behavior is caused by the fact that distant out-of-communication-range cameras can still observe (cover) a common part of the scene (illustrated in Figure 4), which can influence how this protocol selects routing paths in the network. Thus, the communication protocols developed for traditional wireless sensor networks cannot be simply reused in visual sensor networks.

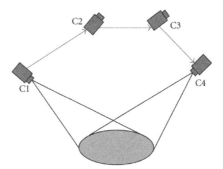

Figure 4. Cameras C1 and C4 observe the same part of the scene, but are not in communication range of each other. Thus, data routing is performed over other camera nodes [30].

An event captured by a visual sensor network can trigger the injection of large amounts of data into the network from multiple sources. Each camera can inject variable amounts of data into the network, depending on the data processing (image processing algorithm, followed by the data compression and error correction). The end-to-end data transmissions should satisfy the delay guarantees, thus requiring stable data routes. At the same time, the choice of routing paths should be performed such that the available network resources (e.g., energy and channel bandwidth) are efficiently balanced across the network.

Beside the energy efficiency and strict QoS constraints, the used data communication model can be influenced by the required quality of the image data provided by the visual sensor network. For example, in [47], Lecuire et al. use an adaptive energy-conserving data transmission model, where nodes, based on their remaining energies, decide whether they will forward packets of a certain priority. The packet priority is defined either based on the resolution level (subband) of the image's wavelet transformation or based on the magnitude of the wavelet coefficients. In order to avoid situations where the data packets are dropped near the data sink, this transmission scheme decreases the probability of packet discarding as the packet approaches the sink. This transmission scheme offers a trade-off in consumed energy versus reconstructed image quality, and it demonstrates the advantage of the magnitude-based prioritization scheme over the resolution level scheme.

Another important aspect in the design of communication protocols for visual sensor networks includes the support for camera collaboration on a specific task. Therefore, the reliable transmission of delay constrained data obtained through collaboration of a number of camera nodes is the main focus of the networking protocols for visual sensor networks. Thus, we further discuss the influence of requirements for reliability, latency, and collaborative processing to the design of data communication protocols for visual sensor networks. Table 2 provides an overview of the networking protocols that are discussed throughout this section with respect to reliability, latency, and collaborative data routing.

Table 2. Representatives of networking protocols used in visual sensor networks.

Criteria	Protocol	Strategy
Reliability		Combined redundant data transmission over multipath routes and error correction algorithms
	Wu and Abouzeid [31]	Multipath cluster based data transmissions combined with error correction at each cluster head
	Chen et al. [32]	Multipath geographical routing and error correction along the routing paths
	Maimour et al. [33]	Comparison of different strategies for load repartition over the multiple routing paths
Delay		Design of delay sensitive MAC and routing protocols, and cross-layer approaches
MAC protocols	DSMAC—Lin et al. [34]	Adjustable sleeping periods of sensor nodes according to the traffic conditions
	DMAC—Lu et al. [35]	Eliminates the delays caused by sleepy nodes that are unaware of current data transmissions
	Ceken [36]	TDMA-based delay aware MAC protocol that provides more time slots for time critical nodes
Routing protocols	SPEED—He et al. [37]	Transmission delay of a packet depends on the distance to the sink and delivery speed
	MMSPEED—Felemban et al. [38]	Multispeed transmission and the establishment of more than one path to the destination
	Lu and Krishnamachari [39]	Joint routing and delay optimization
Cross-layer approaches	Andreopoulos et al. [40]	Capacity-distortion optimization based on several parameters of routing, MAC, and physical layer
	Van der Schaar and Turaga [41]	Packetization and packet retransmission optimization
	Wang et al. [42]	Cross layer protocol for adaptive image transmission for quality optimization of wavelet transformed image
Collaborative image routing		Using spatiotemporal information form multiple correlated data sources
	Obraczka et al. [43]	Communication overhead reduction by collective reasoning based on correlated data
	Medeiros et al. [44]	Cluster-based object tracking

Reliability

Reliable data transport is one of the main QoS requirements of visual sensor networks. In wireless sensor networks, the transport layer of the traditional protocol stack is not fully developed, since the traditional functions of this layer that should provide reliable data transport, such as congestion control, are not a primary concern in low data, low duty-cycle wireless sensor networks. However, the bursty and bulky data traffic in visual sensor networks imposes the need for establishing mechanisms that provide reliable data communication over the unreliable channels across the network.

The standard networking protocols designed to offer reliable data transport are not suitable for visual sensor networks. The commonly used transport protocol TCP cannot be simply reused in wireless networks, since it cannot distinguish between data losses due to network congestion and due to poor wireless channel conditions. In wireless sensor networks, providing reliability oftentimes assumes data retransmissions, which introduce intolerable delays for visual sensor networks. For example, protocols such as Pump Slowly Fetch Quickly (PSFQ) [48] enable the fast recovery of lost data from the local neighborhood using selective NACKs, however, it assumes that the data is lost only due to the channel conditions, and not due to data congestion, basically assuming transmissions of small data amounts through the network.

Data routing over multiple paths is oftentimes considered as a way to reduce the correlations among the packet losses and to spread the energy consumption more evenly among the cameras. Since data retransmissions increase latency in the network, Wu and Abouzeid [31] propose a transport scheme that combines multipath diversity and Reed-Solomon error correction in order to increase data reliability. In their proposed model, the data source transmits several copies of the same data over multiple paths, which converge to the cluster head. Each cluster head compares the received data copies, and it retransmits the error-corrected version of the data over multiple paths toward the next cluster head. Since the error correction is performed at the cluster heads, this transmission scheme improves the quality of the received image data at the sink (measured by PSNR). Another protocol that aims to increase the reliability of transmitted data over multiple paths is presented by Chen et al. [32]. Here, multiple routing paths are established based on the proposed directional geographical routing (DGR) algorithm that, combined with FEC coding, provides more reliable data transmission compared to single-path routing, and it achieves better performance in overall delay and quality of video data at the sink.

Visual sensor networks can experience significant loses of data due to network congestion. As a way to control data congestion in wireless multimedia networks,

Maimour et al. [33] explore several strategies for load repartition on multiple source-sink paths. They compare simple strategies that uniformly distribute the traffic from the data source on all available paths with more complex strategies that use explicit notifications from the congested nodes in order to balance traffic on available paths, while keeping the sending rate unchanged.

Congestion control is a dominant problem in the design of reliable protocols for visual sensor networks. Considering that multimedia data can tolerate a certain degree of loss [49], congestion control mechanisms should provide a trade-off between the quality of the data received from the cameras and the energy expense for transmitting this data. Having concurrent data flows increases the data reliability, but it also greatly increases the transmission cost. Thus, further evaluation is needed to clarify the trade-offs between data reliability and data redundancy in multipath routing schemes for visual sensor networks. Furthermore, most of the described data transmission schemes neglect the requirements for low delays. Thus, we further discuss this QoS requirement of visual sensor networks in the next subsection.

Delay Sensitive Communication Protocols

Real-time data delivery is a common requirement for many applications of visual sensor networks. Data delays can happen in different layers of the network protocol stack, by unsynchronized interaction between different layers of stack, and delay can be further increased by the wireless channel variability. Thus, the design of different communication layers of the network protocol stack should be carefully considered in order to improve the data latency in the network.

The rising needs of delay-sensitive applications in wireless sensor networks have caused the appearance of a number of energy-efficient delay-aware MAC protocols. The main idea behind these protocols is to reduce the sleep delays of sensor nodes operating in duty cycles, and to adapt the nodes' duty cycles according the network traffic. Since there is already a comprehensive survey on the design of MAC protocols for multimedia applications in wireless sensor networks [2], we will not cover these protocols in detail, but instead we will mention some of the most representative delay-aware MAC protocols.

The SMAC [50] protocol developed by Ye et al. was among the first MAC protocols that explored adaptive listening in order to reduce multihop latency due to periodic sleep. (In adaptive listening, a node that overhears its neighbors transmission wakes up at the end of that transmission, so that it can receive a message, if it is the next hop for its neighbor transmission.) In the DSMAC [34] protocol, Lin et al. further improve the latency problem of SMAC by allowing the sensor nodes to dynamically change their sleeping intervals in order to adjust to the current traffic conditions. In this way, the latency is reduced in networks with high traffic load, while still supporting the energy efficiency when network traffic is low. In the DMAC [35] protocol, Lu et al. further explore the adaptive listening mechanism, pointing out the data forwarding interruption problem, which happens due to the limited overhearing range of the nodes, so that a node can be out of range for both sender and receiver and thus unaware of the ongoing data transmission. Such nodes go to sleep, which causes the interruption in data forwarding. The DMAC protocol eliminates the sleeping delays by providing the same schedule (receive-transmit-sleep cycles) to the nodes with the same depth in the data gathering tree. These protocols are contention-based, so they provide only best effort service. Other authors favor scheduling-based MAC protocols, as a way to avoid data delays and data loses due to channel contention and packet collisions. One such MAC protocol is presented by Ceken [36], where sensor nodes follow a TDMA schedule for data transmissions, but the delay-critical sensor nodes can request extra time slots from the central node in the case when their queues exceed a certain threshold.

Finding routing strategies that enable data delivery within a certain time delay is an extremely hard problem. He et al. developed the SPEED protocol [37] for real-time communication in multihop wireless sensor networks. Since the end-to-end delay in a multihop network depends on the distance a packet travels, SPEED routes packets according to the packet's maximum delivery speed, defined as the rate at which the packet should travel along a straight line to the destination. Thus, SPEED determines the transmission delay of the packet considering its end-to-end distance and its delivery speed. However, such a routing scheme is not scalable, as the maximum delivery speed cannot guarantee that the packet will arrive before its delay deadline in larger networks. This issue is addressed in [38], where Felemban et al. propose MMSPEED, where nodes can forward packets with a higher (adjustable) speed over the multiple paths if it appears that the packet cannot meet its delay deadline. However, underlying network management policies (discussed in Section 7) that regulate nodes' activities have a large impact on the packets' delivery latency. Thus, the data latency problem in visual sensor networks should be further analyzed considering the nodes' resource-aware scheduling policies.

Such an approach is taken in [39], where Lu and Krishnamachari look into the joint problem of finding the routes and nodes activity schedules that provide the minimum average latency for current active data flows. It is assumed an FDMA channel model, which enables simultaneous packet transmissions from neighboring nodes with minimized interference. The proposed solution finds a number of disjoint paths over the delay graph constructed by considering the finite delays at each node between the reception and retransmission of a packet in preassigned time slots.

The data delays at different layers of the network protocol stack may be caused by various factors (channel contention, packet retransmissions, long packet queues, nodes' failure, and network congestion). The cross-layer approaches that consider close interactions between different layers of the protocol stack enable the design of frameworks that support delay-sensitive applications of visual sensor networks.

Andreopoulos et al. [40] propose a cross-layer optimization algorithm that aims to find several parameters that maximize the network's capacity-distortion utility function, while considering delay-constrained streaming in a wireless network. The proposed end-to-end optimization algorithm chooses the optimum routing path, the maximum number of retransmissions at the MAC layer as well as the best modulation scheme at the physical layer (considering thereby the available channel bandwidth and data rates). The proposed optimization model assumes the existence of predetermined time reservations per link with contention free access to the wireless channel. Van der Schaar and Turaga [41] propose cross-layer optimized packetization and retransmission strategies constrained by delay requirements for video delivery in wireless networks. Similarly to [40, 41] is based on rate-distortion optimization algorithms, and in both works the energy constrained resources of nodes in the network are not considered. Such a cross-layer resource allocation problem is analyzed in [42], where Wang et al. discuss the adaptive image transmission scheme that optimizes image quality over a multihop network while considering multihop path conditions such as delay constraints and the probability of delay violation. The design guideline of this work lies in the fact that the information about the position of coefficients in a wavelet transformed image have higher importance and thus higher protection levels than the information about the coefficients' magnitudes. Optimizing the image quality over the multihop network involves finding the optimal source coding rates, which can be translated into the maximum source traffic rate with QoS delay bound.

Cross-layer optimization of the protocol stack enables visual sensor networks to meet various QoS constraints of visual data transmissions, including data communication within delay bounds. This cross-layer optimization needs also to include different strategies for intra-camera collaborations, which will lead to a reduction of the total data transmitted in the network. We discuss this problem further in the next subsection.

Collaborative Image Data Routing

In current communication protocols, the camera nodes compete for the network resources, rather than collaborate in order to effectively exploit the available network resources. Thus, the design of communication protocols for visual sensor networks needs to be fundamentally changed, in order to support exchanges of information regarding camera nodes' information contents, which will help to reduce the communication of redundant data and to distribute resources equally among the camera nodes.

Collaboration-based communication should be established between cameras with overlapped FoVs that, based on the spatial-temporal correlation between their images, collectively reason about the events and thus reduce the amount of data and control overhead messages routed through the network [43]. Such a collaboration-based approach for communication is oftentimes used in object tracking applications, where camera nodes are organized into clusters, as for example shown in [44]. Here, the formation of multiple clusters is triggered by the detection of objects. The cluster head node tracks the object, and the cluster head role is assigned to another cluster member once the object is out of the viewing field of the current cluster head. However, in visual sensor networks collaborative clusters can be formed by cameras that have overlapped FoVs, although they can be distant from each other, which can raise questions about the network connectivity. In wireless sensor networks, two nodes are connected if they are able to exchange RF signals. Zhang and Hou [51] prove that if the communication range is at least twice the sensing range, then the complete coverage of a convex area implies that the nodes are connected. However, relation between connectivity and coverage in visual sensor networks needs further investigation, considering the fact that 3D coverage needs to be satisfied and that the area of a camera's coverage usually does not overlap with the transmission range of the camera node.

Finally, supporting data priority has a large effect on the application QoS of visual sensor networks. Camera nodes that detect an event of interest should be given higher priority for data transmissions. In collaborative data processing, camera nodes should collectively decide on data priorities from cameras that provide the most relevant information regarding the captured event. Therefore, protocols that provide differentiated service to support prioritized data flows are needed and must be investigated.

Sensor Management

In redundantly deployed visual sensor networks a subset of cameras can perform continuous monitoring and provide information with a desired quality. This subset of active cameras can be changed over time, which enables balancing of the cameras' energy consumption, while spreading the monitoring task among the cameras. In such a scenario the decision about the camera nodes' activity and the duration of their activity is based on sensor management policies. Sensor management policies define the selection and scheduling (that determines the activity duration) of the camera nodes' activity in such a way that the visual information from selected cameras satisfies the application-specified requirements while the use of camera resources is minimized. Various quality metrics are used in the evaluation of sensor management policies, such as the energy-efficiency of the selection method or the quality of the gathered image data from the selected cameras. In addition, camera management policies are directed by the application; for example, target tracking usually requires selection of cameras that cover only a part of the scene that contains the non-occluded object, while monitoring of large areas requires the selection of cameras with the largest combined FoV.

While energy-efficient organization of camera nodes is oftentimes addressed by camera management policies, the quality of the data produced by the network is the main concern of the application. Table 3 compares several camera management policies considering energy efficiency and bandwidth allocation as two quality metrics for camera selection in two common applications—target tracking and monitoring of large scenes.

Table 3. Comparison of sensor management policies.

Sensor management policy	QoS criteria		Application		Goal of sensor management metric
	Energy efficiency	Bandwidth allocation	Large scene monitoring	Object tracking	
Dagher et al. [52]	Yes	No	Yes	No	Battery lifetime optimization
Park et al. [53]	No	No	Yes	No	Quality of view for every 3D point
Soro and Heinzelman [54]	Yes	No	Yes	No	Exploring trade-offs between the image quality of reconstructed views and energy efficiency
Zamora and Marculescu [55]	Yes	No	No	Yes	Coordinated-wake up policies for energy conservation
Yang and Nahrstedt [56]	No	Yes	No	Yes	Proposed several sensor selection policies (random, event-based, view-based, priority-based) that consider bandwidth constraints
Pahalawatta et al. [25]	Yes	No	No	Yes	Maximize sum of information utility provided by the active sensors subjected to the average energy that can be used by the network
Ercan et al. [29]	No	No	No	Yes	Object occlusions avoidance

Monitoring of large areas (such as parking lots, public areas, large stores, etc.) requires complete coverage of the area at every point in time. Such an application is analyzed in [52], where Dagher et al. provide an optimal strategy for allocating parts of the monitored region to the cameras while maximizing the battery lifetime of the camera nodes. The optimal fractions of regions covered by every camera are found in a centralized way at the base station. The cameras use JPEG2000 to encode the allocated region such that the cost per bit transmission is reduced according to the fraction received from the base station. However, this sensor management policy only considers the coverage of a 2D plane, without occlusions and perspective effects, which makes it harder to use in a real situation.

Oftentimes the quality of a reconstructed view from a set of selected cameras is used as a criterion for the evaluation of camera selection policies. Park et al. [53] use distributed look-up tables to rank the cameras according to how well they image a specific location, and based on this they choose the best candidates that provide images of the desired location. Their selection criterion is based on the fact that the error in the captured image increases as the object gets further away from the center of the viewing frustum. Thus, they divide the frustum of each camera into smaller unit volumes (subfrustums). Then, based on the Euclidian distance of each 3D point to the centers of subfrustums that contain this 3D point, they sort the cameras and find the most favorable camera that contains this point in its field of view. The look-up table entries for each 3D location are propagated through the network in order to build a sorted list of favorable cameras. Thus, camera selection is based exclusively on the quality of the image data provided by the selected cameras, while the resource constraints are not considered.

A similar problem of finding the best camera candidates is investigated in [54]. In this work, we propose several cost metrics for the selection of a set of camera nodes that provide images used for reconstructing a view from a user-specified view point. Two types of metrics are considered: coverage-aware cost metrics and quality-aware cost metrics. The coverage-aware cost metrics consider the remaining energy of the camera nodes and the coverage of the indoor space, and favor the selection of the cameras with higher remaining energy and more redundant coverage. The quality-aware cost metrics favor the selection of the cameras that provide images from a similar view point as the user's view point. Thus, these camera selection methods provide a trade-off between network lifetime and the quality of the reconstructed images.

In order to reduce the energy consumption of cameras Zamora and Marculescu [55] explore distributed power management of camera nodes based on coordinated node wake-ups. The proposed policy assumes that each camera node is awake for a certain period of time, after which the camera node decides whether it should enter the low-power state based on the timeout statuses of its neighboring nodes. Alternatively, camera nodes can decide whether to enter the low-power state based on voting from other neighboring cameras.

Selection of the best cameras for target tracking has been discussed often [25, 29]. In [25] Pahalawatta et al. present a camera selection method for target tracking applications used in energy-constrained visual sensor networks. The camera nodes are selected by minimizing an information utility function (obtained as the uncertainty of the estimated posterior distribution of a target) subject to energy constraints. However, the information obtained from the selected cameras can be lost in the case of object occlusions. This occlusion problem is further discussed in [29], where Ercan et al. propose a method for camera selection in the case when the tracked object becomes occluded by static or moving occluders. Finding the best camera set for object tracking involves minimizing the MSE of the object position's estimates. Such a greedy heuristic for camera selection shows results close to optimal and outperforms naive heuristics, such as selection of the closest set of cameras to the target, or uniformly spaced cameras. The authors here assume that some information about the scene is known in advance, such as the positions of static occluders, and the object and dynamic occluders' prior probabilities for location estimates.

Although a large volume of data is transmitted in visual sensor networks, none of the aforementioned works consider channel bandwidth utilization. This problem is investigated in [56] where Yang and Nahrstedt provide a bandwidth management framework which, based on different camera selection policies and video content, dynamically coordinates the bandwidth requirements among the selected cameras' flows. The bandwidth estimation is provided at the MAC layer of each camera node, and this information is sent to a centralized bandwidth coordinator that allocates the bandwidth to the selected cameras. The centralized bandwidth allocator guarantees that each camera has the minimum bandwidth required, but the flexibility of distributed bandwidth allocation is lost.

In visual sensor networks, sensor management policies are needed to assure balance between the oftentimes opposite requirements imposed by the wireless networking and vision processing tasks. While reducing energy consumption by limiting data transmissions is the primary challenge of energy-constrained visual sensor networks, the quality of the image data and application QoS improve as the network provides more data. In such an environment, the optimization methods for sensor management developed for wireless sensor networks are oftentimes hard to directly apply to visual sensor networks. Such sensor management policies usually do not consider the event-driven nature of visual sensor networks, nor do they consider the unpredictability of data traffic caused by an event detection.

Thus, more research is needed to further explore sensor management for visual sensor networks. Since sensor management policies depend on the underlying networking policies and vision processing, future research lies in the intersection of finding the best trade-offs between these two aspects of visual sensor networks. Additional work is needed to compare the performance of different camera node scheduling sensor policies, including asynchronous (where every camera follows its own on-off schedule) and synchronous (where cameras are divided into different sets, so that in each moment one set of cameras is active) policies. From an application perspective, it would be interesting to explore sensor management policies for supporting multiple applications utilizing a single visual sensor network.

Hardware Architectures for Visual Sensor Networks

A typical wireless sensor node has an 8/16-bit microcontroller, limited memory, and it uses short active periods during which it processes and communicates collected data. Limiting a node's "idle" periods (long periods during which a node listens to the channel) and avoiding power-hungry transmissions of huge amounts of data keep the node's energy consumption sufficiently small, so that it can operate for months or even for years. It is desirable to keep the same low-power features in the design of camera nodes, although in this case more energy will be needed for data capture, processing and transmission. Here, we provide an overview of works that analyze energy consumption in visual sensor networks, as well as an overview of current visual sensor node hardware architectures and testbeds.

Energy Consumption

The lifetime of a battery-operated camera node is limited by its energy consumption, which is determined by the hardware and working mode of the camera node. In order to collect data about energy consumption and to verify camera node designs, a number of camera node prototypes have been recently built and tested. Energy consumption has been analyzed on camera node prototypes built using a wide range of imagers, starting from very low-power, low-resolution camera nodes [57, 58], to web cameras [59, 60] to advanced, high-resolution cameras.

An estimation of the camera node's lifetime can be done based on its power consumption in different tasks, such as image capture, processing, and transmission. Such an analysis is provided in [60], where Margi et al. present results obtained for the power consumption of a visual sensor network testbed consisting of camera nodes built using a Crossbow Stargate [61] board and a Logitech webcam. Each task has an associated power consumption cost and execution time. Several interesting results are reported in [60]. For example, in their setup the time to acquire and process an image takes 2.5 times longer than the time to transmit the compressed image. The energy cost of analyzing the image (via a foreground detection algorithm) and compression of a portion of the image (when an event is detected) is about the same as compression of the full image. Also, they found that transitioning between states can be expensive in terms of energy and time.

In [62] Jung et al. analyze how different operation modes, such as duty-cycle mode and event-driven mode, affect the lifetime of a camera node. The power consumption specifications of the camera node (which consisted of an iMote2 [63] wireless node coupled with an Omnivision OV7649 camera) consider the power consumption profiles of the main components (CPU, radio, and camera) in different operational modes (sleep, idle, and working). The generic power consumption model provided in [62] can be used for the comparison of different hardware platforms in order to determine the most appropriate hardware solution/working mode for the particular application.

Considering the fact that data transmission is the most expensive operation in terms of energy, Ferrigno et al. [64] aim to find the most suitable compression method that provides the best compromise between energy consumption and the quality of the obtained image. Their analysis is drawn from the results of measurements of the current consumption for each state: standby, sensing, processing, connection, and communication. The authors compare several lossy compression methods, including JPEG, JPEG2000, Set Partitioning in Hierarchical Trees (SPIHT), Subsampling (SS) and Discrete Cosine Transform (DCT). The choice of the most suitable compression technique was between SPIHT, which gives the best compression rate and SS, which requires the smallest execution time, has the simplest implementation and assures the best compromise between the compression rate and processing time.

Analysis of the energy consumption of a camera node when performing different tasks [60] and in different working modes [62] is essential for developing effective resource management policies. Understanding the trade-offs between data processing and data communication in terms of energy cost, as analyzed in [64], helps in choosing the best vision processing techniques that provide data of a certain quality while the lifetime of the camera node is prolonged. Analysis of the energy consumption profile helps the selection of hardware components for the specific application. However, the variety of hardware, processing algorithms and networking protocols used in various testbeds makes the comparison of existing camera nodes difficult. Today, there is no systematic overview and comparison of different visual sensor network testbeds from the energy consumption perspective. Therefore, further research should focus on comparing different camera node architectures and visual sensor network testbeds, in order to explore the energy-performance trade-offs.

Visual Sensor Node Platforms

Today, CMOS image sensors are commonly used in many devices, such as cell phones and PDAs. We can expect widespread use of image sensors in wireless sensor networks only if such networks still preserve the low power consumption profile. Because of energy and bandwidth constraints, low-resolution image sensors are actually preferable in many applications of visual sensor networks. Table 4 compares several prototypes of visual sensor nodes with respect to the main hardware components such as processors, memory, image sensor, and RF transceiver.

Table 4. Comparison of different visual sensor node architectures.

Camera node architecture	Processing unit	Memory	Image sensor	RF transceiver
MeshEye [5]	Atmel ARM7TDMI Thumb (32-bit RISC), 55 MHz	64 KB SRAM and 256 KB Flash; external MMC/SD Flash	Two kilopixel imagers Agilent Technologies ADNS 3060 30×30 pixels (grayscale) and one ADCM 2700 VGA (color)	Chipcon CC2420 IEEE 802.15.4
Cyclops [58]	Atmel ATmega128L and CPLD—Xilinx XC2C256 CoolRunner	512 KB Flash 64 KB SRAM	ADCM-1700 Agilent Technology	IEEE 802.15.4 compliant (MICA2 Mote [65])
SIMD (Single-instruction-multiple-data)-based architecture [66]	Philips IC3D Xetal (for low-level image processing), 8051 MCU (local host for high level image processing and control)	1792B RAM and 64 KB Flash internal on 8051 MCU; dual port RAM 128 KB (shared memory by both processors)	VGA Image Sensor (one or two)	Aquis Grain Zigbee module based on Chipcon CC2420
CMUCam3 [67]	ARM7TDMI (32-bit) 60 MHz	64 KB RAM and 128 KB Flash on MCU, 1 MB AL4V8M440 FIFO Frame Buffer Flash (MMC)	Omnivision OV6620, 352×288 pixels	IEEE 802.15.4 compliant (Telos mote)

Compared with processors used for wireless sensor nodes, the processing units used in visual sensor node architectures are usually more powerful, with 32-bit architectures and higher processing speed that enables faster data processing. In some architectures [58, 66] a second processor is used for additional processing and control. Since most procesors have small internal memories, additional external Flash memories are used for frame buffering and permanent data storage. Image sensors also tends to provide small format images (CIF format and smaller). However, some implementations [5, 66] use two image sensors to provide binocular vision. For example, the Mesheye architecture [5] uses two low resolution image sensors (kilopixels) and one high resolution (VGA) image sensor located in between the two low resolution image sensors. With one kilopixel imager the camera node can detect the presence of an object in its FoV. Stereo vision from two kilopixel imagers enables estimation of object position and size, thereby providing the region of interest. Finally, a high resolution image of the region of interest can be obtained using the VGA camera.

It is evident that all camera node prototypes shown in Table 4 use IEEE 802.15.4 RF transceivers, which is commonly used in wireless sensor nodes as well. The Chipcon CC2420 radio supports a maximum of 250Kb/s data rate, although the achievable data rate is often much smaller due to packet overhead and the transient states of the transciever. Since such insufficient data rates can be a bottleneck for vision-based applications, future implementations should consider other radio standards with higher data rates, at the cost of increased energy dissipation. Also, by providing a simpler programming interface, the widespread use of visual sensor nodes can be expected. Such an interface is described in [57] where Hengstler and Aghajan present a framework called Wireless Image Sensor Network Application Platform (WiSNAP) for research and development of applications in wireless visual networks. This Matlab-based application development platform contains APIs that provide a user with interfaces to the image sensor and the wireless node. The WiSNAP framework enables simulations of this visual sensor node platform in different applications.

VSN Architectures – Testbed Research

Testbed implementations of visual sensor networks are an important final step in evaluating processing algorithms and communication protocols. Several architectures for visual sensor networks can be found in the literature.

Among the first reported video-based sensor network systems is Panoptes [59], which consisted of video sensors built from COTS components and software that supports different functions including image capture, compression, filtering, video buffering, and data streaming. Panoptes supports a priority-based streaming mechanism, where the incoming video data is mapped to a number of priorities defined by the surveillance application. Panoptes provides storage and retrieval of video data from sensors, it handles queries from users, and it controls the streaming of events of interest to the user. However, the system does not have real-time support—a user can only select to see past events already stored in the system. Also, there is no interaction between the cameras.

In [68], Kulkarni et al. present SensEye—a heterogeneous multitier camera sensor network consisting of different nodes and cameras in each tier. The SensEye system is designed for a surveillance application, thus supporting tasks such as object detection, recognition, and tracking. These tasks are performed across three network tiers. The lowest layer, which supports object detection and localization, is comprised of Mote nodes [69], and low-fidelity CMUCam camera sensors. The second tier contains Stargate nodes [61] equipped with web cameras, which are woken up on demand by the camera nodes from the lower tier to continue the object recognition task. The third tier contains sparsely deployed high-resolution pan-tilt-zoom cameras connected to a PC, which performs the object tracking. The SensEye platform proves that task allocation across tiers achieves a reduction in energy compared with a homogeneous platform, while the latency of the network response is close to the latency achieved by an always-on homogeneous system.

Researchers from Carnegie Melon University present a framework for a distributed network of vision-enabled sensor nodes called FireFly Mosaic [70] (illustrated in Figure 5). The FireFly platform is built from FireFly sensor nodes enhanced with vision capabilities using the CMUCam3 vision processing board

[67]. The CMUCam3 sensor supports a set of built-in image processing algorithms, including JPEG compression, frame differencing, color tracking, histogramming, and edge detection. Tight global synchronization throughout the network is supported by using an out-of-band AM carrier current radio transmitter and on-board AM radio receiver.

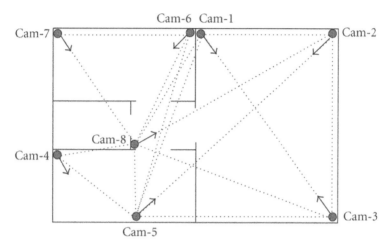

Figure 5. Topology of the visual sensor network, that is, used for testing the FireFly system [70]. The dotted lines represent the communication links between the cameras.

The communication and collaboration of camera nodes is scheduled using a collision free, energy-efficient TDMA-based link layer protocol called RT-Link [71]. In order to support camera group communication (among the cameras with overlapped FoVs) both the network connectivity graph (that considers the links between nodes within communication range, shown in Figure 6(a)) and the camera network graph (that considers the relationships between the cameras' FoVs, Figure 6(b)) are considered. In this way cameras that share part of the view, but are out of each other's communication range can still communicate via other nodes.

The size of the transmitted images with a given resolution is controlled by the quality parameter provided in the JPEG standard, which is used for image compression. The authors noticed that JPEG processing time does not vary significantly with the image quality level, but it changes with image resolution, mostly due to the large I/O transfer time between the camera and the CPU. The authors also measured the sensitivity of the system's tracking performances with the respect to the time jitter, that is, added to the cameras' image capturing time.

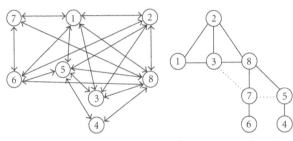

(a) Connectivity graph of the camera nodes from the previous figure. Marked links correspond to the camera network graph

(b) Camera network graph—adjacent links between the cameras indicate that cameras have overlapped FoVs. The dotted lines correspond to the case when the cameras have overlapped views, but cannot communicate directly. The communication schedule must provide message forwarding between these cameras

Figure 6. Connectivity graph and camera network graph of the FireFly system [70].

Middleware Support

The increased number of hardware and software platforms for smart camera nodes has created a problem in how to network these heterogeneous devices and how to easily build applications that use these networked devices. The integration of camera nodes into a distributed and collaborative network benefits from a well-defined middleware that abstracts the physical devices into a logical model, providing a set of services defined through standardized APIs that are portable over different platforms. In wireless sensor networks, middleware provides abstractions for the networking and communication services, and the main challenges are associated with providing abstraction support, data fusion and and managing the limited resources [72].

In the case of visual sensor networks, the development of middleware support is additionally challenged by the need for high-level software for supporting complex and distributed vision processing tasks. In [73] this support is provided using agent-oriented middleware, where different image processing tasks are carried out by different agents. The agents are responsible for task execution at the processing unit, they can create new agents, and they can remotely create new agents at other cameras, which is fundamental for distributed organization of a smart camera network.

In [74], Detmold et al. propose using a Blackboard-based middleware approach instead of the popular multiagent approach. In this model, the results of processing of input video streams are published at the distributed Blackboard component. Thus, the Blackboard acts as a repository of information, where computations are triggered in response to published results. The Blackboard has several interacting levels. The "single scene analysis" provides information derived from object detection and activity analysis (e.g., it produces a "left luggage" hypothesis). The "multi scene analysis" draws conclusions about tracked objects, such as the tracks of people throughout the scene. The "reasoning level" provides higher level hypotheses regarding unusual behavior. Each level contains drivers that process inputs and add them to the level's information space. The information are propagated upwards and shared among the Blackboard levels.

In the future, it is expected that the number of cameras in smart surveillance applications will scale to hundreds or even thousands—in this situation, the middleware will have a crucial role in scaling the network and in integrating the different software components into one automated vision system. In these systems, the middleware should address the system's real-time requirements, together with the other resource (energy and bandwidth) constraints.

Open Research Problems in Visual Sensor Networks

The extensive research has been done in the many directions that contribute to the visual sensor networks. However, the real potential of these networks can be reached through a cross-disciplinary research approach that considers all the various aspects of visual sensor networks: vision processing, networking, sensor managemen, and hardware design.

However, in many cases of the existing work there is no coherence between the different aspects of visual sensor networks. For example, networking protocols used in visual sensor networks are mainly adapted from the routing protocols used in traditional wireless sensor networks, and thus do not provide sufficient support for the data-hungry, time-constrained, collaborative communication of visual sensor networks. Similarly, embedded vision processing algorithms used in visual sensor networks are based on existing computer vision algorithms, and thus they rarely consider the constraints imposed by the underlying wireless network.

Thus, future efforts should be directed toward finding ways to minimize the amount of data that has to be communicated, by finding ways to describe captured events with the least amount of data. Additionally, the processing should be lightweight—information rich descriptors of objects/scenes are not an option.

Hence, the choice of the "right" feature set, as well as support for real-time communication will play a major role in a successfully operated task.

In order to keep communication between cameras minimal, the cameras need to have the ability to estimate whether the information they provide contributes to the monitoring task. In a postevent detection phase, sensor management policies should decide, based on known information from the cameras and the network status, whether more cameras need to be included in the monitoring. In addition, data exchanged between camera nodes should be aggregated in-network at one of the camera nodes, and the decision about the most suitable data fusion center should be dynamic, considering the best view and the communication/fusion cost. However, considering the oftentimes arbitrary deployment of camera nodes, where the cameras' positions and orientations are not known, the problem is to find the best ways to combine these arbitrary views in order to obtain useful information.

In the current literature distributed source coding (DSC) has been extensively investigated as a way to reduce the amount of transmitted data in wireless sensor networks. In DSC, each data source encodes its data independently, without communicating with the other data sources, while joint data decoding is performed at the base station. This model, where sensor nodes have simple encoders and the complexity is brought to the receiver's end, fits well the needs of visual sensor networks. However, many issues have to be resolved before DSC can be practical for visual sensor networks. For example, it is extremely hard to define the correlation structure between different images, especially when the network topology is unknown or without a network training phase. Also, DSC requires tight synchronization between packets sent from correlated sources. Since DSC should be implemented in the upper layers of the network stack, it affects all the other layers below [75]. Thus, the implementation of DSC will also require careful reconsideration of existing cross-layer designs.

From the communication perspective, novel protocols need to be developed that support bursty and collaborative in-network communication. Supporting time-constrained and reliable communication are problems at the forefront of protocol development for visual sensor networks. In order to support the collaborative processing, it is expected that some cameras acts as a fusion centers by collecting and processing raw data from several cameras. Having several fusion centers can affect the data latency throughout the network as well as the amount of the postfusion data. Thus, further research should explore the trade-offs between the ways to combine (fuse) data from multiple sources and latency introduced by these operations.

Furthermore, in order to preserve network scalability and to cope with time-constrained communication, there is a need for developing time-aware sensor management policies that will favor utilization of those cameras that can send data over multihop shortest delay routes. Such communication should support priority differentiation between different data flows, which can be determined based on vision information and acceptable delays for the particular data.

In the future we can expect to see various applications based on multimedia wireless networks, where camera nodes will be integrated with other types of sensors, such as audio sensors, PIRs, vibration sensors, light sensors, and so forth. By utilizing these very low-cost and low-power sensors, the lifetime of the camera nodes can be significantly prolonged. However, many open problems appears in such multimedia networks. The first issue is network deployment, whereby it is necessary to determine network architecture and the numbers of different types of sensors that should be used in a particular application, so that all of the sensors are optimally utilized while at the same time the cost of the network is kept low. Such multimedia networks usually employ a hierarchical architecture, where ultra-low power sensors (such as microphones, PIRs, vibration, or light sensors) continuously monitor the environment over long periods of time, while higher-level sensors, such as cameras sleep most of the time. When the lower-level sensors register an event, they notify higher-level sensors about it. Such a hierarchical model (as seen in [68], e.g.) tends to minimize the amount of communication in the network. However, it is important to reduce the number of false and missed alarms at the low-level sensors, so that the network reliability is not jeopardized. Thus, it is important to precisely define an event at the lower-level sensors that cameras can interpret without ambiguity. A high-level node acting as a data collector should be able to perform multimodal fusion of data received from different types of sensors, in order to reason about captured events and decide an appropriate course of action. The reliability of multimodal data fusion thus depends on the accuracy of the data provided by each sensor modality, so the data from different types of sensors can be associated with different weights before the data fusion.

The growing trend of deploying an increasing number of smart sensors in people's everyday lives poses several privacy issues. We have not discussed this problem in this paper, but it is clear that this problem is a source of concern for many people who can benefit from visual sensor networks, as information about their private life can be accessed through the network. The main problem is that the network can take much more information, such as private information, than it really needs in order to perform its tasks. As pointed out in [76], there are several ways to work around this problem. The most radical solution is to exclude cameras from the network, using only nonimaging sensors. However, many situations cannot be resolved without obtaining image data from the area. Thus, the solutions where cameras perform high-level image analysis and provide descriptive information instead of raw images are favorable. The user can be contacted by the system only on occasions when the system is not sure how to react (e.g., if an unknown face is detected in the house). In the future, people will most probably need to sacrifice a bit of their privacy if they want to benefit from smart applications of visual sensor networks. However, privacy and security should be seriously addressed in all future designs of visual sensor networks.

Based on the work reviewed in this paper, we notice that current research trends in visual sensor networks are divided into two directions. The first direction leads toward the development of visual sensor networks where cameras have large processing capabilities, which makes them suitable for use in a number of high-level reasoning applications. Research in this area is directed toward exploring ways to implement existing vision processing algorithm onto embedded processors. Oftentimes, the networking and sensor management aspects are not considered in this approach. The second direction in visual sensor networks research is motivated by the existing research in wireless sensor networks. Thus, it is directed toward exploring the methods that will enable the network to provide small amounts of data from the camera nodes that are constrained by resource limitations, such as remaining energy and available bandwidth. Thus, such visual sensor networks are designed with the idea of having data provided by the network of cameras for long periods of time.

We believe that in the future these two directions will converge toward the same path. Currently, visual sensor networks are limited by their hardware components (COTS) that are not fully optimized for embedded vision processing applications. Future development of faster, low-power processing architectures and ultra low-power image sensors will open a door toward a new generation of visual sensor networks with better processing capabilities and lower energy consumption. However, the main efforts in the current research of visual sensor networks should be directed toward integrating vision processing tasks and networking requirements. Thus, future directions in visual sensor networks research should be aimed at exploring the following interdisciplinary problems.

(i)   How should vision processing tasks depend on the underlying network conditions, such as limited bandwidth, limited (and potentially time-varying) connectivity between camera nodes or data loss due to varying channel conditions?

(ii) How should the design of network communication protocols be influenced by the vision tasks? For example, how should different priorities be assigned to data flows to dynamically find the smallest delay route or to find the best fusion center?

(iii) How should camera nodes be managed, considering the limited network resources as well as both the vision processing and networking tasks, in order to achieve application-specific QoS requirements, such as those related to the quality of the collected visual data or coverage of the monitored area?

In the end, widespread use of visual sensor networks depends on the programming complexity of the system, which includes implementation of both vision processing algorithms as well as networking protocols. Therefore, we believe that development of middleware for visual sensor networks will have a major role in making these networks widely accepted in a number of applications. We can envision that in the future visual sensor networks will consist of hundreds or even thousands of camera nodes (as well as other types of sensor nodes) scattered throughout an area. The scalability and integration of various vision and networking tasks for such large networks of cameras should be addressed by future developments of distributed middleware architectures. Middleware should provide an abstraction of underlying vision-processing, networking and shared services (where shared services are those commonly used by both the vision processing and networking tasks and include synchronization service, localization service, or neighborhood discovery service, e.g.). By providing a number of APIs, the middleware will enable easy programming at the application layer, and the use of different hardware platforms in one visual sensor network.

Conclusions

Transmission of multimedia content over wireless and wired networks is a well-established research area. However, the focus of this paper is to survey a new type of wireless networks, visual sensor networks, and to point out the unique characteristics and constraints that differentiate visual sensor networks from other types of multimedia networks. We present an overview of existing work in several research areas that support visual sensor networks. In the coming era of low-power distributed computing, visual sensor networks will continue to challenge the research community because of their complex application requirements and tight resource constraints. We discussed many problems encountered in visual sensor network research caused by the strict resource constraints, including embedded vision processing, data communication, camera management issues, and development of effective visual sensor network testbeds. However, visual sensor networks' potential to provide a comprehensive understanding of the environment and their ability to provide visual information from unaccessible areas will make them indispensable in the coming years.

Many problems still need to be addressed through future research. We discussed some of the open issues not only in the different subfields of visual sensor networks, but, more importantly, in the integration of these areas. Real breakthroughs in visual sensor networks will occur only through a comprehensive solution that considers the vision, networking, management, and hardware issues in concert.

Acknowledgement

This work was supported by the National Science Foundation under Grant #ECS-0428157.

References

1. P. Bolliger, M. Köhler, and K. Römer, "Facet: towards a smart camera network of mobile phones," in Proceedings of 1st ACM International Conference on Autonomic Computing and Communication Systems (Autonomics '07), 2007.

2. S. Misra, M. Reisslein, and G. Xue, "A survey of multimedia streaming in wireless sensor networks," IEEE Communications Surveys and Tutorials, vol. 10, pp. 18–39, 2008.

3. Y. Charfi, N. Wakamiya, and M. Murata, "Challenging issues in visual sensor networks," Advanced Network Architecture Laboratory, Osaka University, 2007.

4. I. F. Akyildiz, T. Melodia, and K. R. Chowdhury, "A survey on wireless multimedia sensor networks," Computer Networks, vol. 51, no. 4, pp. 921–960, 2007.

5. S. Hengstler, D. Prashanth, S. Fong, and H. Aghajan, "MeshEye: a hybrid-resolution smart camera mote for applications in distributed intelligent surveillance," in Proceedings of the 6th International Symposium on Information Processing in Sensor Networks (IPSN '07), pp. 360–369, 2007.

6. W. Wolf, B. Ozer, and T. Lv, "Smart cameras as embedded systems," Computer, vol. 35, no. 9, pp. 48–53, 2002.

7. M. Chen, S. Gonzalez, and V. C. M. Leung, "Applications and design issues for mobile agents in wireless sensor networks," IEEE Wireless Communications, vol. 14, no. 6, pp. 20–26, 2007.

8. M. Chen, T. Kwon, Y. Yuan, Y. Choi, and V. C. M. Leung, "Mobile agent-based directed diffusion in wireless sensor networks," EURASIP Journal on Advances in Signal Processing, vol. 2007, 13 pages, 2007.

9. M. Wu and C. W. Chen, "Multiple bitstream image transmission over wireless sensor networks," in Proceedings of 2d IEEE International Conference on Sensors, vol. 2, pp. 727–731, Toronto, Canada, October 2003.

10. R. Hartley and A. Zisserman, Multiple View Geometry in Computer Vision, Cambridge University Press, Cambridge, UK, 2000.

11. K. Römer, P. Blum, and L. Meier, "Time synchronization and calibration in wireless sensor networks," in Handbook of Sensor Networks: Algorithms and Architectures, I. Stojmenovic, Ed., pp. 199–237, John Wiley & Sons, New York, NY, USA, 2005.

12. D. Ganesan, B. Greenstein, D. Perelyubskiy, D. Estrin, and J. Heidemann, "Multi-resolution storage and search in sensor networks," ACM Transactions on Storage, vol. 1, pp. 277–315, 2005.

13. P. Remagnino, A. I. Shihab, and G. A. Jones, "Distributed intelligence for multi-camera visual surveillance," Pattern Recognition, vol. 37, no. 4, pp. 675–689, 2004.

14. T. He, S. Krishnamurthy, L. Luo, et al., "VigilNet: an integrated sensor network system for energy-efficient surveillance," ACM Transactions on Sensor Networks, vol. 2, no. 1, pp. 1–38, 2006.

15. O. Schreer, P. Kauff, and T. Sikora, 3D Video Communication, John Wiley & Sons, New York, NY, USA, 2005.

16. N. J. McCurdy and W. Griswold, "A system architecture for ubiquitous video," in Proceedings of the 3rd Annual International Conference on Mobile Systems, Applications, and Services (Mobisys '05), 2005.

17. S. Hengstler and H. Aghajan, "Application-oriented design of smart camera networks," in Proceedings of the 1st ACM/IEEE International Conference on Distributed Smart Cameras (ICDSC '07), pp. 12–19, 2007.

18. A. Barton-Sweeney, D. Lymberopoulos, and A. Savvides, "Sensor localization and camera calibration in distributed camera sensor networks," in Proceedings of the 3rd International Conference on Broadband Communications, Networks and Systems (BROADNETS '06), 2006.

19. S. Funiak, M. Paskin, C. Guestrin, and R. Sukthankar, "Distributed localization of networked cameras," in Proceedings of the 5th International Conference on Information Processing in Sensor Networks (IPSN '06), pp. 34–42, 2006.

20. C. J. Taylor, "A scheme for calibrating smart camera networks using active lights," in Proceedings of the 2nd International Conference on Embedded Networked Sensor Systems (SenSys '04), p. 322, 2004.

21. D. Devarajan, R. J. Radke, and H. Chung, "Distributed metric calibration of ad hoc camera networks," ACM Transactions on Sensor Networks, vol. 2, no. 3, pp. 380–403, 2006.

22. D. B. Yang, H. H. González-Baños, and L. J. Guibas, "Counting people in crowds with a real-time network of simple image sensors," in Proceedings of the 9th IEEE International Conference on Computer Vision, vol. 1, pp. 122–129, Nice, France, October 2003.

23. D. Yang, J. Shin, A. Ercan, and L. Guibas, "Sensor tasking for occupancy reasoning in a network of cameras," in Proceedings of 2nd IEEE International Conference on Broadband Communications, Networks and Systems (BaseNets '04), 2004.

24. A. Lipton, H. Fujiyoshi, and R. Patil, "Moving target classification and tracking from real-time video," in Proceedings of IEEE Image Understanding Workshop, 1998.

25. P. V. Pahalawatta, T. N. Pappas, and A. K. Katsaggelos, "Optimal sensor selection for video-based target tracking in a wireless sensor network," in Proceedings of the International Conference on Image Processing (ICIP '04), vol. 2, pp. 3073–3076, 2004.

26. S. Fleck, F. Busch, and W. Straßer, "Adaptive probabilistic tracking embedded in smart cameras for distributed surveillance in a 3D model," EURASIP Journal of Embedded Systems, vol. 2007, Article ID 29858, 17 pages, 2007.

27. F. Lau, E. Oto, and H. Aghajan, "Color-based multiple agent tracking for wireless image sensor networks," in Proceedings of the Advanced Concepts for Intelligent Vision Systems (ACIVS '06), pp. 299–310, 2006.

28. T. H. Ko and N. M. Berry, "On scaling distributed low-power wireless image sensors," in Proceedings of the 39th Annual Hawaii International Conference on System Sciences, 2006.

29. A. Ercan, A. E. Gamal, and L. Guibas, "Camera network node selection for target localization in the presence of occlusions," in Proceedings of the ACM SenSys Workshop on Distributed Smart Cameras, 2006.

30. S. Soro and W. B. Heinzelman, "On the coverage problem in video-based wireless sensor networks," in Proceedings of the 2nd International Conference on Broadband Networks (BROADNETS '05), pp. 9–16, 2005.

31. H. Wu and A. A. Abouzeid, "Error resilient image transport in wireless sensor networks," Computer Networks, vol. 50, no. 15, pp. 2873–2887, 2006.

32. M. Chen, V. C. M. Leung, S. Mao, and Y. Yuan, "Directional geographical routing for real-time video communications in wireless sensor networks," Computer Communications, vol. 30, no. 17, pp. 3368–3383, 2007.

33. M. Maimour, C. Pham, and J. Amelot, "Load repartition for congestion control in multimedia wireless sensor networks with multipath routing," in Proceedings of the 3rd International Symposium on Wireless Pervasive Computing (ISWPC '08), pp. 11–15, 2008.

34. P. Lin, C. Qiao, and X. Wang, "Medium access control with a dynamic duty cycle for sensor networks," in Proceedings of the IEEE Wireless Communications and Networking Conference (WCNC '04), vol. 3, pp. 1534–1539, 2004.

35. G. Lu, B. Krishnamachari, and C. S. Raghavendra, "An adaptive energy-efficient and low-latency MAC for data gathering in wireless sensor networks," in Proceedings of the 18th International Parallel and Distributed Processing Symposium (IPDPS '04), pp. 3091–3098, Santa Fe, NM, USA, April 2004.

36. C. Ceken, "An energy efficient and delay sensitive centralized MAC protocol for wireless sensor networks," Computer Standards and Interfaces, vol. 30, no. 1-2, pp. 20–31, 2008.

37. T. He, J. A. Stankovic, C. Lu, and T. Abdelzaher, "SPEED: a stateless protocol for real-time communication in sensor networks," in Proceedings of the International Conference on Distributed Computing Systems (ICDCS '03), pp. 46–55, 2003.

38. E. Felemban, C.-G. Lee, and E. Ekici, "MMSPEED: multipath multi-SPEED protocol for QoS guarantee of reliability and timeliness in wireless sensor networks," IEEE Transactions on Mobile Computing, vol. 5, no. 6, pp. 738–753, 2006.

39. G. Lu and B. Krishnamachari, "Minimum latency joint scheduling and routing in wireless sensor networks," Ad Hoc Networks, vol. 5, no. 6, pp. 832–843, 2007.

40. Y. Andreopoulos, N. Mastronarde, and M. van der Schaar, "Cross-layer optimized video streaming over wireless multi-hop mesh networks," IEEE Journal on Selected Areas in Communications, vol. 24, pp. 2104–1215, 2006.

41. M. van der Schaar and D. S. Turaga, "Cross-layer packetization and retransmission strategies for delay-sensitive wireless multimedia transmission," IEEE Transactions on Multimedia, vol. 9, no. 1, pp. 185–197, 2007.

42. W. Wang, D. Peng, H. Wang, and H. Sharif, "Adaptive image transmission with p-v diversity in multihop wireless mesh networks," International Journal of Electrical, Computer, and Systems Engineering, vol. 1, no. 1, 2007.

43. K. Obraczka, R. Manduchi, and J. Garcia-Luna-Aceves, "Managing the information flow in visual sensor networks," in Proceedings of the 5th International Symposium on Wireless Personal Multimedia Communication, 2002.

44. H. Medeiros, J. Park, and A. Kak, "A light-weight event-driven protocol for sensor clustering in wireless camera networks," in Proceedings of the 1st ACM/ IEEE International Conference on Distributed Smart Cameras (ICDSC '07), pp. 203–210, 2007.

45. T. Teixeira, D. Lymberopoulos, E. Culurciello, Y. Aloimonos, and A. Savvides, "A lightweight camera sensor network operating on symbolic information," in Proceedings of 1st Workshop on Distributed Smart Cameras, Held in Conjunction with ACM SenSys, 2006.

46. H. Aghajan and C. Wu, "From distributed vision networks to human behavior interpretation," in Proceedings of the Behaviour Monitoring and Interpretation Workshop at the 30th German Conference on Artificial Intelligence, 2007.

47. V. Lecuire, C. Duran-Faundez, and N. Krommenacker, "Energy-efficient transmission of wavelet-based images in wireless sensor networks," EURASIP Journal on Image and Video Processing, vol. 2007, no. 1, 15 pages, 2007.

48. C.-Y. Wan, A. T. Campbell, and L. Krishnamurthy, "Pump-slowly, fetch-quickly (PSFQ): a reliable transport protocol for sensor networks," IEEE Journal on Selected Areas in Communications, vol. 23, no. 4, pp. 862–872, 2005.

49. M. van der Schaar and P. Chou, Multimedia over IP and Wireless Networks: Compression, Networking, and Systems, Academic Press, New York, NY, USA, 2007.

50. W. Ye, J. Heidemann, and D. Estrin, "An energy-efficient MAC protocol for wireless sensor networks," in Proceedings of 21st International Annual Joint Conference of the IEEE Computer and Communications Societies (INFOCOM '02), vol. 3, pp. 1567–1576, 2002.

51. H. Zhang and J. C. Hou, "Maintaining sensing coverage and connectivity in large sensor networks," International Journal of Wireless Ad Hoc and Sensor Networks, vol. 1, no. 2, pp. 89–124, 2005.

52. J. C. Dagher, M. W. Marcellin, and M. A. Neifeld, "A method for coordinating the distributed transmission of imagery," IEEE Transactions on Image Processing, vol. 15, no. 7, pp. 1705–1717, 2006.

53. J. Park, P. Bhat, and A. Kak, "A look-up table based approach for solving the camera selection problem in large camera networks," in Proceedings of the International Workshop on Distributed Smart Cameras (DCS '06), 2006.

54. S. Soro and W. Heinzelman, "Camera selection in visual sensor networks," in Proceedings of the IEEE Conference on Advanced Video and Signal Based Surveillance (AVSS '07), pp. 81–86, 2007.

55. N. H. Zamora and R. Marculescu, "Coordinated distributed power management with video sensor networks: analysis, simulation, and prototyping," in Proceedings of the 1st ACM/IEEE International Conference on Distributed Smart Cameras (ICDSC '07), pp. 4–11, 2007.

56. Z. Yang and K. Nahrstedt, "A bandwidth management framework for wireless camera array," in Proceedings of the International Workshop on Network and Operating System Support for Digital Audio and Video (NOSSDAV '05), pp. 147–152, 2005.

57. S. Hengstler and H. Aghajan, "WiSNAP: a wireless image sensor network application platform," in Proceedings of the 2nd International Conference on Testbeds and Research Infrastructures for the Development of Networks and Communities (TRIDENTCOM '06), pp. 7–12, 2006.

58. M. Rahimi, R. Baer, O. I. Iroezi, et al., "Cyclops: in situ image sensing and interpretation in wireless sensor networks," in Proceedings of the 3rd International Conference on Embedded Networked Sensor Systems, 2005.

59. W.-C. Feng, B. Code, E. Kaiser, M. Shea, W.-C. Feng, and L. Bavoil, "Panoptes: scalable low-power video sensor networking technologies," in Proceedings of the 11th ACM International Multimedia Conference and Exhibition (MM '03), pp. 562–571, Berkeley, Calif, USA, November 2003.

60. C. B. Margi, R. Manduchi, and K. Obraczka, "Energy consumption tradeoffs in visual sensor networks," in Proceedings of 24th Brazilian Symposium on Computer Networks (SBRC '06), 2006.

61. Crossbow Stargate platform, http://www.xbow.com/.

62. D. Jung, T. Teixeira, A. Barton-Sweeney, and A. Savvides, "Model-based design exploration of wireless sensor node lifetimes," in Proceedings of the 4th European Conference on Wireless Sensor Networks, pp. 277–292, 2007.

63. L. Nachman, "New Tinyos platforms panel: iMote2," in Proceedings of the Second International TinyOS Technology Exchange, 2005.

64. L. Ferrigno, S. Marano, V. Paciello, and A. Pietrosanto, "Balancing computational and transmission power consumption in wireless image sensor networks," in Poceedings of the IEEE International Conference onVirtual Environments, Human-Computer Interfaces, and Measurement Systems (VECIMS '05), pp. 61–66, 2005.

65. "Mica2 wireless sensor node," http://www.xbow.com/Products/Product_pdf_files/Wireless_pdf/MICA2_Datasheet.pdf.

66. R. Kleihorst, B. Schueler, A. Danilin, and M. Heijligers, "Smart camera mote with high performance vision system," in Proceedings of ACM SenSys Workshop on Distributed Smart Cameras (DSC '06), 2006.

67. A. Rowe, A. Goode, D. Goel, and I. Nourbakhsh, "CMUcam3: an open programmable embedded vision sensor," Carnegie Mellon Robotics Institute, 2007.

68. P. Kulkarni, D. Ganesan, P. Shenoy, and Q. Lu, "SensEye: a multi-tier camera sensor network," in Proceedings of the ACM Multimedia, 2005.

69. "Crossbow wireless sensor platform," http://www.xbow.com/Products/wproductsoverview.aspx.

70. A. Rowe, D. Goel, and R. Rajkumar, "FireFly Mosaic: a visionenabled wireless sensor networking system," in Proceedings of 28th IEEE International Real-Time Systems Symposium (RTSS '07), 2007.

71. A. Rowe, R. Mangharam, and R. Rajkumar, "RT-Link: a time synchronized link protocol for energy constrained multi-hop wireless networks," in Proceedings of IEEE Communications Society Conference on Sensor, Mesh and Ad Hoc Communications and Networks (SECON '06), 2006.

72. M. M. Molla and S. I. Ahamed, "A survey of middleware for sensor network and challenges," in Proceedings of the International Conference on Parallel Processing Workshops, pp. 223–228, 2006.

73. B. Rinner, M. Jovanovic, and M. Quaritsch, "Embedded midddleware on distributed smart cameras," in Proceedings of the IEEE International Conference on Acoustics, Speech, and Signal Processing (ICASSP '07), vol. 4, pp. 1381–1384, Honolulu, Hawaii, USA, April 2007.

74. H. Detmold, A. Dick, K. Falkner, D. S. Munro, A. van den Hengel, and R. Morrison, "Middleware for video surveillance networks," in Proceedings of the Middleware for Sensor Networks (MidSens '06), pp. 31–36, 2006.

75. Z. Xiong, A. D. Liveris, and S. Cheng, "Distributed source coding for sensor networks," IEEE Signal Processing Magazine, vol. 21, no. 5, pp. 80–94, 2004.

76. S. Meyer and A. Rakotonirainy, "A survey of research on contextaware homes," in Proceedings of the Australasian Information Security Workshop Conference on ACSW Frontiers, Australian Computer Society, Inc., 2003.

A Family of Tools for Supporting the Learning of Programming

Guido Rößling

ABSTRACT

Both learning how to program and understanding algorithms or data structures are often difficult. This paper presents three complementary approaches that we employ to help our students in learning to program, especially during the first term of their study. We use a web-based programming task database as an easy and risk-free environment for taking the first steps in programming Java. The Animal algorithm visualization system is used to visualize the dynamic behavior of algorithms and data structures. We complement both approaches with tutorial videos on using the Eclipse IDE. We also report on the experiences with this combined approach.

Keywords: algorithm animation; Animal; programming support; WebTasks

Introduction

Programming is a fundamental part of Computer Science. Educators therefore typically expect that graduates of a CS course, or courses close to CS, will be able to program. However, many studies and the experiences of a large number of teachers agree that "programming is not easy," and that learning to program is also not easy, see, e.g., [1].

Some effort has been put into investigating what factors contribute to this difficulty. For example, the problems seem not to depend on gender, but are correlated with problem solving skills and the first language of the student [2].

Over the last two decades, several tools for supporting the process of teaching or learning programming have appeared. Tools like BlueJ [3–5], Alice [6,7], DrScheme [8–10], Greenfoot [11–13] or Academic Java [14] address programming in their own unique way. For example, while both BlueJ and Alice target novices in object-oriented programming, BlueJ is based on UML and Java, while Alice uses a built-in drag-and-drop interface to program a 3D world with a high degree of interaction. DrScheme is used for teaching the fundamentals of how to design (good) programs in a set of pedagogically motivated teaching languages based on the functional language Scheme, while Greenfoot offers a framework for two-dimensional grid assignments in Java together with an IDE usable by novice programmers. Academic Java finally provides an interface to a large number of small programming examples that previous research had indicated covered both important and often misunderstood concepts in Java.

On the other hand, there have been a number of approaches to help students better grasp programs by visualizing the program itself ("program visualization"), or to present the dynamic behavior of algorithms of data structures ("algorithm visualization"). These systems include for example Jeliot 3 [15], which can visualize Java programs stepwise, or Leonardo [16], which can execute and also reverse the execution of C programs. The tools for visualizing or animating algorithms and data structures include ANIMAL [17] and JHAVE [18].

In this paper, we present a small family of tools that are used for teaching programming, algorithms, and data structures at the TU Darmstadt. These tools consist of a large database with easy to moderately difficult Java programming tasks, a system for visualizing algorithms and data structures, and recordings of tutorials on using the Eclipse IDE. Additionally, we outline our plans to integrate these features into the Moodle [19] open source distributed learning environment.

In the following Sections, we will present the current state of these components and outline the integration of the tools and learning materials that we are working on.

WebTasks: Programming Tasks Database

Testing the programs written by students for syntactic and semantic correctness, functionality or style is common today. Some of the established systems for accomplishing this include Boss [20], CourseMarker [21], and Web-CAT [22].

In 2006, we were looking for a system that supports students with little to no previous programming experience in learning to solve simple Java programming tasks. At the same time, we wanted to have a large pool of possible tasks covering the spectrum from "extremely easy" to "moderately difficult," in order to address both novice programmers and those with some previous exposure, but perhaps in a different programming language. At this stage, we did not yet expect students to be able to write their own tests, so that the test-driven development approach supported by Web-CAT did not apply to our students. In fact, we do not expect our students be able to write a full-fledged Java class including a main method: most tasks only require students to fill in the body of a prepared method.

At the same time, the system was supposed to assist, not assess, students. For example, the results of a student's submission are not taken into account for measuring the same student's accomplishments in the CS 1 course. While we encourage our students to use the system to get some hands-on practice in solving simple Java tasks, their submissions are not monitored and the use of the system is completely voluntary. Plagiarism or "cheating" are thus also not seen as a concern, as the students cannot benefit from this, but only succeed in cheating themselves.

To further lower the barrier in using the system, the system was supposed to run completely in the web browser, without requiring any software installation or even a Java SDK on the students' computers.

For these reasons, the established systems such as Boss [20], CourseMarker [21], and Web-CAT [22] did not perfectly match our expectation. We instead used a competitive programming lab to develop our own solution, called WebTasks, based on the best of four competing systems.

WebTasks [23] runs as a set of JSP pages on an Apache Tomcat server. As the contents mainly cover comparatively simple tasks, the target audience typically consists of students attending courses such as CS 1. No special algorithmic knowledge is required by most tasks, only a basic understanding of the Java programming language.

WebTasks currently contains 118 Java programming tasks. Only six of these tasks require the user to upload a complete class file, while the others require only that the body of a prepared method is implemented correctly. In this way, the student's workload is reduced, and many potentially problematic issues, such as the correct use of the Java main method, can be avoided. This also makes using

WebTasks significantly easier for novices to Java, while at the same time improving the control we have over the submissions.

Figure 1 shows a typical example of a programming task. Note that parts of this web page are in German, as the system was developed to support our local students; however, some tasks including the one shown here have been translated into English. Additionally, an internationalization of the user interface would not be difficult to do. The task shown requires the student to implement a variation on the Pascal triangle, where two initial values are passed in as an array of size 2. The student has to compute the nth step of a Pascal triangle based on this initial input, and return it as an array of int values.

The difficulty level of the task is indicated by a colored difficulty bar. The task in Figure 1 is thus ranked as rather difficult, based on the assumed programming skills of an average student in the first year of CS.

Figure 2 presents the basic work flow for a student working with WebTasks. The student will first pick an assignment and submit a solution proposal. This will be compiled by the server, and, if the compilation was successful, it will automatically be tested for correctness. A correct solution will be submitted to the internal forum. We will now take a closer look at these steps.

If the student decides on implementing the task, he will be taken to an input field as shown in Figure 3. Here, the student sees the predefined method header and return statement, and only needs to provide the correct implementation of the method body. In the Figure, a (slightly incorrect) solution proposal has already been filled in.

Once students think that their code should solve the task, they can press the "Abschicken" (Submit) button to submit their solution. The solution will then be automatically validated using JUnit [24,25]. If the tests are not successful, the result will be shown to the student, as indicated in Figure 4. Here, the system informs the user that test 2 out of 7 has failed, because the last value in the result was 2, not 1. Note that the tests are aborted once one test has failed. Thus, in Figure 4, only the tests Test1 and Test2 were executed. This was done to avoid overwhelming programming novices with a large number of failing tests in the initial submissions: novices shall be able to tackle one problem after the other.

The most popular programming assignment asks students to determine the average value for an array of int values. This task currently has 627 valid solutions. 617 students solved a second tasks that asked them to "append" an int to an array of int values, requiring them to create a new array of the proper size and copy all "old" values accordingly. In total, the 118 programming tasks have received more than 10,000 solutions so far. Note that this number ignores the failed submissions—only successful submissions that passed all internal JUnit tests are counted.

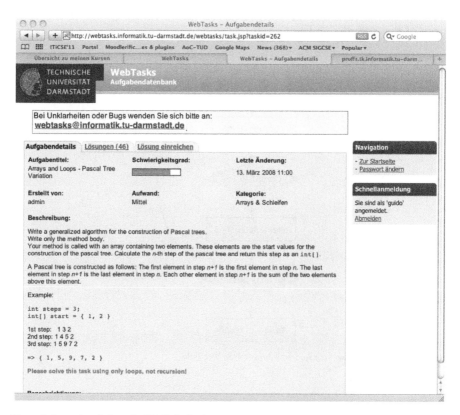

Figure 1. Example task from the WebTasks database.

Once a task has been solved by a student, he or she is able to view the solutions of other students, and may comment on them. The underlying rationale for this feature is that students may learn much from peer solutions, especially if those use clever "tricks" that the student had not thought of before. These "tricks" can for example include the use of System.arraycopy to copy the elements in an array, the use of iterators or the modified "for each" version of the Java for loop.

To use the system, a user first has to log in with the credentials of the CS Department of the TU Darmstadt, or register inside the system. While the first option is only available to students who take courses from our department, the system-internal registration is available to all interested users. The use of the system is encouraged within our CS 1 course as an easy way to get fast feedback on the correctness of programs. Compared to regularly submitted programming tasks which are corrected by a teaching assistant, the delay between submission and access to the result when using WebTasks is only a few seconds: the time needed for the server to compile and test the submission and then provide the output of the compiler and test system.

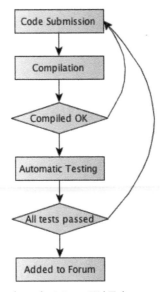

Figure 2. Schematic workflow for a student submission to WebTasks.

```
1st step:  1 3 2
2nd step: 1 4 5 2
3rd step: 1 5 9 7 2

=> { 1, 5, 9, 7, 2 }

Please solve this task using only loops, not recursion!
```

```
1  public static int[] studentsMethod(int[] array_in, final int steps) {
2
    int currentLevel = 0;
    int[] old = array_in;
    int[] result = null;

    if (steps == 1 || array_in == null)
      result = array_in;

    // loop over the target levels
    for (int level = 1; level <= steps; level++) {
      // create array
      result = new int[old.length + 1];
3
4
5    return result;
6  }
```

Abschicken   Zurück

Figure 3. Example student code for a given WebTasks task.

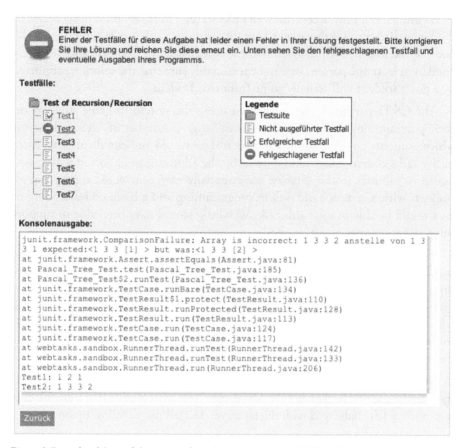

FEHLER
Einer der Testfälle für diese Aufgabe hat leider einen Fehler in Ihrer Lösung festgestellt. Bitte korrigieren Sie Ihre Lösung und reichen Sie diese erneut ein. Unten sehen Sie den fehlgeschlagenen Testfall und eventuelle Ausgaben Ihres Programms.

Testfälle:

Test of Recursion/Recursion
- Test1
- Test2
- Test3
- Test4
- Test5
- Test6
- Test7

Legende
Testsuite
Nicht ausgeführter Testfall
Erfolgreicher Testfall
Fehlgeschlagener Testfall

Konsolenausgabe:

```
junit.framework.ComparisonFailure: Array is incorrect: 1 3 3 2 anstelle von 1 3
3 1 expected:<1 3 3 [1] > but was:<1 3 3 [2] >
at junit.framework.Assert.assertEquals(Assert.java:81)
at Pascal_Tree_Test.test(Pascal_Tree_Test.java:185)
at Pascal_Tree_Test$2.runTest(Pascal_Tree_Test.java:136)
at junit.framework.TestCase.runBare(TestCase.java:134)
at junit.framework.TestResult$1.protect(TestResult.java:110)
at junit.framework.TestResult.runProtected(TestResult.java:128)
at junit.framework.TestResult.run(TestResult.java:113)
at junit.framework.TestCase.run(TestCase.java:124)
at junit.framework.TestCase.run(TestCase.java:117)
at webtasks.sandbox.RunnerThread.runTest(RunnerThread.java:142)
at webtasks.sandbox.RunnerThread.runTest(RunnerThread.java:133)
at webtasks.sandbox.RunnerThread.run(RunnerThread.java:206)
Test1: 1 2 1
Test2: 1 3 3 2
```

Zurück

Figure 4. Example validation failure output for code submitted to the WebTasks database.

The database also contains 50 multiple choice tests. The topics covered in the tests include questions about various tree structures (Heaps, spanning trees, B-and AVL trees), complexity, maximum flow problems, hashing, shortest path problems, boolean and binary operators and sorting algorithms. All these topics belong to the first two Introduction to Computer Science courses taught at the TU Darmstadt, the core courses for teaching programming concepts, programming languages, object orientation, algorithms and data structures.

It should be pointed out that the system as it is is not meant for official grading of student submissions. Although students have to log in, no authentication beyond the login and password is done, so that no valid proof of identity can be guaranteed. WebTasks also offers an "exam" mode in which the access to the system is limited to the computers from our central CS computer pool (with about 100 terminals). Additionally, the pool network is manually reconfigured so that each terminal can only access the WebTasks server, effectively preventing access to the home directory (as this might contain solutions), other computers inside the pool, or the Internet. Thus, given that the students in the pool will also be supervised by at least one person, we can be reasonably sure that the solution submitted by a given student will actually come from that student.

The CS Department also considered using the system to grade students on their programming skills. The idea was to assign a number of "exam" dates for which students could register. Each such date would present them with three to five tasks chosen either randomly or by the educator, to be solved within two hours. As all tasks in the database are essentially easy, one would expect that all students with a certain basic skill in programming and a basic understanding of Java would be able to solve this task. WebTasks would have been able to support this testing in a special testing mode.

However, after some internal discussions, the CS Department dropped these considerations in favor of a mandatory CS 1 programming project and a mentoring system. This was done to place more emphasis on supporting students than on using exams to distinguish between "sufficiently qualified" students and those who were not allowed to continue. As the goal of WebTasks is to assist, not monitor or evaluate, students in taking the first steps in programming Java in a threat-free environment, we were glad that the plans were ultimately dropped.

We initially also included an automatic and rigorous checking of the code quality with the use of CheckStyle [26]. Since our target users are programming novices who already felt challenged with the tasks, we decided not to follow up on this.

Visualizing and Animating Algorithms and Data Structures

The WebTasks database described in Section 2 is meant to provide students with little programming experience in Java with an easy and fault-tolerant environment for working on simple programming tasks. Another problematic area in programming is understanding common algorithms and data structures. Topics such as searching and sorting algorithms are usually taught in a CS 2 course, together with data structures such as binary trees, graphs, or more complex data structures such as AVL trees.

The main problem here is often not that the students have to program these algorithms or data structures. Rather, the students first have to be able to understand the behavior of these structures. For this purpose, the field of algorithm and program visualization has been active in implementing tools and providing guidelines for supporting the understanding of algorithms and data structures.

Our basic credo is that the highly dynamic nature of the underlying data structures or algorithms should also be presented dynamically, as getting a firm grasp of the "inner workings" based solely on the (static) code is difficult for many students. Besides supporting students by showing them how a given data structure or algorithm behaves, it has increasingly been recognized that it is also important to actively engage the learners. A seminal report by a set of experts in the field [27] has defined a taxonomy of "levels of engagement," which has been referenced in more than 100 publications and has caused some follow-up research with similar results including [18,28]. The report was further supported by a survey of successful evaluations [29].

One of the most elaborate systems for visualizing (almost) arbitrary content is ANIMAL [17,30]. ANIMAL presents contents based on a set of built-in flexible graphical primitives and animation effects. It does not "understand" the underlying "code," but usually processes programs written in the ANIMALSCRIPT visualization scripting language [31]. This notation allows the placement of objects in relation to each other, e.g., at an offset from another object's top left corner. It also supports a number of computer science-specific data structures, such as arrays, lists or code blocks including indentation and highlighting.

What sets ANIMAL apart from other related systems is the flexibility of providing content to the user. The presentation controls allow easy access in both directions and optionally also offer a "table of contents" for each animation—provided that the animation author has populated this. More importantly, there are several ways how animation content can be generated:

- Even novices can generate contents manually using drag and drop. While this may initially seem to be almost as time-consuming as doing it in programs such as PowerPoint, the support for data structures makes the process faster. Additionally, since each animation frame builds on the previous frame, the user does not have to copy all current elements to the next slide, as would be needed in presentation software such as PowerPoint or Keynote.

- Content can be written directly in ANIMALSCRIPT. ANIMAL provides an online reference to the language, so that writing a syntactically correct program is not difficult.

- Animations can be generated from a program by adding appropriate statements that will create ANIMALSCRIPT output at "interesting places."

- Programs can also be enriched by using the AlgoAnim API. This API will also create ANIMALSCRIPT output, but provides a far cleaner interface than incorporating the associated output statements into existing code [32].

- By placing output-producing programs into the generator framework, the associated programs can be run directly inside ANIMAL [33]. Additionally, this allows the end-user to adjust parameters, such as the concrete values to be sorted or inserted, as well as visual properties, such as the color chosen for individual elements.

Figure 5 shows an example screenshot of ANIMAL visualizing a version of Bubble Sort. The animation shows the array and the current values for the array index variables i and j. It also includes the complete source code with indentation below the array. The currently executing code line, in this case the inner "for" loop, is highlighted to make it easier for the user to link the code with the visualized contents. Additionally, the value for the boolean variable "isSorted" is shown and the number of assignments and comparisons ("Zuweisungen" and "Vergleiche" in German, respectively) are visualized at the top.

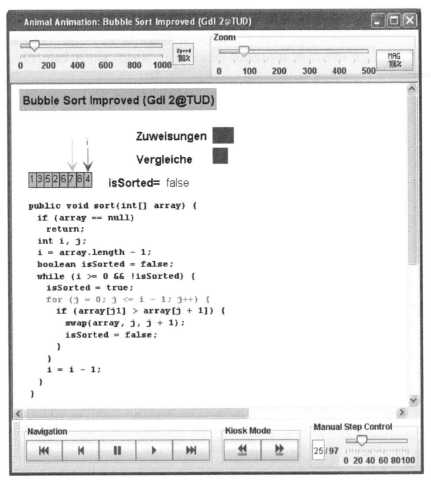

Figure 5. Example screenshot from the ANIMAL user front-end animating BubbleSort.

The user can navigate the animation using the basic navigation controls at the bottom left. Note that this also includes jumping to the start of the animation or taking one step backwards. ANIMAL places no limit on the number of steps to be taken backwards; users could easily jump to the end of the animation and then walk through it backwards if they wanted to do so.

The "kiosk mode" buttons put the animation on continuous play until the end, or in reverse mode the beginning, of the animation has been reached. Users can also type in the number of the step they want to jump to, or drag the ruler to some point in the animation. Note that the ruler is always normalized to the percentage of the animation shown, and thus will always stay between 0 and 100 (for 100%). Dragging the ruler from left to right gives a "fast fly-by overview" of the animation.

One key aspect for the acceptance of algorithm visualization in a course is the integration of the visualization with the other lecture materials [34,35]. The report of an international expert group recommended what they termed as a visualization-based computer science hypertextbook (VizCoSH), which would have a structure similar to a textbook but would tightly integrate the teaching and learning materials with algorithm or program visualizations [34].

We have developed a VizCoSH prototype as an activity for the Moodle distributed learning environment [19]. This activity emulates a regular "textbook," separated into chapters and paragraphs. However, it also provides several additional features. For example, each paragraph can be discussed in a separate "thread" [35].

Figure 6 shows a screenshot of this activity. The top of the screen shows a screenshot of the animation. One click on this image will lead to an information page about the animation, and a second click will cause the ANIMAL system to start up, load the animation from the web server, and display to the end user. Below, links to other animations are included, illustrating the way the algorithm—here, Insertion Sort—will behave on data placed in ascending, descending or alternating order. Additionally, users can start the built-in generator to generate an animation portraying how "their" custom input data will be sorted using Insertion Sort. The icons to the right of the main text provide access to the discussion about the current paragraph. The 3 next to the orange bubble indicates that three comments have been posted about this paragraph (visible to the right), while the 0 next to the blue icon shows that there are no private posts for this element.

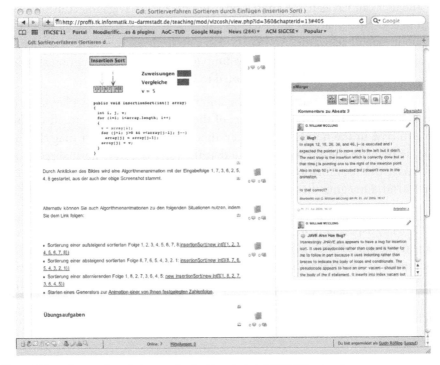

Figure 6. Example screenshot of a hypertextbook with an included ANIMAL animation.

In addition to commenting on paragraphs, users can also use a text marker, included above the comment threads on the right, to highlight individual words or passages in the text. The navigation between chapters is accomplished using the table of contents shown at the top of each page (missing on the screenshot), as well as the pair of back/forward buttons at the top and bottom of each page. Finally, users can print the complete "book" or a single chapter comfortably.

The large benefit of the integration into Moodle is that the animations of algorithms and data structures can now be placed together with the other learning materials, such as slides, exercise sheets, or homework submission and correction facilities. All these activities are placed in the same Moodle course, allowing students to access them whenever needed without having to "switch context."

Tutorials for Teaching the Use of Eclipse

To further enable our students to work with the comfortable but also complex Eclipse Java IDE, we have produced a small number of (German) screen recordings as tutorials. The videos were produced using the excellent Camtasia [36] software, partially under Windows (Camtasia Studio 6) and under Mac OS X (Camtasia 1.0.1).

Since the software is very easy to use and records the complete desktop or a part thereof, we first wrote a script of things we wanted to show. We defined five videos to be provided as tutorials:

- Eclipse Basics presents the basics of using Eclipse: starting the IDE, explaining the initially visible icons, and taking a walk through the "Hello World" tutorial. During the programming, we have intentionally introduced a bug, in order to illustrate how Eclipse will highlight errors and how they can be fixed using the "Quick Fix" option.

- Implementing a new class shows the implementation of a class, based on a basic piece of code. We show how code can be indented and formatted, and how mistakes can be addressed (in this case, by renaming a mistyped variable). We also implement the toString() method and use code completion as well as the generation of get-and set-methods including comments. The use of the code outline and the "Problems" and "JavaDoc" view is explained. The tutorial ends by discussing the look-up of definitions using the F3 key, using quick fixes, formatting source code, adding and organizing imports, and sorting members.

- Implementing and testing a sample calculator presents a simple implementation of a basic calculator that is developed "live." The tutorial starts by creating a new project, package, and class, and implementing several simple calculator methods, complete with some intentional bugs. We then show how a JUnit test can be implemented in a separate package, and how test methods are annotated with the @Test notation. The development of tests is done in parallel with re-runs of the existing and new tests. We then add an initialization method and show how methods not yet ready for testing can be ignored, how expected exceptions can be checked, and how infinite loops can be prevented during testing.

- Extending classes illustrates how a new class can be defined to extend an existing class. We show one example each using an abstract and a concrete base class. We then repeat this by having a class implement an interface.

- Debugging is illustrated in a separate video. Here, we use JUnit tests to pinpoint the offending method and code line, and then use breakpoints to narrow down the possible lines of code. The tutorial also shows how variables can be inspected and how (changed) method code can be re-run.

Summary and Conclusions

We have presented our tools for assisting students to learn programming Java. These consist of a web-based database of easy to moderately difficult programming tasks, a system for visualizing the behavior of algorithm and data structures, and tutorials on how to use the Eclipse IDE.

Our WebTasks system [23] has been in use since 2006. The system provides a set of programming tasks that mostly require the student to provide a method body. In this way, we can prevent a number of typical problems that novices to Java face, such as the correct use of the main method. Submissions are tested on upload, providing feedback within a few seconds of submitting a solution. Students who have solved a given task are granted access to all solutions for this task, so that they can look at what their peers did. They can also comment on other students' solutions. The system has seen much use since its inception, with currently more than 10,000 (correct) submitted solutions to the more than 100 programming tasks.

To make understanding the dynamic behavior of algorithms and data structures easier, we provide the ANIMAL system [17,30]. ANIMAL offers full reversibility of the contents and thus makes following the display easier. ANIMAL animations typically also show the underlying source code and highlight the currently executing line, making it easier to connect the code with the visualized representation.

Finally, the difficulties that especially novice programmers face when working with a full-fledged IDE like Eclipse are addressed by tutorial videos that illustrate the use of Eclipse.

Our experiences with the tool support so far are very encouraging. Student feedback for the CS 1 lecture in which the tools are used has been very good, including winning the prize for the best lecture in the summer term 2009 based on student evaluation results. Students also stated that using the tools had been a great help in getting ready to program Java and understand the presented algorithms. However, some students also stated that they would have preferred to have a single base system, rather than a set of independent elements.

To provide better access to our materials, we are working on integrating both the WebTasks database, the algorithm visualizations and the tutorial materials into the Moodle Learning Management System [19]. This will allow students to use a single login to access all course materials, exercise their programming skills, and watch and interact with visualizations of algorithms and data structures. Currently, the visualization of ANIMAL content has already been implemented, and we are working on integrating the WebTasks database into Moodle. Once this integration has been accomplished, we will be glad to share the materials with interested educators.

Acknowledgements

We gratefully acknowledge the assistance of our students who implemented parts of the system described in this paper, in alphabetical order: Tobias Ackermann, Sebastian Hartte, Stephan Mehlhase, Jens Pfau, Anselmo Stelzer, and Teena Vellaramkalayil.

References

1. McCracken, M.; Almstrum, V.; Diaz, D.; Guzdial, M.; Hagan, D.; Kolikant, Y.B.D.; Laxer, C.; Thomas, L.; Utting, I.; Wilusz, T. A multi-national, multi-institutional study of assessment of programming skills of first-year CS students. SIGCSE Bull. 2001, 33, 125–180.

2. Pillay, N.; Jugoo, V.R. An investigation into student characteristics affecting novice programming performance. SIGCSE Bull. 2005, 37, 107–110.

3. Kouznetsova, S. Using BlueJ and Blackjack to teach object-oriented design concepts in CS1. J. Comput. Small Coll. 2007, 22, 49–55.

4. Kölling, M., Using BlueJ to introduce programming. In Reflections on the Teaching of Programming: Methods and Implementations; Springer-Verlag: Berlin, Heidelberg, Germany, 2008; pp. 98–115.

5. Barnes, D.J.; Kölling, M. Objects First with Java: A Practical Introduction Using BlueJ, 4th ed.; Prentice Hall: Upper Saddle River, NJ, USA, 2008.

6. Dann, W.P.; Cooper, S.; Pausch, R. Learning to Program with Alice; Prentice Hall: Upper Saddle River, NJ, USA, 2006.

7. Rodger, S.H.; Hayes, J.; Lezin, G.; Qin, H.; Nelson, D.; Tucker, R.; Lopez, M.; Cooper, S.; Dann, W.; Slater, D. Engaging middle school teachers and students with Alice in a diverse set of subjects. In SIGCSE '09: Proceedings of the 40th ACM Technical Symposium on Computer Science Education; ACM: New York, NY, USA, 2009; pp. 271–275.

8. Page, R.; Eastlund, C.; Felleisen, M. Functional programming and theorem proving for undergraduates: a progress report. In FDPE '08: Proceedings of the 2008 International Workshop on Functional and Declarative Programming in Education; ACM: New York, NY, USA, 2008; pp. 21–30.

9. Bieniusa, A.; Degen, M.; Heidegger, P.; Thiemann, P.; Wehr, S.; Gasbichler, M.; Sperber, M.; Crestani, M.; Klaeren, H.; Knauel, E. HtDP and DMDA in the battlefield: A case study in first-year programming instruction. In FDPE '08: Proceedings of the 2008 International Workshop on Functional and

Declarative Programming in Education; ACM: New York, NY, USA, 2008; pp. 1–12.

10. Felleisen, M.; Findler, R.B.; Flatt, M.; Krishnamurthi, S. How to Design Programs—An Introduction to Programming and Computing; MIT Press: Cambridge, MA, USA, 2001.

11. Gallant, R.J.; Mahmoud, Q.H. Using Greenfoot and a Moon Scenario to teach Java programming in CS1. In ACM-SE 46: Proceedings of the 46th Annual Southeast Regional Conference; ACM: New York, NY, USA, 2008; pp. 118–121.

12. Al-Bow, M.; Austin, D.; Edgington, J.; Fajardo, R.; Fishburn, J.; Lara, C.; Leutenegger, S.; Meyer, S. Using Greenfoot and games to teach rising 9th and 10th grade novice programmers. In Sandbox '08: Proceedings of the 2008 ACM SIGGRAPH Symposium on Video Games; ACM: New York, NY, USA, 2008; pp. 55–59.

13. Kölling, M. Greenfoot: a highly graphical IDE for learning object-oriented programming. In ITiCSE '08: Proceedings of the 13th Annual Conference on Innovation and Technology in Computer Science Education; ACM: New York, NY, USA, 2008; pp. 327–327.

14. Academic Java. Availible online: http://academicjava.com/ (accessed on 25 March 2010).

15. Moreno, A.; Myller, N.; Sutinen, E.; Ben-Ari, M. Visualizing Programs with Jeliot 3. In Proceedings of the Working Conference on Advanced Visual Interfaces (AVI 2004); ACM Press: New York, NY, USA, 2004; pp. 373–380.

16. Demetrescu, C.; Finocchi, I. A portable virtual machine for program debugging and directing. In SAC '04: Proceedings of the 2004 ACM Symposium on Applied Computing; ACM: New York, NY, USA, 2004; pp. 1524–1530.

17. Rößling, G.; Freisleben, B. ANIMAL: A System for Supporting Multiple Roles in Algorithm Animation. J. Visual Lang. Computing 2002, 13, 341–354.

18. Naps, T. JHAVÉ—Addressing the Need to Support Algorithm Visualization with Tools for Active Engagement. IEEE Comput. Graph. Appl. 2005, 25, 49–55.

19. Rice IV, W.H.; Nash, S.S. Moodle 1.9 Teaching Techniques -Creative ways to build powerful and effective online courses; Packt Publishing: Birmingham, UK, 2010.

20. Joy, M.; Griffiths, N.; Boyatt, R. The Boss online submission and assessment system. J. Educ. Resour. Comput. 2005, 5, 2.

21. Higgins, C.A.; Gray, G.; Symeonidis, P.; Tsintsifas, A. Automated assessment and experiences of teaching programming. J. Educ. Resour. Comput. 2005, 5, 5.

22. Edwards, S.H.; Perez-Quinones, M.A. Experiences using test-driven development with an automated grader. J. Comput. Small Coll. 2007, 22, 44–50.

23. Rößling, G.; Hartte, S. WebTasks: Online Programming Exercises Made Easy. In Proceedings of the 13th Annual SIGCSE Conference on Innovation and Technology in Computer Science Education (ITiCSE 2008); ACM Press: New York, NY, USA, 2008; p. 363.

24. Wick, M.; Stevenson, D.; Wagner, P. Using testing and JUnit across the curriculum. In SIGCSE '05: Proceedings of the 36th SIGCSE Technical Symposium on Computer Science Education; ACM: New York, NY, USA, 2005; pp. 236–240.

25. Object Mentor. JUnit.org Resources for Test Driven Development. Available online: http://www. junit.org (accessed on 25 March 2010).

26. Burn, O. Checkstyle 5.0. Availible online: http://checkstyle.sourceforge.net/ (accessed on 25 March 2010).

27. Naps, T.L.; Rößling, G.; Almstrum, V.; Dann, W.; Fleischer, R.; Hundhausen, C.; Korhonen, A.; Malmi, L.; McNally, M.; Rodger, S.; Velazquez-Iturbide, J. A. Exploring the Role of Visualization and Engagement in Computer Science Education. ACM SIGCSE Bullet. 2003, 35, 131–152.

28. Grissom, S.; McNally, M.; Naps, T.L. Algorithm Visualization in Computer Science Education: Comparing Levels of Student Engagement. In Proceedings of the First ACM Symposium on Software Visualization; ACM Press: New York, NY, USA, 2003; pp. 87–94.

29. Urquiza-Fuentes, J.; Velazquez-Iturbide, J.A. A survey of successful evaluations of program visualization and algorithm animation systems. Trans. Comput. Educ. 2009, 9, 1–21.

30. Rößling, G. Animal-Farm: An Extensible Framework for Algorithm Visualization; VDM Verlag Dr. Mucken, Germany, 2008.

31. Rößling, G.; Gliesche, F.; Jajeh, T.; Widjaja, T. Enhanced Expressiveness in Scripting Using ANIMALSCRIPT V2. In Proceedings of the Third Program Visualization Workshop, Warwick, UK, July 2004; pp. 15–19.

32. Rößling, G.; Mehlhase, S.; Pfau, J. A Java API for Creating (not only) ANIMALSCRIPT. Electron. Note Theor. Comput. Sci. 2009, 224, 15–25.

33. Rößling, G. Electr. Noteoßling, G.; Ackermann, T. A Framework for Generating AV Content on-the-fly. Theor. Comput. Sci. 2007, 178, 23–31.

34. Rößling, G.; Naps, T.; Hall, M.S.; Karavirta, V.; Kerren, A.; Leska, C.; Moreno, A.; Oechsle, R.; Rodger, S.H.; Urquiza-Fuentes, J.; Velazquez-Iturbide, J. A. Merging Interactive Visualizations with Hypertextbooks and Course Management. SIGCSE Bullet. inroad 2006, 38, 166–181.

35. Rößling, G. A Visualization-Based Computer Science Hypertextbook; Vellaramkalayil, T. Prototype. ACM Trans. Comput. Educat. 2009, 9, 1–13.

36. Aman, J.; Wilson, B.; Shirvani, S. Maintaining lecture context in a blended course. J. Comput. Small Coll. 2007, 23, 56–63.

InfoVis Interaction Techniques in Animation of Recursive Programs

J. Ángel Velázquez-Iturbide and Antonio Pérez-Carrasco

ABSTRACT

Algorithm animations typically assist in educational tasks aimed simply at achieving understanding. Potentially, animations could assist in higher levels of cognition, such as the analysis level, but they usually fail in providing this support because they are not flexible or comprehensive enough. In particular, animations of recursion provided by educational systems hardly support the analysis of recursive algorithms. Here we show how to provide full support to the analysis of recursive algorithms. From a technical point of view, animations are enriched with interaction techniques inspired by the information visualization (InfoVis) field. Interaction tasks are presented in seven categories, and deal with both static visualizations and dynamic animations. All of these features are implemented in the SRec system, and visualizations generated by SRec are used to illustrate the article.

Keywords: program animation; program visualization; information visualization; recursion; human-computer interaction

Introduction

Recursion is a fundamental concept in Computer Science education, especially in programming courses. Its role varies from course to course. It is one of the concepts learnt in introductory courses to programming, but it is a programming construct applied in algorithm courses. For example, dynamic programming algorithms are usually stated recursively in a first phase and transformed into a tabulated, iterative version in a second phase. As a consequence, an animation system of recursion may be a valuable tool for any course where recursion plays an important role, in particular in algorithm courses.

Teaching and learning algorithms are often assisted by animations. Animations typically assist in understanding algorithms, but they could also assist in their analysis. We are not using the word "analysis" in any restricting sense (e.g., "complexity analysis"), but in the more general sense used by Bloom et al. [1]:

"The student is able to distinguish, classify and relate hypothesis and evidences of the information given, as well as decomposing a problem into its parts."

We are interested in using animations to assist in analyzing interactively the behavior of recursive algorithms: in other words, we seek a kind of "software oscilloscope" [2] for recursion. Support for the analysis of algorithms is typically provided by debuggers, which are very flexible, complex systems. Therefore, animations for the analysis of recursive algorithms must exhibit as powerful visualization features as debuggers do. We show that such analysis power can be feasibly achieved by using interaction techniques inspired by the information visualization (InfoVis) field.

In this article, we discuss and illustrate interaction techniques aimed at giving flexible, comprehensive support to recursion analysis in animation systems. Section 2 shows common, effective visualizations of recursion, in general and also as supported by different systems, especially by the SRec system [3]. Section 3 shows interaction techniques tailored to the interactive analysis of recursive algorithms. These techniques are classified into seven categories, and they deal with both static visualizations and dynamic animations. Finally, we summarize our conclusions in Section 4.

Visualization of Recursion

In this section, we first present different visualizations of recursion. We then present the visualizations supported by the SRec system. Finally, we survey different visualization systems of recursion, and show the very limited facilities they pro-vide to the user to interact with visualizations. In order to keep the discussion short, we restrict our survey to the imperative paradigm.

Visualizations of Recursion

There is no single visualization of recursion. A small number of visualizations can be found in the literature, for instance, traces, the control stack and recur-sion trees (e.g., [4]). Another visualization, used in visualization systems, is called "multiple copies" (e.g., [5]) and shows a different copy of either code or data for each recursive call.

We also find additional visualizations or variants of the visualizations cited above for specific cases of recursion. For instance, Stern and Naish [6] propose three visualizations for different recursive operations; their main feature is that they combine control and data. The most important class of recursive algorithms is divide-and-conquer. Variants of either traces or recursion trees have also been used to better illustrate divide-and-conquer algorithms [7 (p.158),8]; at each step, they focus on a part of the main data structure. It has also been noticed that some visualizations are effective both to show the inductive definition and the run-time behavior of divide-and-conquer algorithms, for instance, a sequence of visualiza-tions of the main data structure [8].

No matter the quality of visualization, it will have merits and drawbacks and will be more useful for some aims. For instance, traces are good for novices, as they can easily follow the sequential flow of execution. Therefore, a system will probably be more useful if it provides multiple views, so that the user is able to choose the most adequate for the task she wants to perform.

Visualizations of Recursion in SRec

In this article, we focus on the visualizations generated by the SRec animation system. SRec supports visualization and animation of recursion in any Java algo-rithm, with the only restriction of using primitive data types. Versions 1.0 and 1.1 of SRec provided three general views (namely, traces, the control stack, and recursion trees) [3]. Version 1.1 enhanced substantially its interaction facilities, as shown here. Finally, version 1.2 of SRec supports three additional visualizations, specific to divide-and-conquer algorithms [8]; the system is currently capable of simultaneously showing two views. This evolution is partially due to the results of usability evaluations it has been subject to. SRec is a program animation sys-tem that generates animations (semi)automatically. The user may load any file containing Java source code, and it is preprocessed. If the file contains any divide-and-conquer algorithms, the user must identify them in a dialog. Then, the user may launch any method invocation, and during its execution a trail of relevant events is generated. After completion, the user may freely interact with its visualization and animation, which is automatically generated from the trail. The user has available five visualizations for divide-and-conquer algorithms and three visualizations for general recursive algorithms. We do not describe here implementation details, as they can be found elsewhere [9].

In the rest of the article, we use the well-known function fib for the Fibonacci series to illustrate recursive algorithms in general, and mergesort for divide-and-conquer algorithms.

The three general visualizations are briefly described:

- Recursion tree. This visualization allows display of the complete history of a recursive process as a tree. The root corresponds to the initial invocation. The children of a node are the recursive calls that it has invoked, from left to right in chronological order. Leaves represent calls corresponding to base cases. Every node is displayed with two areas, where the top area contains input values of parameters and the bottom one the result of the invocation (if the method does not return any value, the output state of parameters can be displayed). For example, Figure 1(a) displays the computation state for fib (5) where most recursive calls finished their execution, but the active call fib (1) and pending calls fib (3) and fib (5). In SRec, two states are displayed for every invocation: immediately after the invocation entry, and immediately before the invocation exit. The node framed in black in Figure 1(a) is the active node, so its computation is close to exit. Nodes framed in red correspond to pending invocations. In the figure, input values have a blue background and output values have a green background.

- The control stack. The control stack is an internal data structure of the virtual machine that makes possible the execution of programs with subroutines. In SRec, records of the control stack only contain input and output values, so they have the same structure as the nodes of recursion trees. The control stack initially contains the first invocation. On entry of a method invocation, a new record is pushed at the top of the stack, becoming the active record. This new record contains input values, but the output area is empty. On exit of a method invocation, the output area of the record at the top is filled with the call results and it is later popped. Figure 1(b) displays the control stack at the same instant as Figure 1(a). Visualizations of the control stack can be quite complex [10]. Notice however that the control stack, as displayed by SRec, is isomorphic to the rightmost branch of its associated recursion tree.

- Trace. A trace is a textual description of the sequence of events that take place during the execution of an algorithm, here entry or exit of every method invocation. Each entry (or exit) is represented as a text line that contains an indication that it is an entry (or exit), the method name and its actual parameters (or results). Using a color convention allows differentiating entry and exit invocations. In addition, indentation is commonly used to represent the level of nesting of invocations. Figure 1(c) contains a trace of the same computation of fib (5). Notice that the trace is isomorphic to a traversal of the recursion tree, where input values are printed inorder and ouput values are printed postorder.

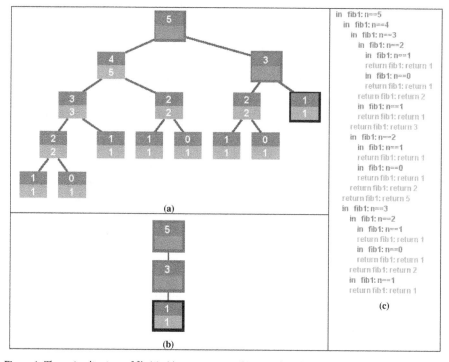

Figure 1. Three visualizations of fib (5): (a) recursion tree, (b) control stack, and (c) trace.

Three additional representations, specific for divide-and-conquer algorithms, are supported by SRec. We briefly explain them below:

- Divide-and-conquer recursion tree. Divide-and-conquer algorithms typically manipulate a large data structure, but in most recursive calls, the focus of interest is limited to a part of it (i.e. a substructure). An effective variant of recursion trees for divide-and-conquer algorithms consists of displaying the whole structure with the relevant substructure highlighted. SRec supports this additional display for vectors and matrices. Figure 2(a) shows this representation when mergesorting the array {0,4,9,6,8,3}.

- Sequence of visualizations of the data structure. This representation consists of a sequence of visualizations of the state of the data structure, displayed top-down. It can be considered a variant of the trace visualization, which differs in the layout and in the amount of information displayed. Every time a recursive call is invoked, the array state is displayed. In order to better illustrate the algorithm behavior, each line only shows the subarray delimited in the recursive call. Every time a recursive call exits, the output state of its associated subarray is displayed adjacent to its input state. Again, the relative placement and the use of colors allow differentiating input and output states of subarrays. Figure 2(b) shows this view at the same state as Figure 2(a).

- Colored data structure. This is a mixed view that displays both the state of the data structure to manipulate and hints about the recursive process. In particular, if the data structure is a vector, a set of bars is displayed below the vector. The bars mirror the recursive process by underlining the subarray delimited in each recursive call. A coloring scheme that distinguishes input and output is also applied here. For each underlying bar, the coloring scheme indicates whether the corresponding recursive call is pending or finished. For each subarray, the scheme indicates whether the last update of its state by a recursive invocation was made with input or output values. Tones are also used to represent the distance in the activation tree to the active call. Figure 2(c) shows this representation at the same instant as Figure 2(a).

Systems for Recursion Animation

Programming environments fully support the analysis of execution, but they hardly support specific analysis of recursion. These are the most promising systems to analyze recursion, as they have available all the information on program execution, which should be rendered and interacted with adequate user interfaces. We point out ETV [11], a tool that allows visualizing the execution of a C++ program from the trace generated in execution time.

Some systems were specifically designed to learn recursion. Most of them are based on the "copies model" of recursion, that is, they show a different copy of either code or data for each recursive call. We may cite Recursion Animator [5], SimRECUR [12], Function Visualizer [13] and EROSI [14]. Flopex 2 [15] is an Excel extension for visual programming. EROSI, Recursion Animator and Sim-RECUR have been successfully evaluated.

We have compared SRec to these systems with respect to several issues: generality, effort to construct animations, visualization and animation features, and interaction features. We used two features to characterize system generality, namely methods to visualize, and range of types and input data supported. With respect to the methods visualized, Function Visualizer and Recursion Animator only visualize the first written method, while ETV and SRec are more flexible as they allow selecting any method. Only SRec allows changing interactively the set of visualizable methods. With respect to the range of types and input data supported, the literature reports that EROSI and SimRECUR are (again) very restrictive, SRec supports primitive data types, and the rest of the systems "seem" to allow any Java data type.

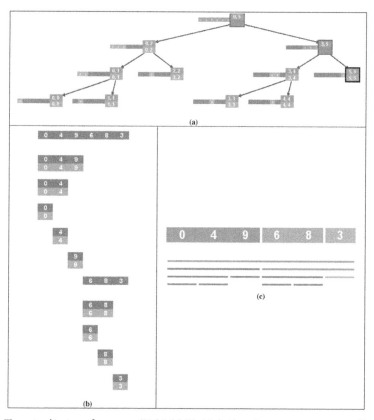

Figure 2. Three visualizations of mergesort ({0,4,9,6,8,3}): (a) divide-and-conquer recursion tree, (b) sequence of visualizations of a data structure, and (c) colored data structure.

The second feature we compared was the effort required for constructing animations. EROSI and SimRECUR only visualize predefined examples, Flopex 2 requires user construction of the recursion visualization, and the other four systems (including SRec) are automatic, which is the most comfortable method to construct animations.

The comparison with respect to visualization and animation features can be found in Table 1. Notice that SRec is the system that offers more views and has the most complete set of animation controls.

Finally, we found very few interaction facilities in most systems (with the exception of SRec). According to the system descriptions available in the literature, these systems do not have interaction facilities except for animation. The exception is ETV, which allows expanding/contracting nodes in the recursion tree, and transferring control to the entry of a function call.

Table 1. Comparison of visualization and animation features in several animation systems of recursion.

System	Visualizations	Animation controls
EROSI	Copies model (variables)	Step forwards Automatic play Exit
ETV	Copies model (code) Traces Recursion tree	Step/complete Forwards/backwards Manual Restart/finish Exit
Flopex 2	Control stack Recursion tree	Step forwards Automatic play Restart
Function Visualizer	Copies model (code and variables)	Step forwards Automatic play Exit
Recursion Animator	Copies model (variables)	Step by step Forwards/backwards Manual/automatic Exit
SimRECUR	Copies model (code) Control stack Recursion tree	Step forwards Manual/automatic Exit
SRec	Traces Control stack Recursion tree (general and divide-and-conquer) Colored data structure Sequence of visualizations of the data structure	Step/step over/complete Forwards/backwards Manual/automatic Restart/finish Exit

Interacting with Visualizations and Animations of Recursion

Effective algorithm analysis demands more than static visualizations, but advanced interaction to give the user the capability to enquire flexibly. As there are many ways of interacting with visualizations, we need a framework to analyze interaction support. Consequently, we adopt a comprehensive framework [16] from information visualization, a very demanding field in this regard. The authors classify different kinds of interaction into seven categories, namely encode, connect, filter, abstract/elaborate, explore, reconfigure, and select.

However, we must bring attention to an important issue. Program visualization can be considered a subfield of information visualization, but it also has some specific features. In particular, programs may be visualized statically "in space" (i.e., their declaration or their state), but also dynamically "in time" (i.e., evolution of its state during execution). This feature is called program animation, and the most common interaction techniques are animation controls. As we are dealing with program visualizations, we take this duality space-time into account.

In the following, we show how the categories can be effectively used to interact with recursion. Each category is first introduced by quoting a sentence from [16] that summarizes its meaning. Then, we present techniques of that category that allow interacting with recursion visualizations, both static and dynamic.

Encode

"Encode interaction techniques enable users to alter the fundamental visual representation of the data including visual appearance (e.g., color, size, and shape) [16]."

According to this definition, the most straightforward alteration consists of changing visual appearance. For example, Figure 3(a) displays the same computation state as Figure 1(a), close to execution termination. Changing colors and line and border styles leads to Figure 3(b).

More drastic variations lead to different graphical representations of the same information, i.e., multiple views. We identified alternative views of recursion in Sections 2.1 and 2.2. Figure 4 shows two views, as displayed by the SRec system, of a computation state of fib (11). The views are contained in the central and right panels; corresponding to a recursion tree and control stack, respectively. The left panel contains the algorithm source code.

Connect

"Connect refers to interaction techniques that are used to (1) highlight associations and relationships between data items that are already represented, and (2) show hidden data items that are relevant to a specified item [16]."

The most important relationship in recursion connects caller and called invocations. No special interaction must be provided to the user since this relationship is explicitly shown in the different views (see Figure 1). The control stack and recursion trees encode it with arcs or arrows. Traces suggest it with typographic means, especially indentation.

Another relationship connects input and output values of a given invocation. Again, this connection is explicitly shown. The control stack and recursion trees encode it as the two halves of a given node. Traces represent it with typographic means, especially indentation.

Multiples views are not independent of each other, but they are coordinated. Coordination may be shown in two ways. Firstly, by synchronizing the information displayed in the views during an animation. Secondly, by having the views sharing visual conventions in the different representations used for the same objects. The two views in Figure 4 represent the same state of computation. They share color conventions and spatial orientation.

Finally, relevant events in an animation are usually connected by means of the animation controls. For instance, entry and exit of an invocation can be animated adjacent in time by means of a "step over" control.

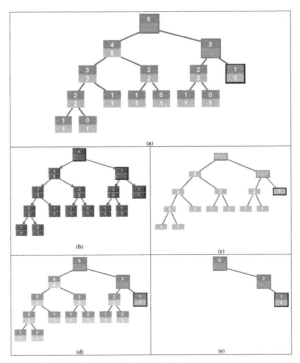

Figure 3. Recursion tree for fib (5): (a) basic visualization (b–e) variants.

Filter

"Filter interaction techniques enable users to change the set of data items being presented based on some specific conditions [16]."

Filtering can be applied to recursion trees in several ways. Firstly, we may omit input or output values. By displaying input, we give information about the recursive structure of the algorithm, while also showing output gives the computation results. Leaving visible only the output can be useful for prediction exercises. For instance, Figure 3(c) is obtained from Figure 3(a) by omitting input. Notice that the two pending calls, squared in red, have no value inside.

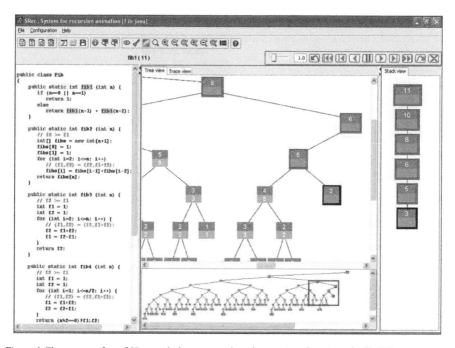

Figure 4. The user interface of SRec, with the source code and two views of recursion for fib (11).

Secondly, past recursive calls that have finished execution can be filtered. Showing all the nodes in the recursion tree displays the complete history of the algorithm. Alternatively, showing only pending nodes and the active one produces a display of the current state of execution. An intermediate display consists of blurring finished nodes. Figure 3(d) and Figure 3(e) show the two latter possibilities.

A related kind of filter can be applied to recursive invocations produced by a particular invocation. In the recursion tree, they generate a subtree with the particular invocation as the root. An animation control to "step over" can either display or omit the resulting subtree; in any of these cases, its result is displayed.

Finally, filtering can be applied to the parameters, return values and methods to visualize. For instance, the three recursion trees shown in Figure 5 were generated on mergesorting the array {0,4,9,6,8,3}.

Figure 5(a) is a comprehensive picture of the computation actually performed. It displays an initial call to the main method (in the figure, s for sort) and calls to a recursive method (ms for msort) and to an auxiliary method (me for merge). In order to keep the visualization manageable, only some input values are displayed, namely the original array in the main method and the indices that bound the subarray in each call in the other two methods.

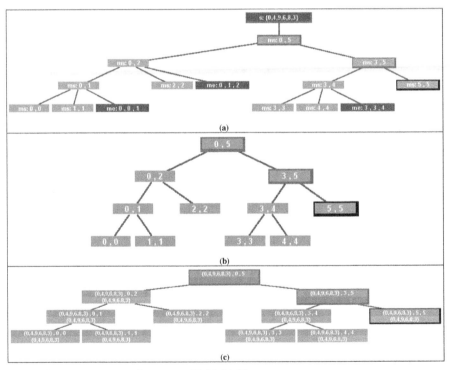

Figure 5. Recursion tree variants for mergesort({0,4,9,6,8,3}).

Figure 5(b) is similar, but focuses on the recursive structure of msort by filtering the other two methods. As the resulting recursion tree is smaller, we may display more input values and also output values. Thus, Figure 5(c) shows the resulting recursion tree, where each node contains two occurrences of the array to sort: its input state and its output state.

A facility complementary to filtering is semantic zoom, which can be applied to obtain full information of a given node. Positioning the mouse over the node and pressing the left button results in popping-up a small window that contains the values of all its parameter and result values. Figure 6 illustrates the effect of semantically zooming a given node of the recursion tree displayed in Figure 5(b).

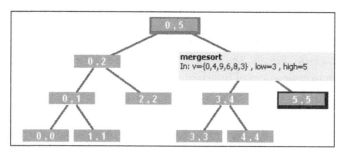

Figure 6. Semantic zoom on a node of the recursion tree for mergesort({0,4,9,6,8,3}).

Abstract/Elaborate

"Abstract/elaborate interaction techniques provide users with the ability to change the level of abstraction of a data representation [16]."

The level of abstraction is always kept equal in visualizations of recursion. However, we may achieve a higher level of abstraction by displaying on demand global information about the number of several kinds of nodes in an animation (e.g., visible nodes, past nodes, highlighted nodes, etc.). Semantic zooming can also be used to give global information about a given node (e.g., its relative number of invocation or the number of descendant nodes that descend from it).

Explore

"Explore interaction techniques enable users to examine a different subset of data cases [16]."

This category is especially important to handle large visualizations. SRec supports two ways of selecting a subset of information in a visualization of recursion:

- Panning+scrolling. Panning is another name for geometric zooming, which allows changing the scale of the visualization and therefore the amount of information that fits the screen. When a visualization does not fit its enclosing panel, a scroll bar may be provided to allow the user to select the part that she wishes to focus on.

- Overview+detail. Panning+scrolling allows navigating, but if the visualization is much larger than the part visible in a panel, the user may get lost. An overview+detail interface provides two complementary views: the "detail" view makes readable a part of the visualization and the "overview" gives a sketch of the global view of the visualization, identifying the position of the "detail" view.

Figure 4 contains visual cues of the first two of these interaction techniques. Several icons for zooming (that display a lens) can be identified at the right of the icon bar. The panels for traces and for recursion trees have their scrolling bars activated to navigate. Finally, the recursion tree panel is split into two parts, jointly providing an overview+detail interface.

Interaction techniques to explore time are typically provided as animation controls. Figure 4 shows a computation state close to its end. Program animation is controlled with the animation bar available at the top right corner. As the animation advances, new recursion nodes are generated. Nodes corresponding to finished calls may be kept or disappear from the visualization, depending on the particular view or user settings.

Reconfigure

"Reconfigure interaction techniques provide users with different perspectives onto the data set by changing the spatial arrangement of representations [16]."

The visualizations can be slightly reconfigured with certain customization options, e.g., distances between sibling nodes in a recursion tree. However, reconfiguring can be produced by other criteria, for example, where to place subarrays in the sequence of visualizations of the data structure. Figure 7 shows two chronological sequences of subarrays of {0,4,9,6,8,3} on call entry and exit. Figure 7(a) keeps entry and exit states of subarrays joint for each call, while in Figure 7(b) they are separated and strict chronological order is used to display subarrays.

Reconfiguration also makes sense in relation to multiple views. The screen usually only provides space for displaying a few views in an understandable way. The user should be allowed to choose the views to display and their relative position. In Figure 4, the user selected two views and to display them vertically. This layout allows optimizing the space necessary to display the control stack, thus leaving more space for the recursion tree.

Select

"Select interaction techniques provide users with the ability to mark a data item of interest to keep track of it [16]."

A user of a program visualization system may be interested in selecting information either in space or in time. A case of selection in space consists of identifying multiple occurrences of a given node in a redundant algorithm, such as fibonacci. A dialog is enough to enter the input or output values that identify the target nodes. Figure 8 shows the recursion tree included in Figure 4, corresponding to fib (11), after selecting nodes corresponding to fib (3). The selected nodes are highlighted in orange.

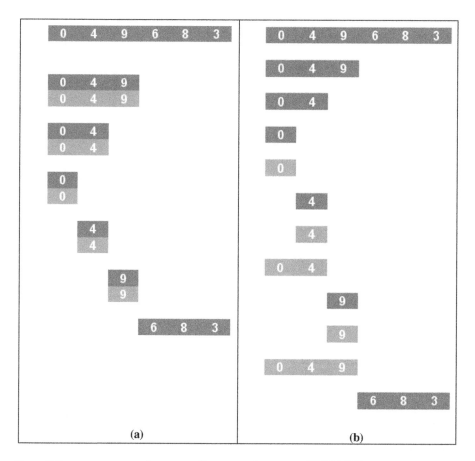

(a)   (b)

Figure 7. Two rearrangements of a sequence of array states for mergesort({0,4,9,6,8,3}).

With respect to time, the user may be interested in moving to a particular instant of the animation. The interaction may consist in positioning the mouse over a node of the recursion tree and pressing the right bottom to make it the active node in the animation.

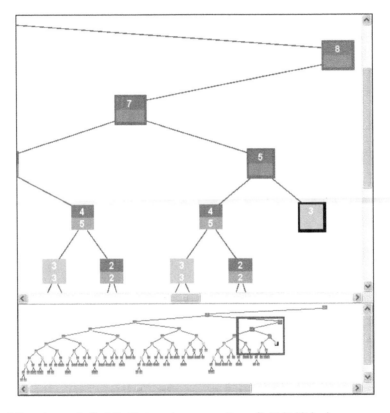

Figure 8. Recursion tree for fib (11) with the nodes corresponding to fib (3) highlighted.

Conclusions

This article demonstrates techniques to support flexible analysis of recursive algorithms by means of enhanced interaction features. All of these features are implemented in the SRec system and were illustrated in the paper. We have also shown that interaction facilities in other animation systems of recursion are very limited. The SRec system and related information and documentation (including user manual and the results of usability evaluations) are freely available at the following URL: http://lite.etsii.urjc.es/srec.

Much effort has been devoted in the two last decades to educational uses of algorithm animations. Their main drawbacks for general adoption have been identified elsewhere [17]:

- Lack of evidence of their educational efficiency.
- Heavy workload posed on animation constructors (typically, the instructors).

Our current study dealt with both these problems. With respect to the issue of educational effectiveness, notice that educational effectiveness of animations requires student engagement [17,18]. Our proposal for enhanced interactivity provides attractive visual tools to engage students in analysis tasks.

The issue of construction effort is also addressed by our contribution. In effect, automation and interaction are two of the four issues identified in a previous proposal [19] to identify "effortless" systems. The issue of improving interaction is clearly addressed in our study. With respect to automation, our approach to deliver program visualizations more easily supports flexible interaction by using processing language techniques. Program processing generates an annotated, intermediate representation of the program that allows gathering relevant information in run-time. Execution information can be displayed by the animation system to the user by means of its interaction facilities. User effort is then reduced to interacting with the system.

studying how to enhance visualization and interaction in animation systems to assist different user tasks is promising for programming education. We also plan to extend this work in several directions. Firstly, the comparison between SRec and other systems included one general program animation system (namely ETV), but the comparison should be extended to other general systems. Secondly, SRec can benefit from some additional interaction facilities; the work of Yi et al. [16] provides a good framework to identify such improvements. Finally, it would be very valuable for instructors to design a more structured mapping between interaction techniques and learning tasks.

Acknowledgements

This work was supported by project TIN2008-04103 of the Spanish Ministry of Science and Innovation.

References

1. Bloom, B.; Furst, E.; Hill, W.; Krathwohl, D.R. Taxonomy of Educational Objectives: Handbook I, The Cognitive Domain; Longmans: New York, NY, USA, 1959.

2. Böcker, H.D.; Fisher, G.; Nieper, H. The enhancement of understanding through visual representations. In Proceedings of the ACM SIGCHI Conference on Human Factors in Computing, Boston, MA, USA, April 1986; pp. 44–50.

3. Velázquez-Iturbide, J.Á.; Pérez-Carrasco, A.; Urquiza-Fuentes, J. SRec: An animation system of recursion for algorithm courses. In Proceedings of the 13th Annual Conference Innovation and Technology in Computer Science Education, Madrid, Spain, June 2008; pp. 225–229.

4. Haynes, S.M. Explaining recursion to the unsophisticated. ACM SIGCSE Bulletin 1995, 27, 3-6 and 14.

5. Wilcocks, D.; Sanders, I. Animating recursion as an aid to instruction. Comput. Educ. 1994, 23, 221–226.

6. Stern, L.; Naish, L. Visual representations for recursive algorithms. In Proceedings of the 33rd SIGCSE technical symposium on Computer science education, Cincinnati, KY, USA, February 2002; pp. 196–200.

7. Software Visualization; Stasko, J.T., Domingue, J., Brown, M.H., Price, B.A., eds.; MIT Press: Cambridge, MA, USA, 1997.

8. Velázquez-Iturbide, J.Á.; Pérez-Carrasco, A.; Urquiza-Fuentes, J. A design of automatic visualizations for divide-and-conquer algorithms. Electr. N. Theor. Comput. Sci. 2009, 224, 113–120.

9. Fernández-Muñoz, L.; Pérez-Carrasco, A.; Velázquez-Iturbide, J.Á.; Urquiza-Fuentes, J. A framework for the automatic generation of algorithm animations based on design techniques. In Proceedings of the Second European Conference on Technology Enhanced Learning, Crete, Greece, September 2007; pp. 475–480.

10. Velázquez-Iturbide, J.Á. Formalization of the control stack. ACM SIGPLAN Notices 1989, 24, 46–54.

11. Terada, M. ETV: A program trace player for students. In Proceedings of the 10th Annual Conference Innovation and Technology in Computer Science Education, Monte da Caparica, Portugal, June 2005; pp. 118–122.

12. Wu, C.C.; Lin, J.M.C.; Hsu, I.Y.W. Closed laboratories using SimLIST and SimRECUR. Comput. Educat. 1997, 28, 55–64.

13. Dershem, H.L.; Parker, D.E.; Weinhold, R. A Java function visualizer. J. Comput. Small Coll. 1999, 15, 220–230.

14. George, C.E. EROSII Visualizing recursion and discovering new errors. In Proceedings of the SIGCSE'00, Austin, TX, USA, March 2000; pp. 305–309.

15. Eskola, J.; Tarhio, J. On visualization of recursion with Excel. In Proceedings of the Second Program Visualization Workshop, HornstrupCentret, Denmark, June 2002; pp. 45–51.

16. Yi, J.S.; Kang, Y.; Stasko, J.; Jacko, J.A. Toward a deeper understanding of the role of interaction in information visualization. IEEE Trans. Visualiz. Comput. Graph. 2007, 13, 1224–1231.

17. Naps, T.; Roessling, G.; Almstrum, V.; Dann, W.; Fleischer, R.; Hundhausen, C.; Korhonen, A.; Malmi, L.; McNally, M.; Rodger, S.; Velázquez-Iturbide, J.Á. Exploring the role of visualization and engagement in computer science education. ACM SIGCSE Bulletin 2003, 35, 131–152.

18. Hundhausen, C.; Douglas, S.; Stasko, J. A meta-study of algorithm visualization effectiveness. J. Vis. Lang. Comput. 2002, 13, 259–290.

19. Ihantola, P.; Karavirta, V.; Korhonen, A.; Nikander, J. Taxonomy of effortless creation of algorithm visualization. In Proceedings of the International Workshop on Computing Education Research, Seattle, WA, USA, October 2005; pp. 123–133.

Towards a Serious Game to Help Students Learn Computer Programming

Mathieu Muratet, Patrice Torguet, Jean-Pierre Jesse
and Fabienne Viallet

ABSTRACT

Video games are part of our culture like TV, movies, and books. We believe that this kind of software can be used to increase students' interest in computer science. Video games with other goals than entertainment, serious games, are present, today, in several fields such as education, government, health, defence, industry, civil security, and science. This paper presents a study around a serious game dedicated to strengthening programming skills. Real-Time Strategy, which is a popular game genre, seems to be the most suitable kind of game to support such a serious game. From programming teaching features to video game characteristics, we define a teaching organisation to experiment if a serious game can be adapted to learn programming.

Introduction

Since the first boom of video games in the 80s, the gaming industry has held an important place in the world market. According to the Entertainment Software Association figures (http://www.theesa.com/facts/pdfs/ESA_EF_2008.pdf) accessed 26 August 2008, in 2007 the market of U.S. computer and video games amounts to $9.5 billion. This is almost equal to the U.S. movie market (http://www.the-numbers.com/market/2007.php) accessed 26 August 2008 ($9.6 billion in 2007). Students currently in university were born with video games, which are as much a part of their culture as TV, movies, or books.

However, to progress in video games, the player must at the same time play and learn. Serious games use this feature to interest players in specific topics, teach some specific educational content, or train workers to specific tasks. The idea is that entertainment can lead to learning if some specific constraints are respected.

On the other hand, all over the world, students are becoming less interested in science. In computer science, for example, according to Crenshaw et al. [1] and Kelleher [2], the number of students is shrinking. Moreover, "colleges and universities routinely report that 50% or more of those students who initially choose computer science study soon decide to abandon it" [3, page 39]. Our university experiences the same phenomenon with a decrease of 16.6% over the last four years in students studying computer science.

Therefore, in the computer science education research field, there is an important area directed to the recruitment and retention of students [4]. A promising way explored by this specific research is using games to teach and learn programming [5]. It allows students to better learn in a familiar and playful environment. Moreover, it promotes collaborative learning and spurs student to learn.

We propose to study if serious games, which can be collaborative learning games, could be of value in order to teach programming and to attract and keep computer science students. The question is: Is it interesting to use a serious game for teaching programming?

To achieve this goal, we propose the methodology of design experiments [6]: "prototypically, design experiments entail both "engineering" particular forms of learning and systematically studying those forms of learning within the context defined by the means of supporting them. This designed context is subject to test and revision, and the successive iterations that result play a role similar to that of systematic variation in experiment." The intent of this methodology in educational research is to investigate the possibilities for educational improvement by bringing about new forms of learning in order to study them. Because designs are typically test-beds for innovation, the nature of the methodology is highly interventionist, involving a research team, one or more teachers, at least one student, and eventually school administrators. Design contexts are conceptualized as interacting systems and are implemented with a hypothesized learning process and the means of supporting it. Although design experiments are conducted in a limited number of settings, they aim to develop a relatively humble theory that targets a domain specific learning process. To prepare a design experiment, the research team has to define a theoretical intent and specify disciplinary ideas and forms of teaching that constitute the prospective goals or endpoints to student learning. The challenge is to formulate a design that embodies testable conjectures about both significant shifts in student learning and the specific means of supporting those shifts. In our experiment, the theory we attempt to develop is the process of learning programming through serious games. In this paper, we discuss how to build a design context that will allow us to construct several conjectures to test our theory about an original form of programming teaching.

In the rest of this paper, we define briefly what a serious game is and what its learning aims are. After presenting programming teaching features and associated environment, we analyse some of them in reference to learning objectives and serious games features. Because there is currently no serious game dedicated to this field and suitable to design experiments, the rest of the paper presents the serious game we built. Section 4 presents how we chose the video game that supports our serious game. Section 5 details the implementation of our serious game. Section 6 describes how learning objectives are mapped into the game from the student, teacher, and knowledge points of view. Section 7 explains how we will conduct our first experiment.

Serious Games

Definitions

For Zyda [7], a serious game is "a mental contest, played with a computer in accordance with specific rules, that uses entertainment to further government or corporate training, education, health, public policy, and strategic communication objectives." Thus, any video game built to differ from pure entertainment can be considered as a serious game. Serious games represent, therefore, a wide range of digital games. Blackman [8] gives a synopsis of the gaming industry and its applications. Sophisticated video game graphic engines are nowadays used for nongame applications because they offer real-time rendering and physical models. Applications such as simulators can use such video game technologies. Serious games are not restricted to video games; they can also be based on simulators. Figure 1 illustrates the relationship between video games, simulators, and serious games.

Figure 1. Relation between video games, simulators, and serious games.

Example of Serious Games

To highlight the relationship between the target public and serious game objectives we present three examples of serious games following different aims: "Darfur is Dying" (http://www.darfurisdying.com/) accessed 30 November 2008, "Tactical Language & Culture" (http://www.tacticallanguage.com/) accessed 30 November 2008, and "America's Army" (http://www.americasarmy.com/) accessed 30 November 2008; "Darfur is Dying" is a game developed in partnership with the Reebok Human Rights Foundation and the International Crisis Group. The purpose of this game is to increase public awareness of the crisis in Darfur. The player controls a Darfurian who forages for water and develops his/her camp. Because the objective was to reach a maximum of people, "Darfur is Dying" is a minigame based on a platform game genre easy to play even for nongamers. It is free and accessible by everyone.

"Tactical Language & Culture" is a game started in 2003 as a research project at the University of Southern California's Information Sciences Institute under funding from the Defence Advanced Research Projects Agency (DARPA). Its purpose is to teach foreign languages and cultural knowledge needed to conduct tasks effectively and safely during both daily life and military missions. Currently, it offers courses in Iraqi Arabic language and culture (Tactical Iraqi), Pashto language and culture for the Pashtun regions of Afghanistan (Tactical Pashto), and French as spoken in the countries of Sahel Africa (Tactical French). "Tactical Language & Culture" is a complex game targeted for servicemen. It is based on a role-playing game genre to enable an immersive communication with virtual avatars in the game. It is played in interaction with a virtual tutor who evaluates the learner's speech and gives feedback on errors.

"America's Army" is a game launched in July 2002 designed by the Modelling, Virtual Environments, and Simulation (MOVES) Institute at the Naval Postgraduate School in Monterey, Calif, USA. It was initially built as a recruiting tool for the United States of America's army. However it became the first really successful serious game and is currently one of the ten most popular PC action games played online. "America's Army" is a complex game based on a shooter game genre to immerse the player in action. It is a free multiplayer game requiring a team effort.

These serious games use entertainment to pursue different learning objectives: "Darfur is dying" tries to raise public awareness; "Tactical Language & Culture" aims to learn foreign languages and cultures; "America's Army" tries to attract young people to join the US Army.

Video Games

Serious games are mainly based on video games that define their usability. According to the aims of the serious game, the video games characteristics of game genre, game mode, and game complexity define the target audience. The game genre is used to classify video games. Some examples are "shooters" like "Doom" series or "Counter Strike" (players combat several characters with projectile weapons, such as guns or missiles), "sports" like "Pro Evolution Soccer" or "Virtual Tennis" series (emulates the playing of traditional physical sports), "strategy" like "Age of Empires" or "Civilization" series (players control an army and command it to achieve objectives), or "role-playing" like "Final Fantasy" series or "World of Warcraft" (players are cast in the role of one or more "adventurers" to progress through a predetermined storyline).

We define the game mode as the networked nature of the game. Single player refers to a game, where only one player can interact with the game. The player plays against preprogrammed challenges and/or opponents controlled by Artificial Intelligences (AI). A multiplayer mode allows players to interact with each other. Partnerships, cooperation, competitions, or rivalries emerge to provide a form of social communication.

The Game complexity refers as in [9] to the duration of the game. Minigames or trivial games take less than one hour to complete, treat only one subject, puzzle, or game play type in a small way. Complex games take more than ten hours to complete, provide a sophisticated mixture of difficult challenges that typically intertwine and support each other. Main features of complex games are levelling-up, adaptability, clear and worthwhile goals, interaction with other players, and shared experiences.

The choice of a game genre, a game mode, and the complexity of the video game is a crucial point to be in agreement with the target audience and the serious game objectives.

Serious Games and Learning

The critical point of serious games is the relationship between the game and the educational content: Zyda [7] wrote that "Pedagogy must be subordinate to story—

the entertainment component comes first." A hypothesis is that if the game is attractive, fun, and stimulating, and encourages the player to progress, then she/he will automatically learn skills from the game and will absorb a lot of information. What about serious games devoted to teaching how to program? Is there a need for such tools?

Programming Fundamentals Learning

In order to determine if serious games can be useful for teaching programming, we present educational features, bring to light problems encountered by students, and expose different solutions proposed by teachers. Among the developed tools devoted to this field, we chose to analyse some of them in reference to learning objectives and serious games features.

Features

An ACM/IEEE report [3] provides an overview of the different kinds of undergraduate degree curricula in computing. This report divides computing in five major disciplines: Computer Engineering (CE), Computer Science (CS), Information Systems (IS), Information Technology (IT), and Software Engineering (SE). It shows that the most important requirement for all these disciplines is the "Programming Fundamentals" topic, and the ability to "Do small-scale programming" is the most expected performance capability. The requirements of "Programming fundamentals" (PFs) are detailed in another report [10], which defines precisely the features of programming courses and outlines a set of recommendations for undergraduate curricula. It is divided in 5 core units: fundamental programming constructs (PF1), algorithms and problem solving (PF2), fundamental data structures (PF3), recursion (PF4), and event-driven programming (PF5). There are no recommendations on the programming language used for teaching. The main topics taught in PF are variables, types, expressions, assignments, simple Input/Output, conditional and iterative control structures, functions, parameter passing, arrays, and records.

Problems

Programming fundamentals are hard skills to learn, especially for novices, for several reasons. First, students encounter some unexpected epistemological obstacles, like learning looping constructs [11, 12], conditionals, or assembling programs out of base components: "Data structure and algorithms [...] are often difficult issues, since capturing the dynamic nature of abstract algorithms is not a straight-forward task" [13]. Thus, "the lack of student programming skill even after a year of undergraduate studies in computer science was noted and measured in the early 80's [14] and again in this decade [15]" [4, page 127].

Second, the computer environment they use daily, to play or chat for example, is very different from the one they use for learning and they do not immediately see the connection between the two universes: "People studying pedagogical techniques agree that students who are new to computer science typically find the field full of theoretical, technical, or even tedious concepts" [16].

Third, learning how to program assumes lectures, classes, and practice sessions. To be able to program, students need to know programming skills and concepts, but to learn those skills and concepts they have to practice programming. Dealing with this paradox, Greitzer et al. [9] explain in particular that "an effective approach is to encourage learners to work immediately on meaningful, realistic tasks."

Some Solutions

To the question as to what makes programming easier for novices and what helps students to acquire programming fundamentals, a great many answers are proposed in the literature. For example, Stevenson and Wagner [17] analyse assignments from textbooks and historical usage to look for student's problems and propose a set of characteristics and assignments that should be a "good programming assignment" in CS1: (1) be based on a real-world problem; (2) allow the students to generate a realistic solution to that problem; (3) allow them to focus on current topic(s) from class within the context of larger programs; (4) be challenging; (5) be interesting; (6) make use of one or more existing application programming interfaces (APIs); (7) have multiple levels of challenge and achievement, thus supporting possible refactoring; (8) allow some creativity and innovation. To implement this assignment, the authors propose a CS1 project based on a web crawler and a spam evaluator.

Another trend, studying how students relate to computer science and why they quit, has shown that a lack of meaning and relevance is key issues that create distaste for the discipline [4, page 150]. One answer is to develop specific interesting and relevant computational artefacts that have meaning for students. In this direction, three approaches exist: (1) building novice-programming environments, using (2) programming contests or (3) video games.

Many novice-programming environments have been built. Most of them use block-based graphical languages. This programming metaphor allows students to forget syntax and directly experiment with programming. Here are a few examples.

(i) StarLogo The Next Generation [18] uses computer game design as the motivation and theme to introduce programming to middle or high school students. It is a modelling and simulation software. Students and teachers use agents-based programming and 3D graphics to create and understand simulations and complex systems.

(ii) Scratch [19] is a programming language that makes it easy to create interactive stories, animations, games, music, and art and share them through the web. It is designed to help young people (ages 8 and up) develop learning skills from several disciplines. As they create Scratch projects, young people learn important mathematical and computational ideas, while also gaining a deeper understanding of the process of design.

(iii) Alice2 [20] is a programming environment designed for teaching programming while building 3D virtual worlds. This drag and drop programming system allows users to experiment with the logic and programming structures taught in introductory programming classes without making syntax errors. It allows users to experiment with conditionals, loops, variables, parameters, and procedures.

(iv) Cleogo [21] is a groupware environment that allows several users to simultaneously develop programs through any mixture of three alternative programming metaphors: a direct manipulation language for programming by demonstration an iconic language and a standard text-based language. Cleogo is motivated by the pedagogical values of peer learning and of collaborative problem solving, at home and at work.

The second approach consists in using competition to motivate students. Robocode (http://robocode.sourceforge.net/) accessed 17 April 2007, is a Java programming game, where the goal is to develop a robot battle tank to battle against other tanks programmed by other players. It is designed to help people learn Java programming. The robot battles are running in real-time and on-screen. It is suitable to all kind of programmers from beginners (a simple robot can be written in just a few minutes) to experts (perfecting an AI can take months).

The last approach uses video games in order to hook the player and bring him/her to programming. Two uses have been experimented: implementing new video games and playing video games. For example, in [22], students are required to implement in C++, through a collaborative project, a small-to-medium scale interactive computer game in one semester, making use of a game framework. In [23], a case study based on EEClone is proposed. EEClone is an arcade-style computer game implemented in Java: students analysed various design patterns within

EEClone, and from this experience, learned how to apply design patterns in their own game software. In [5], a "Game First" approach is used to teach introductory programming. These authors believe that game programming motivates most new programmers. They use 2D game development as a unifying theme.

Another solution is to let students learn when they play a game. Two games use this approach: the Wireless Intelligent agent Simulation Environment (WISE) [24] and Colobot (http://www.ceebot.com/colobot/index-e.php) accessed 21 September 2007. WISE combines activities from virtual and physical versions of the Wumpus World game. It allows physically distributed agents to play an interactive game and provides a dynamic learning environment that can enhance a number of computer science courses: it can be used as a medium for demonstrating techniques in lectures; in the classes students can work on laboratory exercises that test, expand, or modify the simulator. The Wumpus World game can be played cooperatively or competitively. But WISE requires a great number of resources (e.g., space, robots, and so on) for the physical version.

Colobot is the only example that we know, of a complete video game, which mixes interactivity, storytelling, and programming. In this game, the user must colonize a planet using some robots that she/he is able to program in a specific object oriented programming language similar to C++. The only drawback in our opinion is that Colobot has no multiplayer mode.

Conclusion

"Although there is a weak theoretical basis and few techniques for measuring learning in computer science" [21, page 151], several environments for teaching programming have been developed. Stevenson and Wagner [17] define a set of characteristics for a "good assignment." All the studied environments agree with the criteria number two (generate a realistic solution), three (focus on current topics from class), four (be challenging), five (be interesting), seven (offers multiple levels of challenge), and eight (allow creativity and innovation). However none is based on real-world problems. But when students use Robocode, EEClone, and Colobot, they use complex APIs.

Novice programming environments (StarLogo, Scratch, Alice2, and Cleogo) are not games and cannot be considered as serious games. In [5, 22, 23], since students have to build a game and not to play, these approaches cannot be considered as games. Among the others, only Robocode, WISE, and Colobot use a gaming activity to stimulate the player. However, only Colobot allows the player to interactively program in game. But it is not free and cannot be adapted to different teaching context. Indeed, it is devoted to a specific programming language and cannot be adapted to specific pedagogical choices. Since in [10] there is no recommendation about the programming language, there is no consensus about the choice of a language. Indeed for pedagogical reasons, some teachers develop their own programming languages. Moreover, it is not easy for a teacher to introduce new exercises into the game. Since our experiment lies on design experiments, we need to test a serious game dedicated to teaching programming in several contexts with different teachers and students. The existing games do not allow that, and thus we decided to build our own serious game.

What Kind of Video Game for Our Serious Game?

The usability of a serious game is based on the compatibility between the learning objectives and the target public. Since we want to build a serious game for students in computer science, we have to base it on one of their most played video games. Our first step was thus to ask what kind of video games our students practice, and to find the most suitable one to motivate students to program.

Students and Video Games

To check the interest of our students in the kind of game they practice, we submitted a survey: 181 students were questioned (154 males and 27 females) in three different curricula (two on computer science and one on civil engineering). The average age is 21 years old (see Figure 2 for distribution).

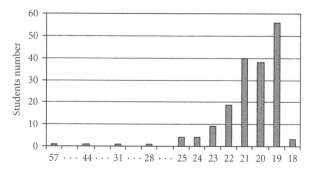

Figure 2. Age of students.

The first analysis verifies ESA's results about the student interest in games at our university. Figure 3 shows the percentage of students who play (males and females). More players are males but a small majority of females also play video games. We infer from these figures that video games are widely played by our students, even for females. These results corroborate the potential of serious games for these students.

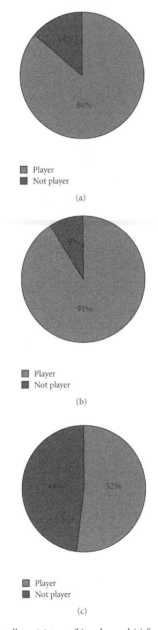

Figure 3. (a) Players' percentage for all participants, (b) males, and (c) females.

The second analysis identifies the most used game genre played by our students. Figure 4 shows the percentage of players who play each game genre. The most played game genre is strategy games. We notice that this game genre is also appreciated by females (57% of female players play strategy games).

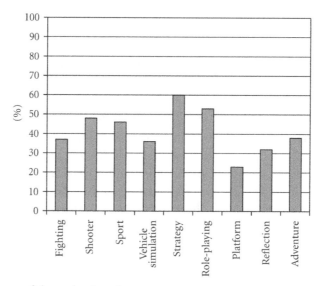

Figure 4. Percentage of players who play each game genre.

Figure 5 shows the percentage of students who used multiplayer games. As we can see, most of them use this type of game.

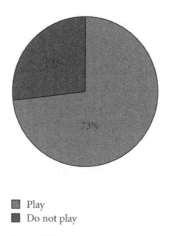

Play
Do not play

Figure 5. Percentage of players who play multiplayer games.

Thus, to be adapted to our target audience, our serious game should be based on a multiplayer strategy game.

What is a Strategy Game?

Strategy games are, by and large, represented by Real-Time Strategy (RTS) games. In this game genre players evolve in a virtual environment, where resources are scattered on a map. RTS is traditionally structured around three main phases closely linked: harvesting resources, building structures and units, and fighting opponents. To win a game, the player has to destroy all structures and units of opponents or achieve a specific goal. To build a strong army, a good economy is required and protection of strategic areas is essential.

A strong player should show abilities in planning and know how to anticipate and react. She/he has to command hundreds of units, which leads to a large cognitive load. Moreover, RTSs have an important feature: the "fog of war." This hides the movements and actions of opponents until they come into the line of sight of one of the player troops. The player evolves in a virtual world with incomplete information, which increases the game interest.

Traditionally, RTSs provide two types of game: Campaign and Skirmish. Campaigns attract the player and teach him/her how to play, and skirmishes extend the life of the game. A campaign is divided in missions that gradually introduce game contents and complexity. Skirmishes require a better control of the game. The player fights against computer AIs or other players. Moreover, to increase the game challenge, it is always possible to find better or equivalent players on the Internet.

In RTS games, a player gives orders to his/her units to carry out operations (i.e., moving, building, etc.). Typically, these instructions are given by clicking on a map with the mouse. An RTS game, where such instructions can be given through programs, might be the answer to our serious game. The idea is to stimulate the player to give orders through programs. These programs will assist the student/player during the game and should increase his/her probability of winning, if they are efficient, relevant, and suitable to the game. Moreover, when they test their programs, students will still use the same environment (the game).

Are Strategy Games Compatible with Teaching Programming?

As we have seen before, serious games for teaching programming already exist and are used. In particular, Colobot is based on a sort of RTS. In Colobot, teaching is provided through an interactive library available for consultation but a teacher using Colobot cannot modify or adapt it to his/her courses. And there is only one course level for novice programmers (PF).

Learning how to program requires writing programs. A priori, RTS and programming activities are incompatible: real-time games are dynamics and have a strong interactivity with the player, and programming tasks require time for design and implementation of programs. Integrating programming activities in an RTS should then modify foundations of the game. Colobot and Robocode found two different solutions to solve this problem.

(i) Colobot is based on a modified RTS to enable in-game programming. The common rules of the game are modified by this fact, and it demands a specific skill from the player. For example, the player cannot control several entities in the game at the same time.

(ii) Robocode distinguishes beteen programming and playing activities. First, the player writes an AI, and then she/he runs them. Thus the player is inactive during the simulation and is merely a spectator of his/her AI.

Implementation

RTSs are very complex programs, with more than tens of thousands of code lines. Because our goal was not to develop a new RTS, we decided to use an existing engine. This engine had to be open sourced to allow us to develop the specific features of the serious game.

Game Engine Choice

We found two open source multiplayer 3D RTS engines: the Spring project (http://spring.clan-sy.com/) accessed 2 February 2007, and Open Real-Time Strategy (ORTS). ORTS [25, 26] has been developed to provide a programming environment for discussing problems related to AI. This game is designed to allow the user to easily program and integrate his/her AIs. It is aimed at users who already know how to program. Spring is a project aiming to create a new and versatile RTS Engine which was built to reuse some game data from a commercial game called Total Annihilation. Currently, Spring is more successful than ORTS. A gamer community plays Spring everyday on the Internet. This community helps to discover bugs, which are fixed by a development group. This process is not present in ORTS which is experimental. We chose the Spring engine instead of ORTS because of this community.

Characteristics of Spring

Along with the Spring engine, several "mods" exist (http://spring.clan-sy.com/wiki/Mods) accessed 26 August 2008, (mods constitute additions to a game that change the way it works). For our experiment, we chose to use "Kernel Panic" (http://spring.clan-sy.com/wiki/Kernel_Panic) accessed 26 August 2008; Figure 6 presents a screenshot of Kernel Panic, where three players (red, green, and pink) fight on a map. Kernel Panic uses computer science metaphors, like bits and pointers, which is an asset for our training purposes. Moreover, Kernel Panic is a simplified RTS with the following features: there is no resource management except for time and space; all units are free to create; it has a small technology improvement tree with less than ten units; it uses low-end vectorial graphics, which match the universe. These characteristics emphasize strategy and tactics in an action-oriented game while always remaining user friendly.

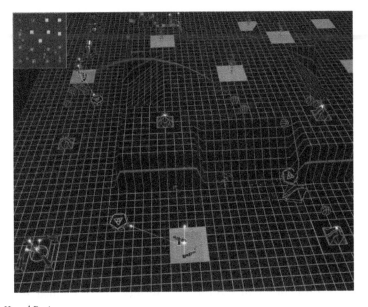

Figure 6. Kernel Panic.

Serious Game Implementation

To adapt the Spring engine to the serious game we wanted to build, we had to take into account some constraints: (i) allow players to write code plugged dynamically into the game; (ii) protect the game engine against player's code bugs; (iii) hide the complexity of the game engine; (iv) support different programming languages. The integration of the player's code in the engine must be interactive (without stopping the game) in order to maintain the progress and coherence of the game.

In some previous works [27] we used an implementation based on a dynamic library. Use of dynamic libraries turned out to be inadaptable to interpreted languages. Indeed, dynamic libraries solve problems in a single process: the game engine. This process controls student's computer programs. But interpreted languages also require an interpreter which is carried out in its own process. Thus, we discovered limits of the use of a dynamic library containing the player's code.

Considering this drawback, we designed a new system. Students' programs are not included in a dynamic library loaded and performed by the game but are running in an independent process and communicate with the game. This enables the use of compiled or interpreted languages. A set of techniques exist for exchanging data among processes. We needed a portable and fast solution designed for process communication and not just threads communication. We chose to use the Boost interprocess library (http://www.boost.org/doc/libs/1_37_0/doc/html/interprocess.html) accessed 26 November 2008, that provides shared memory functionality. Moreover, this library offers the possibility to use complex data, like vectors or maps, in the shared memory.

The UML component diagram in Figure 7 expresses the dependencies between the player's program and the game engine. These two components interact through the Game Engine Interface (GEI). The "Supplier GEI" is used by the game engine. We have integrated into the game engine some modifications. When the game starts, it creates the "Supplier GEI," and then the supplier interface can be used through the subroutines in Table 1.

Table 1

GEI_Init	Create the shared memory
GEI_Quit	Close the shared memory
GEI_Update	Make an update if it is required
GEI_ExecPendingActions	Execute pending actions

The "Client GEI" is used by the player's program. After creating the "Client GEI," it can use the client interface to interact with the game engine through the subroutines in Table 2.

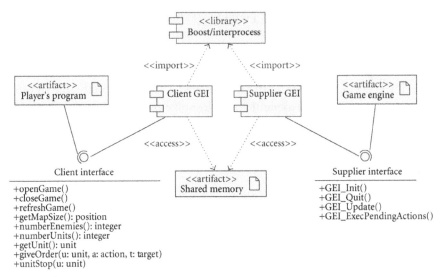

Figure 7. Architecture.

Table 2

openGame	Connect the program to the shared memory
closeGame	Disconnect the program from the shared memory
refreshGame	Ask the game engine to update its data
getMapSize	Get the map size
numberEnemies	Get the number of enemies visible by the player
numberUnits	Get the number of units controlled by the player
getUnit	Get the nth unit of the player
giveOrder	Set an action to the unit on a target
unitStop	Command a unit to stop its current action

GEIs use the Boost interprocess library to interact with the shared memory. GEIs hide the synchronization complexity of the shared memory and make communication with the game easier. At the request of the student program, pertinent data is copied into the shared memory. To avoid incoherent situations, students' programs work on this copy. In this way, at any time, the player can change his/her code and carry it out to use the shared memory and to communicate with the game.

All languages that are able to use a C library can use the "Client GEI" and communicate with the game engine. Currently, we propose interfaces for the "Client GEI" in C, C++, Java, Visual Basic for Application (VBA), and an interpreted language called "Compaglo" (used in a specific course at our university).

Mapping Learning Objectives into the Game

Is the built serious game compatible with learning objectives? Different viewpoints can be envisaged: the student view, the teacher view, and the knowledge view.

The Student Point of View

The first step for a student is to learn how to use the serious game. Especially at the beginning, students have to understand what they can program and how they can do it through the "client GEI." A campaign seems to be very suitable for game appropriation where motivation is maintained by a story.

When players are over with all the missions, they should be able to control the serious game and develop their own AIs for skirmishes. To build these AIs, players need to call upon their skills learned during the campaign. They have to design and implement each AI. The developed AIs span from simpler ones for novices, to very complex ones for experts.

In skirmishes, a student can play against the computer or against his/her friends. Multiplayer sessions encourage them to carry out new challenges. The motivation is maintained by competition between players.

The player defines a strategy, composed by a set of tasks, to win. She/he can choose to carry out some of them through AI. If the developed AIs improve the game, students will be better when they play. They will then perhaps find interest in programming, spend time to perform it and so increase their abilities in programming practice.

The Teacher Point of View

The serious game we built can be adapted to the programming language chosen by the teacher. According to the language characteristics, she/he can build activities for different course levels from PF to complex AI algorithms. Moreover, if s/he chooses to use the multiplayer mode, she/he can use individual, competitive, and collaborative pedagogical methods.

The Knowledge Point of View

Because unlike Colobot, the tool has not an interactive library of programming skills, it cannot be used without an appropriate teaching environment: students need to be assisted by teachers and peers to write their AIs and, after playing, an institutionalization [28] stage is necessary to carry out collaborative learning.

Simon [29] defines institutionalization as a phase where ideas "constructed or modified during problem solving attain the status of knowledge in the classroom community." PF skills are gradually introduced through the missions, which initial aims are to progress in the story.

GEI is a fairly complex Application Programming Interface (API) which is not simple for novices to use. Teachers can develop an overlay adapted to their own subroutines specifications.

First Experiment

Before conducting design experiments with different teachers and students, we decided to test our serious game on some of our students and first define a simplified design experiment. To comply with the traditional game mode of an RTS, we first propose to carry out a campaign and then to develop additional programs usable in multiplayer sessions. We first present an example of a campaign, then we show how to organise a skirmish to ensure learning.

Our Campaign

"Kernel Panic" is only a multiplayer game and does not provide campaigns. Therefore, we built a campaign to gradually introduce learning topics and enable students to learn how to play and to program AIs. We take advantage of the Kernel Panic universe and offer students the following scenario: "For a certain number of years, a secret war is rife inside computers. Steady attacks are led against innocent victims. Today is your turn. Your aggressor captured your mouse controller. You must recover it. Your only solution: programming."

To achieve this objective, five missions are created.

(i) *Mission 1.* "You lost a lot of units in the last attack. Units currently alive are dispersed on the map. You have only one BIT under control. You must go to the rally point at position (1056, 1792) to find other units." To succeed, the player has to make a small program where she/he uses variables, types, assignments, functions, parameter passing, and records. Algorithm 1 shows a solution.

(ii) *Mission 2.* "You just found a BYTE unit. It tells you that other units are reassembled not far. It gives you the position (479, 1825) of a BYTE group that it tries to rally. Moreover, it warns you that a group of BITS is forming at position (1400, 1371). To retrieve these units, command your two units to meet up with their respective groups." In this mission the conditional control structure is introduced to give a target position to each unit according to their type (BYTE or BIT).

(iii) *Mission 3.* "All units you control are weakened. You must repair them before starting a counter attack. A report indicates that an ASSEMBLER is posted at the position (256, 1024). Find it and it will help you." In this mission the iterative control structure is introduced to iterate through each unit and move them on the right position. Algorithm 2 shows a solution.

(iv) *Mission 4.* "You found an ASSEMBLER. Use it to repair your weakened units." This mission is the most complicated and requires overlapping iterative and conditional control structures. The player has to iterate through each units and commands the ASSEMBLER to repair a unit if this unit is weakened and if the ASSEMBLER is inactive.

(v) *Mission 5.* "All units are repaired. Now it is time to fight back. The mouse device is positioned at (1056, 256). Good luck commander." This mission goal is to reward students with a simple fight.

```
program mission1
glossary
    Unit u
    Position p
begin
    openGame()
    p.x ← 1056
    p.y ← 1792
    u ← getUnit(1)
    giveOrder(u, MOVE, p)
    closeGame()
end
```

Algorithm 1: Mission one algorithm.

```
program mission3
glossary
    Unit u
    Position p
    Counter c
begin
    openGame()
    p.x ← 256
    p.y ← 1024
    for c ← 1 to numberUnits() do
        u ← getUnit(c)
        giveOrder(u, MOVE, p)
    endFor
    closeGame()
end
```

Algorithm 2: Mission three algorithm.

Skirmishes

When students finish the campaign, they can write their own AIs and use them during skirmishes. Here are some examples of strategic AIs which could be written by students and give an "in-game" asset to the player: "Search for opponent" to quickly find the enemy in order to adapt one's strategy to the adversary's; "Create a mine field" which may slow down opponents' expansion in order to give more time to develop our own strategy; "Repair" using specific units to keep strategic units in good health; "Withdraw" to protect units when facing a stronger opponent. All these examples support a part of a player strategy and let him/her take charge of the rest, and therefore play the game at the same time.

Algorithm 3 shows the algorithm of "search for opponent" where units search for the enemy. Random target areas are computed to move each unit until an enemy is found. It uses library subroutines, like "giveOrder(u, MOVE, pos)" to move the unit "u" to the position "pos." Usually, the player does this with the mouse and has to select each unit one by one, a long and tedious process. The loop allows the player to perform this operation automatically. Moreover, while the player is selecting the enemy units with the mouse, she/he cannot carry out other tasks. With this program she/he can, for example, develop his/her base while the program explores the map.

```
program search-for-opponents
glossary
    Position pos, map
    Unit u
    Boolean found
    Counter c
begin
    found ← FALSE
    openGame()
    map ← getMapSize()
    while not found do
        refreshGame()
        // Check if an enemy is visible
        if numberEnemies() > 0 then
            // stop all units
            for c ← 1 to numberUnits() do
                unitStop(getUnit(c))
            endFor
            found ← TRUE
        else
            // give random target area to move for each unit
            for c ← 1 to numberUnits() do
                // choose a random target area
                u ← getUnit(c)
                if u.inactive then
                    // choose a random value between 0 and map.x
                    pos.x ← randomValue(map.x)
                    // choose a random value between 0 and map.y
                    pos.y ← randomValue(map.y)
                    giveOrder(u, MOVE, pos)
                endIf
            endFor
        endIf
    endWhile
    closeGame()
end
```

Algorithm 3: "Search for opponent" algorithm.

Organization of the Course

Table 3 shows the schedule of our teaching organization for our first experiment. Two instructors supervise each session: one game specialist and one computer science teacher. During the first session, students play the game to familiarize themselves with it. A discussion about what could be done to improve the game and which are the most efficient strategies for winning is initiated. The second session is a presentation of GEI. The computer science teacher proposes that all students carry out missions. The programming obstacles are dealt in concert with the teacher. During the two next weeks, students work autonomously but can call upon their instructors. They have to develop their own AIs. If they have no idea of what to program, a database of efficient algorithms is proposed such as the "Search for opponent" algorithm. The game specialist guides the students through different game strategies to improve the playing sessions. The computer science instructor deals with installations and programming problems. The students are allowed to communicate with each other. They can then elaborate alliances or cooperation strategies, or simply help each other with programming. When all the programs are completed and operational, the third session occurs: students play using their own programs. The game specialist teacher turns his attention to decipher what really happened during the game: the role of the programs, the activities of the students, and the strategies used. This observation is the base of the last session: students and teachers analyse games and try to find the reasons behind victories and defeats. A discussion about the importance of the programs is held. The learning objective is that our students continue to use by themselves this serious game and improve their programming skills.

Table 3. Teaching organization schedule.

Session 1	Session 2	Two weeks	Session 3	Session 4
Presentation of the initial version of the RTS followed by a multiplayer playing session	Presentation of the API and carrying out the five missions of the campaign	Students develop their own programs by themselves with teachers remote tutoring and if they want with peers	Multiplayer playing using student's programs	Institutionalization

This experiment will be conducted in our university this year with novice students. To evaluate the process we will use several indicators such as student investment, number, quality and pertinence of the written programs, student retention, gained skills and exam results. We also want to evaluate the "feel good" factor as defined in [30].

Conclusion

This paper deals with the compatibility between a serious game and teaching programming. Serious games are more and more popular and can meet learning objectives. On the other hand, computer science students encounter a lot of difficulties while learning programming. Some researchers in computer science education develop programming environments to encourage and retain students. Some of these environments can be considered as serious games but they are not adaptable enough to validate our hypothesis in regards to design experiments, which is why we decided to build an adaptable serious game dedicated to programming.

As a basis for our serious game we chose to use an RTS, because it is the most played game genre for our target audience. Because it was not possible to develop our own RTS engine, we decided to use the Spring game engine and the Kernel Panic game. The implementation of the serious game led to modifying the engine to enable an interactive and secure programming activity through an API. The students can command game entities with their own AIs and have contests with their friends in the multiplayer mode. The game can be adapted to specific programming languages, and teachers can adapt the API to their own specification subroutines. PF skills are mapped on the game through missions. In order to validate the game, we designed a first design experiment with our students.

The next step is to conduct this experimentation and to adapt it to several contexts with different instructors and students in order to apply the iterative process of design experiments. The possible evolution of the serious game is the introduction of teaching facilities, like Colobot, and in order to keep pace with the rapid evolution of video game standards, the use of another mod, or the integration of other RTS game engines.

We hope that these experiments will show us the breadth of teaching applications supported by our system as well as the range of potential audiences and teaching methodologies. Analysis of our experimentation will explore and resolve potential issues concerning usability and effectiveness of learning with serious games. At the same time, it will be important to determine which skills are learned by students when the campaign is finished and how users switch between game play and coding elements. It would also be interesting to evaluate this approach with another video game genre and to compare it with our RTS-based serious game.

References

1. T. L. Crenshaw, E. W. Chambers, and H. Metcalf, "A case study of retention practices at the University of Illinois at Urbana-Champaign," in Proceedings of the

39th ACM Technical Symposium on Computer Science Education (SIGCSE '08), pp. 412–416, Portland, Ore, USA, March 2008.

2. C. Kelleher, "Alice and The Sims: the story from the Alice side of the fence," in The Annual Serious Games Summit (DC '06), Washington, DC, USA, October 2006.

3. ACM/IEEE-Curriculum 2005 Task Force, Computing Curricula 2005, The Overview Report, IEEE Computer Society Press and ACM Press, New York, NY, USA, September 2005.

4. S. Fincher and M. Petre, "Mapping the territory," in Computer Science Education Research, RoutledgeFalmer, pp. 1–8, Taylor & Francis, Boca Raton, Fla, USA, 2004.

5. S. Leutenegger and J. Edgington, "A games first approach to teaching introductory programming," in Proceedings of the 38th SIGCSE Technical Symposium on Computer Science Education (SIGCSE '07), pp. 115–118, Covington, Ky, USA, March 2007.

6. P. Cobb, J. Confrey, A. DiSessa, R. Lehrer, and L. Schauble, "Design experiments in educational research," Educational Researcher, vol. 32, no. 1, pp. 9–13, 2003.

7. M. Zyda, "From visual simulation to virtual reality to games," Computer, vol. 38, no. 9, pp. 25–32, 2005.

8. S. Blackman, "Serious games...and less!," Computer Graphics, vol. 39, no. 1, pp. 12–16, 2005.

9. F. L. Greitzer, O. A. Kuchar, and K. Huston, "Cognitive science implications for enhancing training effectiveness in a serious gaming context," ACM Journal on Educational Resources in Computing, vol. 7, no. 3, article no. 2, 2007.

10. ACM/IEEE-Curriculum 2001 Task Force, Computing Curricula 2001, Computer Science, IEEE Computer Society Press and ACM Press, New York, NY, USA, December 2001.

11. D. Ginat, "On novice loop boundaries and range conceptions," Computer Science Education, vol. 14, no. 3, pp. 165–181, 2004.

12. E. Soloway, J. Bonar, and K. Ehrlich, "Cognitive strategies and looping constructs: an empirical study," Communications of the ACM, vol. 26, no. 11, pp. 853–860, 1983.

13. O. Seppälä, L. Malmi, and A. Korhonen, "Observations on student misconceptions—a case study of the Build Heap Algorithm," Computer Science Education, vol. 16, no. 3, pp. 241–255, 2006.

14. E. Soloway, K. Ehrlich, J. Bonar, and J. Greenspan, "What do novices know about programming?," in Directions in Human-Computer Interaction, pp. 87–122, Ablex, New York, NY, USA, 1982.

15. M. McCracken, V. Almstrum, D. Diaz, et al., "A multi-national, multi-institutional study of assessment of programming skills of first-year CS students," in Working Group Reports from ITiCSE on Innovation and Technology in Computer Science Education (ITiCSE-WGR '01), pp. 125–180, Canterbury, UK, June 2001.

16. S. Stamm, "Mixed nuts: atypical classroom techniques for computer science courses," Crossroads, vol. 10, no. 4, p. 3, 2004.

17. D. E. Stevenson and P. J. Wagner, "Developing real-world programming assignments for CS1," in Proceedings of the 11th Annual SIGCSE Conference on Innovation and Technology in Computer Science Education (ITiCSE '06), pp. 158–162, Bologna, Italy, June 2006.

18. E. Klopfer and S. Yoon, "Developing games and simulations for today and tomorrow's tech savvy youth," TechTrends, vol. 49, no. 3, pp. 33–41, 2005.

19. J. Maloney, L. Burd, Y. Kafai, N. Rusk, B. Silverman, and M. Resnick, "Scratch: a sneak preview," in Proceedings of the 2nd International Conference on Creating, Connecting and Collaborating through Computing, pp. 104–109, Kyoto, Japan, January 2004.

20. C. Kelleher, D. Cosgrove, D. Culyba, C. Forlines, J. Pratt, and R. Pausch, "Alice2: programming without syntax errors," in Proceedings of the 15th Annual Symposium on the User Interface Software and Technology, Paris, France, October 2002.

21. A. Cockburn and A. Bryant, "Cleogo: collaborative and multi-metaphor programming for kids," in Proceedings of the 3rd Asian Pacific Computer and Human Interaction, pp. 189–194, Shonan Village Center, Japan, July 1998.

22. W.-K. Chen and Y. C. Cheng, "Teaching object-oriented programming laboratory with computer game programming," IEEE Transactions on Education, vol. 50, no. 3, pp. 197–203, 2007.

23. P. Gestwicki and F.-S. Sun, "Teaching design patterns through computer game development," ACM Journal on Educational Resources in Computing, vol. 8, no. 1, article no. 2, pp. 1–22, 2008.

24. D. J. Cook, M. Huber, R. Yerraballi, and L. B. Holder, "Enhancing computer science education with a wireless intelligent simulation environment," Journal of Computing in Higher Education, vol. 16, no. 1, pp. 106–127, 2004.

25. M. Buro, "ORTS: a hack-free RTS game environment," in Proceedings of the 3rd International Conference Computers and Games (CG '02), vol. 2883 of Lecture Notes in Computer Science, pp. 280–291, Edmonton, Canada, July 2002.

26. M. Buro and T. Furtak, "On the development of a free RTS game engine," in Proceedings of the 1st Annual North American Game-On Conference (GameOn'NA '05), pp. 1–5, Montreal, Canada, August 2005.

27. M. Muratet, P. Torguet, and J.-P. Jessel, "Learning programming with an RTS based Serious Game," in Serious Games on the Move International Conference, Cambridge, UK, June 2008.

28. G. Brousseau, Theory of Didactical Situations in Mathematics, Kluwer Academic Publishers, Dordrecht, The Netherlands, 1997.

29. M. A. Simon, "Learning mathematics and learning to teach: learning cycles in mathematics teacher education," Educational Studies in Mathematics, vol. 26, no. 1, pp. 71–94, 1994.

30. M. M. Muller and F. Padberg, "An empirical study about the feelgood factor in pair programming," in Proceedings of the 10th International Software Metrics Symposium (METRICS '04), pp. 151–158, Chicago, Ill, USA, September 2004.

Distributed Network, Wireless and Cloud Computing Enabled 3-D Ultrasound; a New Medical Technology Paradigm

Arie Meir and Boris Rubinsky

ABSTRACT

Medical technologies are indispensable to modern medicine. However, they have become exceedingly expensive and complex and are not available to the economically disadvantaged majority of the world population in underdeveloped as well as developed parts of the world. For example, according to the World Health Organization about two thirds of the world population does not have access to medical imaging. In this paper we introduce a new medical technology paradigm centered on wireless technology and cloud computing that was designed to overcome the problems of increasing health technology costs. We demonstrate the value of the concept with an example; the design of a wireless, distributed network and central (cloud) computing enabled three-dimensional (3-D) ultrasound system. Specifically, we demonstrate the feasibility of producing a 3-D high end ultrasound scan at a central computing facility using the raw data acquired at the remote patient site with an inexpensive low end ultrasound transducer designed for 2-D, through a mobile device and wireless connection link between them. Producing high-end 3D ultrasound images with simple low-end transducers reduces the cost of imaging by orders of magnitude. It also removes the requirement of having a highly trained imaging expert at the patient site, since the need for hand-eye coordination and the ability to reconstruct a 3-D mental image from 2-D scans, which is a necessity for high quality ultrasound imaging, is eliminated. This could enable relatively untrained medical workers in developing nations to administer imaging and a more accurate diagnosis, effectively saving the lives of people.

Introduction

During the last century, major advances in medical technology have led to substantial improvements in health care. This has come at a cost; the health care technology has become complex and expensive which, in turn, has led to a very wide disparity in health care delivery between those who have the financial resources to benefit from the advanced medical technology and those that do not. The ultimate outcome of this situation is that the majority of the world population does not have access to advanced medical technology and advanced health care. For instance, according to WHO reports, "Around 95% of medical technology in developing countries is imported, much of which does not meet the needs of national health care systems. Over 50% of equipment is not being used, either because of a lack of maintenance or spare parts, because it is too sophisticated or in disrepair, or simply because the health personnel do not know how to use it." [1]. This situation is particularly acute in the field of medical imaging, which is required for correct diagnostic in about 20% to 30% of cases worldwide and which is not available to over 60% of the world population [2]. The challenges in diagnostic imaging in developing countries include: a severe lack of safe and appropriate diagnostic imaging services because of the cost and complexity of the devices as well as a severe lack of technical skills and trained radiographers/technologists leading to a large number of images being misread or of poor quality and therefore of no diagnostic use [3].

For over a decade, our group has been working on trying to find solutions to the medical technology delivery disparity between those who have the financial resources to purchase and use these technologies and those who do not. We have identified that one major factor affecting the cost and the complexity of advanced medical technologies, such as medical imaging, is the hardware and software for data processing. Currently, medical devices are mostly stand-alone units, with redundant and practically limited computational parts, both software and hardware. The computational part becomes increasingly complex and expensive with an increase in the sophistication of the technology. In the recent years, advances in computer science, telecommunication and the Internet made information technology available at low cost to even remote villages everywhere in the world. Inspired by this fact, we conceived of a similar concept for delivering advanced medical care and medical technology. The key concept is that the computational part (hardware and software) is at a central facility, now called "cloud" which does the data processing and provides the most advanced computational service, at any time, to an unlimited number of users, connected through telecommunication to the central processing facility. The devices at the user site have limited or no data processing facility and are used primarily to transfer the raw data to the central processing facility and to display the processed data. To focus ideas, the remote devices become a dumb terminal for a central computational facility. This removes the cost and limitations of the computation, manipulation and interpretation of data from the vicinity of the patient and uses instead a central and effectively unlimited computational facility. In the vicinity of the patient only the components that directly interact with the patient and which acquire or use the raw data are needed. It should be emphasized that this is different from conventional telemedicine in which the data processing is still done in the vicinity of the patient and the processed images, for example, are sent on. In our concept the majority of the processing is done at the central facility that can be at a completely different geographical location than the patient. The central facility serves a large number of remote users and the telecommunication is used to transfer the raw or minimally processed data to this central processing.

We have demonstrated the feasibility of the concept described above using the Internet and land telecommunication for imaging with electrical impedance tomography (EIT) and for EIT monitored minimally invasive surgery [4], [5]. We have also shown that this concept can be used with cellular phone based wireless technology for remote medical imaging with EIT and that it is valuable to other computationally expensive procedures, such as developing classifiers and data bases for medical data analysis [6], [7], [8]. A review of some of the aspects of our cellular phone based work can be found in a recent Nature news feature [9].

The goal of this study is to elaborate on the fundamental paradigm we developed earlier and to illustrate the value of this paradigm with a new implementation, which could be immediately useful for medical imaging in economically disadvantaged parts of the world. We believe that in addition to EIT, ultrasound is one of the imaging modalities with the best potential to become widely used with this paradigm, due to its relatively small physical dimensions and relatively low-cost. Conventional ultrasound produces a two dimensional image. Successful use of ultrasound relies heavily on understanding the significance of the image displayed and optimal placement of the transducer through hand-eye coordination. The highly trained and experienced users of ultrasound have had to develop hand-eye coordination skills which enable them to create the mental 3D picture of the human body while watching 2D images acquired by the ultrasound system in real-time. They know exactly how to position the ultrasound (US) probe, at what angle to scan and how fast to move it along the patient's body to get a good image. Since medical personnel with such skill-sets are scarce in economically disadvantaged parts of the world, medical imaging is usually not done. In cases when medical imaging is performed the patients may be subject to wrong diagnosis and ultimately wrong treatment or no treatment at all. Three dimensional ultrasound image reconstruction, which is a relative recent addition to ultrasound, removes the need for high quality radiological expertise by allowing the physician to perform the scan without getting into the minute details of the data acquisition process such as the precise probe angle and position [10]. The challenge with industrial 3D ultrasound systems is their prohibitive cost which precludes them from being used in the developing nations, the place they are needed the most. Even in developed countries, small clinics that lack highly trained specialists, which could benefit from owning a 3D-US system, cannot afford purchasing it due to the high market price.

In this work we took the concept of processing at a central facility a step forward by implementing a fully functional 3D ultrasound system in which the 2-D intended raw data acquired at the patient site by a medical untrained person is transferred through telecommunication to a central processing facility, where it can be processed into a 3-D image or, in fact, for any conceivable use. The 3-D processed data can then be made available through communication to the data acquisition site or to an expert at any other location. The idea of coupling an ultrasound device with a communication device such as Wi-Fi adapter or a cellular phone is not new. In [11] Martini et al. have focused on the possibility of utilizing 3 g/WiFi networks for the purpose of video-streaming the acquired and processed ultrasound imaging data to the remote expert station. In [12] Dickson has evaluated several wireless communication options for ultrasound systems focusing on video-streaming capabilities in his analysis. However, to the best of our knowledge no other work has evaluated the feasibility of using telecommunication and wireless technology to transmit raw ultrasound data for processing on the central processing station that serves a large number of users and generates 3D image from the raw data.

We believe that the work presented in this study illustrates the value of our paradigm in a meaningful way. The powerful central processing facility, which can serve unlimited numbers of remote users, allows a remote unskilled user to employ an inexpensive technology and nevertheless obtain a state of the art product in terms of a 3-D ultrasound image, at a fraction of the cost and without the need for complex data processing facilities and software at the user site.

Results

The system architecture aligned with the proposed general paradigm is shown to contain two major components: Mobile Console and Remote Expert System (Fig. 1a). The mobile console with its sensors acts as the data acquisition device which collects the raw data from the patient, and sends it to the remote server for processing. The processing server is capable of transforming the large amount of otherwise meaningless measurements into a human understandable form such as an image or diagnosis.

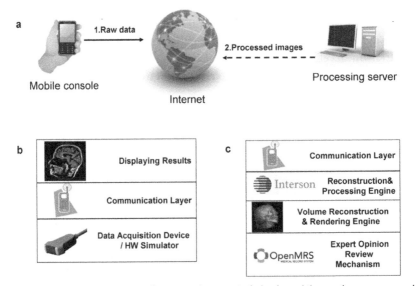

Figure 1. System Architecture. (a) Overall system architecture includes the mobile console component and the remote processing server (Expert System) which performs the computation-extensive work. (b) Mobile Console Architecture. The console has one or more data acquisition devices, a communication module and a display capability. (c) Server Architecture. Contains a communication module, a processing engine, a visualization engine and an expert assessment mechanism.

The mobile console (Fig. 1b) contains a hardware data acquisition device, a display and a communication component able to send raw data and receive results. The Processing Server (Fig. 1c) contains a communication component to receive the raw data, a processing (reconstruction) component to process the data into a useful form and a visualization (rendering) engine which shapes the data in a visually meaningful way. Optionally the server side can contain a human-assessment mechanism, which enables an expert doctor to review the results before sending them back to the mobile console.

The implementation of the general paradigm of Fig. 1 for 3-D ultrasound is given in detail in the Materials and Methods section. Specifically, we have used Lenovo R61 1.5GHz, 2GB RAM Windows XP as our server test bed running the server-side of the application software including the processing engine and OpenMRS server. For the purpose of this study we've focused primarily on a data flow in a typical obstetrics US scan, performed in B-Mode, with spatial resolution of 256×256, maintaining a contrast resolution of 8 bits (256 shades of gray). In such a study, the raw data required for the reconstruction is acquired by driving the transducer in a rectilinear, uniform direction with constant speed [13], [14]. The number of slices acquired depends on the specific application. We've used 80 slices in our study. We've used a standard, very inexpensive 3.5 MHz abdominal ultrasound probe manufactured by Interson Corporation for 2-D ultrasound (http://www.interson.com).

Our system is based on Google's Android platform which we chose because it is fully open source and capable of utilizing all the modern features provided by cellular operators. We have tested the system in two configurations: a) running on HTC G1 mobile phone and b) running in an emulator environment on Asus EEE 1000HE netbook computer.

Since USB host mode is not enabled on the conventional HTC G1 phone, it was not possible to connect the USB ultrasound probe to the mobile phone. For this reason we have designed a frame-grabber software module, which is responsible for capturing the raw data from the ultrasound probe and sending it to the G1 phone over short-range wireless network. We've used the same frame-grabber interface when we tested the system in an Android emulation environment running on Asus netbook. Android-powered netbooks are expected to appear in the nearest future and we envision our system running natively on those computers, getting the ultrasound data directly from the available USB port.

Although they have made great progress in the recent years, the cellular data channels available today are still limited when compared to broad-band Wi-Fi alternatives. Even HSDPA, commonly referred to as 3.5G, provides 14.0 Mbps downlink under optimal conditions and HSUPA, which is the uplink component of 3.5G, provides an uplink of up to 5.76 Mbps. This is especially true in developing nations where available cellular services tend to lag behind the cutting edge technologies available in the developed world. This is important because medical imaging devices are often known for generating large quantities of data.

For this reason it is important that the mobile console provides a buffering zone between the actual sensor and the processing station. Even if the connection channel is low-speed and/or unreliable, given enough storage space, the mobile console will eventually succeed to send the data to the processing station once the connection becomes stable.

An alternative scenario might involve a local health worker acquiring large amounts of data from multiple patients and later, when he is back to the local clinic where wi-fi is available, uploading all the accumulated data to the remote station for processing.

Fortunately, the costs of memory have dropped dramatically in the recent years (a 16 gb micro-sd supported by the G1 costs less than $45) so the buffering problem can be efficiently solved; the mobile device (netbook/cellular phone) would accumulate the data on it's internal memory card until connection for uploading this data is available. The raw data flows from the acquisition device, an US probe in our case, to the mobile device which is a mobile phone acting as a storage device, and then transferred to the processing server when the connection is available (Fig. 2).

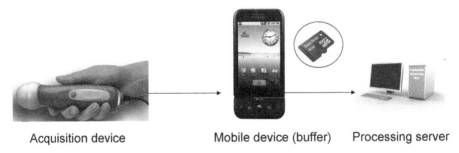

Acquisition device   Mobile device (buffer)   Processing server

Figure 2. Data Storage Mechanism. The raw data flowing from the mobile device which acts as a storage device. Once a connection is available, the data is being transferred to the server for processing.

To demonstrate a typical scan, we have followed an example from [15] and created an agar based box-shaped phantom, sized 3.5"x2.75"x2". During the solidifying process, we've embedded a marble ball, a peach pit and two cherry pits inside the phantom to be able to trace those objects in the resulting ultrasound scan (Fig. 3)

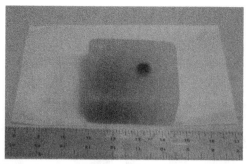

Figure 3. Ultrasound Phantom. Agar based 3.5"x2.75"x2" box shaped phantom with embedded marble ball, peach pit and two cherry pits. The marble ball and the peach pit can be seen from the image.

Since our purpose was to generate 3-dimensional images, we needed some type of system to provide with positional information. We used a hand held steadily moved probe to avoid the need for a more complex positioning system. It has not escaped our attention that for a truly freehand 3D-US a positioning system is preferable, otherwise the image resolution is extremely low and the image is unusable for clinical purposes. Nevertheless we have intentionally chosen to work around the position information problem since the focus of our work is the feasibility of the overall data acquisition and 3-D processing framework. We provide a brief review of possible alternatives for position and orientation estimation later in this paper.

For performance evaluation, relevant measurements are summarized in Table 1.

Table 1. Performances measurements.

Raw data size for a single B-Mode raw image	512 kB
Average raw data transfer for a single B-Mode raw image data (Wi-Fi)	3.9 sec
Volume rendering of 80 slices	28 sec
Snapshot generation for angular resolution of 10 degrees, yielding 36 projections per rotation axis	115 sec
36 Angular snapshot images transfer back to the mobile console (Wi-Fi)	31 sec

As can be seen from the time measurements, we transfer substantial amounts of raw data over the wireless connection, thus the round-trip time is not real-time. Although it is possible to make our system more efficient by using various data compression and channel quality adaptive algorithms, we'd like to emphasize an important point: due to the nature of the 3D ultrasound, the need for real-time feedback is removed because no hand-eye coordination is required anymore. The relatively unskilled health worker can acquire the data in a freehand manner and after the remote processing is done, have the complete 3D volume data available for review and diagnostic purposes.

A snapshot of the 3D reconstructed phantom is presented in multiple projection views (Fig. 4a and 4b). The ROI (region of interest) is shown in higher zoom level (Fig. 4c and 4d) where the marble ball can be seen on the top, the peach pit on the right and two cherry pits on the left part of the scan (Fig. 4c)

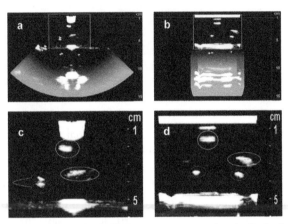

Figure 4. Resulting 3D Volume Visualized. (a) Front projection, axial angle 0°, depth of 15 cm (b) Side projection, axial angle 90°, depth of 15 cm (c) Zoom on ROI from (a): the cherry pits, the peach pit and the marble ball are clearly seen. (d) Zoom on ROI from (b) the cherry pits, the peach pit and the marble ball are clearly seen.

Discussion

We've shown in this work the feasibility of performing a 3D ultrasound scan using an inexpensive ultrasound transducer designed for 2-D, a mobile device, a remote processing station and a wireless connection link between them. Acquiring 3D ultrasound data removes the requirement of having a highly trained expert since hand-eye coordination process becomes obsolete. This enables medical workers in developing nations to administer a more accurate diagnosis, effectively saving the lives of people who would have otherwise been misdiagnosed.

It has to be noted that although our system did not incorporate any position information, due to the relatively steady motion of a US transducer by an untrained US user, we managed to get reasonable 3D results, without any positioning device or hand-eye coordination. To provide the health worker with even higher degree of freedom and flexibility during data acquisition we intend to research cost-effective position information mechanisms which can be embedded in our system as a part of our effort to design an affordable and effective medical imaging mechanism for developing nations.

Although our case study focused on US, the implementation of any another medical technology would be identical in its conceptual essence. We chose US since, due to it's mobility and wide availability, it seems like the natural choice of medical diagnostic modality for the developing world. In addition, ultrasound utilizes the available cellular connection as opposed to EIT described in [7] which sends very little data. We expect medical imaging solutions following the paradigm we've demonstrated in this work to appear in the foreseeable future. Constantly lowering mobile devices costs and communication technology advancements will contribute to this process.

An alternative and conceptually similar solution, might include integrating a data acquisition device such as the ultrasound probe used in our case-study with a cellular-phone chip such as, for example Gobi or Snapdragon technologies by Qualcomm   (http://www.qctconnect.com/products/snapdragon.html,http://gobianywhere.com/). This solution would include a small display which is capable of displaying the diagnostic information after the remote server has finished processing the raw data. This architecture can be utilized in a consumer device. The possible drawback of such architecture is binding the medical device to a specific cellular technology such as CDMA or GSM. A solution to this problem might include a Bluetooth transmitter in the end device which will send the raw data to any standard cellular phone; most modern phones include Bluetooth capabilities in them. This would expand the possible reach of the technology, since now we can leverage any existing cellular infrastructure.

One such possible device could be used to perform the scan by a health worker or even a home user. The raw data acquired by the Data Acquisition Device would be sent to remote station for processing and a diagnostic result in the form of a text message would be displayed on the LCD line: "Healthy" or "Thorough test is required" (Fig. 5).

Figure 5. Integrated breast cancer self-examination device for home use.

A class of such devices for self-diagnosis is the natural extension of our work and having such a device would enable early detection of diseases, such as cancers or internal bleeding, thus potentially saving the lives of many.

Materials and Methods

We will describe here the details of the 3-D ultrasound system implemented in this study using the general raw data transfer and data processing algorithm described in Fig. 1. Ultrasound imaging utilizes acoustic waves for the mapping of internal organs and tissues from changes in acoustic impedance between the tissues. Ultrasound works by sending acoustic pulse waves towards the mapped organ and then reconstructing the echoes of those waves into a visual image used for medical diagnosis. Due to the relatively compact size and low power consumption, ultrasound provides an important alternative to other medical imaging modalities such as CT and MRI.

In classic 2D ultrasound, the trained radiologist views the monitor while constructing a mental 3D image of the patient's body. The quality of the diagnostic is heavily biased in the favor of a well-trained radiologist with excellent hand eye coordination and ability to integrate a sequence the 2-D images into a 3-D mental understanding of the image. In 3D ultrasound systems, computer algorithms reconstruct a 3D image from the acquired 2-dimensional images, and therefore simplify the diagnostics. Since the reconstruction engine needs to position the 2D image in the 3D volume, in addition to the image data itself, the exact position and orientation of the US probe are required for each 2D image taken. Several approaches to estimating position and orientation are described at the end of the materials and methods section.

On a highly abstract level, any typical Ultrasound Imaging System includes 4 primary components: a) Transducer—a unit which emits and receives the acoustic waves and records the correlation between them, b) Control unit—used to control the operation of the transducer, c) Processing unit—which converts the raw data acquired by the transducer into a human usable form, usually a visual image, and d) Imaging—the final stage of the ultrasound scan chain where the visual image is being displayed on the monitor for diagnostic purposes.

The detailed step-by-step implementation of our wireless 3-D ultrasound algorithm as illustrated (Fig. 6):

1. The raw data arrives from the ultrasound probe.
2. The data arrives to the mobile device which stores the information on its internal memory card until a reliable connection channel becomes available.

3. Every once in a while (frequency can be configured trading-off responsiveness vs. battery life) the mobile device tests the available connection in order to detect the right moment to send the data. Once a connection has been established, the data transfer begins to the processing server. The communication protocol between the mobile device and the processing server is based on XML-RPC (http://www.xmlrpc.com/) which in turn is based on the standard HTTP protocol for transport. The data is packaged in a way that supports operating in slow, unreliable connection channels.

3.1 Once all the raw data arrives to the server, the processing stage can begin. The data is grouped by the slice number it belongs to.

3.2 In this stage a stack of parallel slices is being turned into a volume dataset for later manipulation. This can be achieved using the "DICOM Volume Render" open source software module by Mark Wyszomierski which is based on the popular graphics engine VTK.

Digital Imaging and Communications in Medicine (DICOM) is a standard for handling, storing, printing, and transmitting information in medical imaging. In addition to the raw image data, DICOM format enables incorporation of various meta-parameters for example, in our case slice sickness, slice number e.t.c. To design and build a quick prototype, we have decided to skip the direct generation of DICOM files, a process which might easily become mundane. Instead we have downloaded an existing 3D Ultrasound and simply replaced the raw image data with our data, in addition to modifying the relevant parameters.

Once this process of generating the DICOM files is complete, the renderer can process the stack of 2d images in DICOM format and create a volumetric data-set which is later snapshot to generate multiple view projects for 3d visualization.

3.3 Once the volumetric data-set has been created, it is projected in multiple directions to create the effect of 3D viewing on the mobile device. Given a high enough angular resolution, the effect is close to a full 3D manipulation in the commonly used axial, sagittal and coronal planes. It's worth noting that recent technological advances in mobile devices, specifically in CPU power and graphic processing abilities, already allow many cellular phones to perform 3D rendering on the mobile unit itself, as demonstrated by [16]. The trade-off decision of battery life vs. visualization power will have to be taken into account by any application designer in the mobile medical imaging field. We've decided to benefit from both worlds by enabling limited 3D visualization by pre-computed projections.

Once the projections have been generated they are saved as jpeg formatted images which are sent back to the mobile device, again using the XML-RPC over HTTP protocol. By using jpeg images as opposed to sending the volumetric data and rendering the data on the mobile device, we engage only the image-displaying capability of the mobile device as opposed to it's power-hungry 3D engine, thus saving precious battery life.

One minute, yet important aspect of communication has to be noted: due to the nature of a mobile device, its IP address is highly unstable. The cellular network might decide at a certain point that the IP address of a certain mobile device has to be changed to a different one. This makes it difficult for the server to contact the mobile console to notify it that the processing was completed and results are pending. Even if the mobile console sends its ID to the server, in the time period between the raw-data transmission to the termination of the processing phase, the IP address might have been changed. For this reason we've implemented a console-driven polling mechanism. Once the raw data has been sent, every once in a while, the mobile console polls the server if the results are ready. If they are, the console makes a request for them. The frequency of the polling procedure is a system parameter which can be configured to trade off responsiveness vs. battery life. We've found that the value of Tperiod = 30 seconds provides reasonable results.

3.4 Global Expert Opinion: to provide an optional expert opinion to the remote health worker, we have integrated our system with OpenMRS® (http://www.openmrs.org), a popular open source medical records system. Once the raw data has been reconstructed and 3D images are available, the processed images are being displayed in a "pending" queue in OpenMRS. After a medical expert reviews the data and adds his comments, the result is sent to the mobile console for display. Because we adapted the concept of distributing the components of the imaging system, the expert reviewing the diagnostic images can be at any geographic location, unrelated to the location of the health worker or the processing station. What this means is that a local health worker in rural Uganda can perform a scan that is being processed in data servers in

India and an expert radiologist from the U.S. provides a diagnostic opinion which is sent with the results back to the local health worker effectively in real-time.

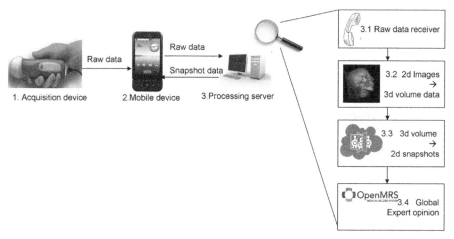

Figure 6. Data flow. The raw data flows from the hardware acquisition device to the mobile console which acts as a storage and communication conduit. Once the data is processed on the server, the results are transferred back to the console for review and diagnosis.

An important aspect of any 3D ultrasound system concerns position and orientation information. During the process of 3-dimensional image reconstruction, every surface element (pixel) from the 2-dimensional images is mapped to a volume element (voxel) in the 3D reconstructed volume. To perform such a mapping accurately, the reconstruction algorithm needs to know the precise position and orientation of the ultrasound probe at the moment of the 2D image acquisition. There are several techniques to this end. Mercier et al. review common technologies for medical instruments tracking [17]. Electro-magnetic and optical technologies for ultrasound probe tracking are the most popular. While those approaches provide good accuracy, they are also relatively bulky and expensive. Since we are working with the needs of developing countries in mind, we want to emphasize more mobile, cost-effective solutions. Abdul Rahni et al. have studied the possible usage of Micro Electro-Mechanical Systems (MEMS) based approach to estimate position and orientation in 3D [18]. In their study, the authors have used an Internal Measurement Unit (IMU) which included an accelerometer and a gyroscope. The advantage of this approach is its simplicity—no external camera or receiver is needed, as in the electromagnetic/optical technology case. The raw physical measurements (acceleration, angular velocity and static orientation) are read from the IMU and processed to calculate the absolute 3D position and orientation. By adding redundant sensors, it is possible to compensate for some of the numeric errors inherent to the process. Another work that has caught our attention has used a conventional digital camera for position and orientation estimation [19]. During the data acquisition process, in addition to the US data, a video clip focusing on the ultrasound probe is captured. After the acquisition process is over, the position and orientation information are extracted by applying machine vision algorithms to the acquired video stream. By using a conventional digital camera, which often comes as an integral part of any modern cell-phone, it is possible to build a low-cost, ultra-mobile 3D position mechanism.

We believe that the approaches presented in [18], [19] can be used as a basis for a cost-effective, mobile position and orientation estimation mechanism which are required by a 3D reconstruction algorithm and we intend to explore those research directions. Since the primary focus of our current work was to illustrate the concept of the overall data acquisition and 3-D processing framework, we've decided to relax the freehand requirement and work around the 3D positioning issue by steadily moving the US probe in a straight line during the data acquisition stage. By sticking to the straight line trajectory, we were able to use a more straightforward reconstruction algorithm since it could simply stack the 2D images one next to each other and still get a 3D images of reasonable quality. In the future we intend to develop relevant variants of the techniques described in [18], [19].

Acknowledgements

We would like to thank Mr. Eric Stein and Google Corporation for donating an HTC G1 mobile phone which made our work possible.

Authors' Contributions

Conceived and designed the experiments: BR. Performed the experiments: AM. Analyzed the data: AM. Wrote the paper: AM BR.

References

1. WHO report (2003) Essential Health Technologies Strategy 2004–2007. World Health Organization. http://www.who.int/eht/en/EHT_strategy_2 004-2007.pdf.

2. WHO report, Essential Diagnostic Imaging. World Health Organization, http://www.who.int/eht/en/DiagnosticImaging.pdf.

3. WHO report, About Diagnostic imaging. World Health Organization, http://www.who.int/diagnostic_imaging/en/.

4. Rubinsky B, Otten D (2004) Method and apparatus for remote imaging of biological tissue by electrical impedance tomography through a communication network. US Patent #6725087.

5. Otten D, Onik G, Rubinsky B (2004) Distributed Network Imaging and Electrical Impedance Tomography of Minimally Invasive Surgery. Technology in Cancer Research and Treatment Vol. 3, No. 2: 1–10.

6. Granot T, Ivorra A, Rubinsky B (2008) A New Concept for Medical Imaging Centered on Cellular Phone Technology. PloS ONE 3(4): e2075.

7. Laufer S, Rubinsky B (2009) "Tissue characterization with a multimodality classifier: electrical spectroscopy and medical imaging" IEEE Trans Biomed Eng Feb;56(2): 525–8.

8. Laufer S, Rubinsky B (2009) Cellular Phone Enabled Non-Invasive Tissue Classifier. PLoS ONE 4(4): e5178. doi:10.1371/journal.pone.0005178.

9. Kwok R (2009) Personal technology: Phoning in data. Nature 458: 959–961.

10. Gee A, Prager R, Treece G, Berman L (2003) Engineering a freehand 3-D ultrasound system. Pattern Recognit Lett vol. 24, no. 4–5: 757–777.

11. Martini MG, Istepanian RSH, Mazzotti M, Philip N (2007) A Cross-Layer Approach for Wireless Medical Video Streaming in Robotic Teleultrasonography. Conf Proc IEEE Eng Med Biol Soc 3082–5.

12. Dickson BW (2008) Wireless Communication Options for a Mobile Ultrasound System, MSc. Thesis, Worcester Polytechnic Institute, http://www.wpi.edu/Pubs/ETD/Available/etd-090208-162440/.

13. Goes CE, Schiabel H, Nunes FLS, Berezowski AT (2006) "Volume Rendering for Ultrasound Computer Phantoms Images by Using Multiplatform Software" IFMBE Proceedings World Congress on Medical Physics and Biomedical Engineering. 2456–2459.

14. Kelly M, Gardener JE, Brett AD, Richards R, Lees WR (1994) Three-dimensional US of the fetus—work in progress. Radiology 192: 253–259.

15. Bude RO, Adler RS (1995) An easily made, low-cost, tissue-like ultrasound phantom material. J Clin Ultrasound 23: 271–273.

16. Moser M, Weiskopf D (2008): Interactive volume rendering on mobile devices. In Vision, Modeling, and Visualization '08 Conference Proceedings 217–226.

17. Mercier L, Langø T, Lindseth F, Collins LD (2005) A review of calibration techniques for freehand 3-D ultrasound systems. Ultrasound in Medicine & Biology Volume 31, Issue 4: 587.

18. Abdul Rahni AA, Yahya I, Mustaza SM (2008) "2D Translation from a 6-DOF MEMS IMU's Orientation for Freehand 3D Ultrasound Scanning," Proceedings of 4th Kuala Lumpur International Conference on Biomedical Engineering.

19. Ali A, Logeswaran R (2007) "A visual probe localization and calibration system for cost-effective computer-aided 3D ultrasound," Computers in Biology and Medicine 37: 1141–1147.

miRMaid: A Unified Programming Interface for Microrna Data Resources

Anders Jacobsen, Anders Krogh, Sakari Kauppinen
and Morten Lindow

ABSTRACT

Background

MicroRNAs (miRNAs) are endogenous small RNAs that play a key role in post-transcriptional regulation of gene expression in animals and plants. The number of known miRNAs has increased rapidly over the years. The current release (version 14.0) of miRBase, the central online repository for miR-NA annotation, comprises over 10.000 miRNA precursors from 115 different species. Furthermore, a large number of decentralized online resources are now available, each contributing with important miRNA annotation and information.

Results

We have developed a software framework, designated here as miRMaid, with the goal of integrating miRNA data resources in a uniform web service interface that can be accessed and queried by researchers and, most importantly, by computers. miRMaid is built around data from miRBase and is designed to follow the official miRBase data releases. It exposes miRBase data as interconnected web services. Third-party miRNA data resources can be modularly integrated as miRMaid plugins or they can loosely couple with miRMaid as individual entities in the World Wide Web. miRMaid is available as a public web service but is also easily installed as a local application. The software framework is freely available under the LGPL open source license for academic and commercial use.

Conclusion

miRMaid is an intuitive and modular software platform designed to unify miRBase and independent miRNA data resources. It enables miRNA researchers to computationally address complex questions involving the multitude of miRNA data resources. Furthermore, miRMaid constitutes a basic framework for further programming in which microRNA-interested bioinformaticians can readily develop their own tools and data sources.

Background

MicroRNAs (miRNAs) are short regulatory RNA molecules that are encoded in the genomes of animals, plants and viruses. They function as post-transcriptional regulators of mRNAs and have gained high interest due to their importance in many biological processes [1-3] and their potential as drug targets [4]. The relatively recent discovery and the main mechanism of action of miRNA-based regulation, which is based on Watson-Crick base pairing, has led to a recent explosion in algorithms, websites and databases that provide different data about microRNAs.

The large number of miRNAs discovered during the last couple of years has been supported by miRBase as the central clearing house for miRNA nomenclature and annotation [5,6]. At the miRBase web site, scientists can submit newly discovered miRNAs and information about sequences and homologies in other species. Today miRBase has become a central and highly useful website for scientists who search for information about specific miRNAs. A number of flat files in different formats are made available with each release of miRBase to support computational analysis. In addition to miRBase, a variety of miRNA data resources has been developed by other research groups. These include resources that deal with genomic contexts and evolutionary conservation of miRNAs (miROrtho [7], miRGen [8], miRfunc [9], microTranspoGene [10]), prediction and validation of miRNA targets (TargetScan [11], miRNAMap [12], microRNA.org [13], miRDB [14], miRecords [15], TarBase [16]) and biological functions and phenotypes of individual miRNAs (miR2Disease [17], DIANA-mirPath [18], MMIA [19]). These miRNA resources are primarily available online as point-and-click web sites.

It is currently a burdensome task to do an integrated computational analysis using data from one or more of the online miRNA resources. For each resource, it requires manually downloading raw data files (if available), understanding the sometimes arcane format and structure of the resource in question and finally, construction of a script to parse the content and various identifiers. The researcher has to go through all these steps, and repeat them each time a resource is updated. A more simple procedure would reduce errors, increase reproducibility of the scientific results and make the data analysis less labor-intensive. miRMaid is a software framework designed to eliminate the aforementioned preprocessing steps. It provides non-redundant, structured and inter-connected data that are accessible both through an object oriented interface (using the Ruby programming language) and as web-based resources that are accessible remotely using most computer programming languages. The web-based resources follow a set of design principles, Representational State Transfer (REST) [20], implying that every resource is uniquely and uniformly addressable using an URL. The effect is that the web resources can be accessed equivalently by computer programs and researchers using a web browser.

Implementation

Core Architecture

miRMaid is built in the Ruby programming language using an open source web application framework, Ruby on Rails (RoR, http://www.rubyonrails.org). RoR allows rapid development of web applications in a Model-View-Controller (MVC) architecture, which isolates business logic from the user interface and facilitates program maintenance and scalability. In the RoR framework, data is stored in a relational database management system (SQLite, PostgreSQL and MySQL are currently supported in miRMaid) and encapsulated in an object-oriented model layer (Figure 1). The models are inter-connected and can be queried directly from the Ruby programming language. When miRMaid is deployed, it automatically (unless a specific miRBase version is stated) fetches the online raw data files from the current miRBase release. This data is restructured to yield the set of miRMaid core data models. An overview of these models and their associations is shown in Table 1.

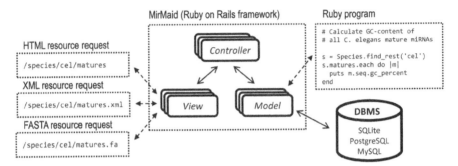

Figure 1. Architecture overview. miRMaid uses a Model-View-controller architecture. The model layer provides object oriented encapsulation of data stored in a relational database. The model layer can be efficiently and directly queried using the Ruby programming language. Each model is additionally exposed as a RESTful web resource. The data returned from a resource URL can be returned as HTML (suitable for web browsers), XML (suitable for computer programs) and for some resources also as FASTA sequence format.

Table 1. Models

Model	Description	Attributes	Relationships
Precursor	The miRNA precursor, processed from longer primary transcripts by endonucleases.	name, accession, description, sequence, comment	**Mature**,**GenomeContext**, **GenomePosition**, Paper, **PrecursorCluster**, Species, PrecursorFamily
Mature	The mature miRNA, processed from the miRNA precursor by Dicer.	name, accession, evidence, experiment, similarity, sequence	Precursor, SeedFamily
Species	The taxonomic species having miRNAs encoded in the genome.	abbreviation, name, division, taxonomy, genome_assembly	**Precursor**
PrecursorFamily	The miRBase grouping of precursors into families.	name, accession, description	**Precursor**
GenomeContext	Other gene models overlapping the miRNA precursor in genome.	overlap_sense, overlap_type, transcript_source, transcript_name	Precursor
GenomePosition	The position of the miRNA precursor in the genome.	xsome, contig_start, contig_end, strand	Precursor
PrecursorCluster (*)	A grouping of precursors occurring close to each other in the genome - presumably transcribed together.	Name	**Precursor**
SeedFamily (*)	A grouping of mature miRNAs based on the 6mer seed (bases 2-7) or 7mer seed (bases 2-8).	name, sequence	**Mature**
Paper	Papers related to the annotation and identification of a miRNA as reported in miRBase.	medline, title, author, journal	**Precursor**

miRMaid data models: miRMaid restructures data in miRBase to yield a set of core data models. The data for the two models highlighted with a (*) is not readily available from miRBase data but is automatically computed when miRMaid is deployed. Each model is semantically related and connected to other models as listed in the last column of the table. Relationships highlighted in bold denote a 'many' relationship: a species has 'many' miRNA precursors, while a miRNA precursor is only related to 'one' species. The attributes and relations on each data object can be accessed in an object-oriented manner (see Figure 5 for an example).

All models are also exposed on the web as read-only RESTful resources, rendering HTML to researchers (using web browsers) and XML or FASTA representations to computer programs. Figure 2 illustrates the miRMaid resources, the associations between resources and how they are addressed by an URL. miRMaid (using RoR) ships with a lightweight, but efficient, web server that can be loaded from the command line, but miRMaid is also easily integrated with an existing Apache web server.

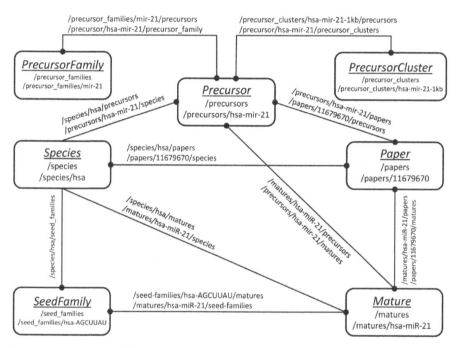

Figure 2. Resource map. Each data model (i.e. 'Precursor') in miRMaid has resource URLs for listing all objects (/precursors) or a single object (/precursors/hsa-mir-21). Relationships (denoted by edges in the figure) between models are captured by nested resource URLs (/matures/hsa-miR-21/papers). A solid circle at the end of an edge denotes a 'many' relationship. For example, a species 'has many' precursors (/species/hsa/precursors), while a precursor is related to only 'one' species (/precursors/hsa-mir-21/species).

Modular Design

A central feature of miRMaid is its modularity. It has a structured, but simple application interface (RESTful web-service or the Ruby object-relational layer) and can be loosely coupled as an independent data component in existing systems. Furthermore, miRMaid is built as a framework that is easy to extend with new data and functionality. We have designed a plugin architecture, where the core miRMaid framework works independently of activated plugins. The plugins can dynamically integrate with and extend miRMaid data and functionality without making changes to the core application. It is a simple procedure to develop an extension or plugin to miRMaid that introduces new data models and resources integrated with the core miRMaid framework (Figure 3). The result is a modular web application, where the core miRMaid framework can be dynamically extended with plugins to provide a unified browsing experience and application interface. Please, refer to the result section for an example of how the plugin integration works in practice.

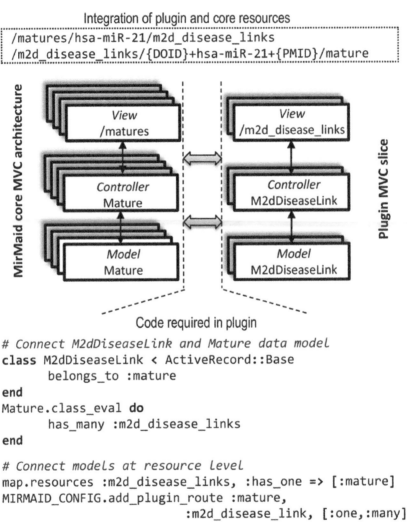

Integration of plugin and core resources

```
/matures/hsa-miR-21/m2d_disease_links
/m2d_disease_links/{DOID}+hsa-miR-21+{PMID}/mature
```

Code required in plugin

```
# Connect M2dDiseaseLink and Mature data model
class M2dDiseaseLink < ActiveRecord::Base
      belongs_to :mature
end
Mature.class_eval do
      has_many :m2d_disease_links
end

# Connect models at resource level
map.resources :m2d_disease_links, :has_one => [:mature]
MIRMAID_CONFIG.add_plugin_route :mature,
                        :m2d_disease_link, [:one,:many]
```

Figure 3. Plugin integration. A miRMaid plugin is implemented as an isolated MVC slice (an 'Engine' in the Ruby on Rails framework). The plugin defines its own data models and the relationships between these models. The integration (model and resource relationships) between the miRMaid core framework and the plugin is configured inside the plugin. The core framework provides hooks where a plugin can register itself. In the example above, the miR2Disease plugin defines two data models, M2dDisease and M2dDiseaseLink, where only the M2dDiseaseLink integrates directly with the core framework (a 'one-many' relationship with the Mature data model and resource). The effect of this integration is that M2dDiseaseLink objects are connected to Mature objects and that these relationships can be queried directly through the data models or by using RESTful resource URLs.

Results and Discussion

Maintenance and Lifecycle of miRMaid

miRBase is the data source of the core miRMaid framework. With every data release of miRBase there will be a corresponding public version of the miRMaid web service) while older miRMaid versions will be kept available for a limited time period. Besides being a public web service, miRMaid can easily be installed locally. When a new version of MirBase is released, a local installation can be updated simply by reinstalling the miRMaid framework (together with optional plugins) using a single command on the command line. The source code for miR-Maid is under the LGPL license and utilizes the Git multi-user versioning system (accessible via http://www.github.com). When changes are committed and released in the miRMaid project repository, it is a simple task to pull the changes and update a local miRMaid installation.

In miRMaid, there are unit tests for all models and RESTful resources. This is done to assist development and so that end-users can verify that their local miRMaid installation behaves as expected. The test suite can be run from the command-line. Plugins must also specify tests for models, RESTful resources and connections between the plugin and the core framework. The plugin unit tests are straightforward to implement and they are automatically evaluated together with the core test suite in miRMaid.

RESTful clients

A major benefit of a RESTful web service is the simplicity by which programs or other web services can retrieve information. Querying a RESTful web service only requires that the program is able to generate a HTTP request to the URL that specifies the resource and then parse the response document—most programming languages have such features readily available. miRMaid can generate HTML and XML response documents for all resource URLs and FASTA documents where it is appropriate. XML documents are suited for computer programs and they are easily handled and parsed in most programming languages. In Figure 4 we give two examples of RESTful clients implemented in the Ruby and Perl programming languages. Both programs perform two simple tasks: 1) retrieving the comment attribute for the cel-let-7 precursor, and 2) retrieving the sequences for the two mature miRNAs (hsa-miR-21 and hsa-miR-21*) in the hsa-mir-21 precursor. In Figure 4, we have also included two examples to illustrate the simplicity of the RESTful interface. We use the R statistical framework [21] and the 'curl' command-line program to issue a HTTP request to retrieve all C. elegans mature sequences in FASTA format. Furthermore, a normal web-browser can be used as a RESTful client to inspect the XML and FASTA response documents for a given URL. There is currently no widely adopted web service description standard for RESTful services. Until a standard has been adopted, the resource API for a given miRMaid instance (including installed plugins) is dynamically documented via the URL http://current.miRMaid.org/described_routes.txt (also available as an XML document). This feature is further documented on the miRMaid community site.

Ruby RESTful client

```ruby
1  require 'rubygems'
2  require 'activeresource'
3
4  @@url = 'http://current.mirmaid.org'
5  class Precursor < ActiveResource::Base; self.site = @@url; end
6  class Mature < ActiveResource::Base; self.site = @@url; end
7
8  # 1) Get the 'comment' attribute for the cel-let-7 precursor
9  puts Precursor.find('cel-let-7').comment
10
11 # 2) Get the mature sequences for the hsa-mir-21 precursor
12 Mature.find(:all, :from => '/precursors/hsa-mir-21/matures').each do |m|
13   puts m.sequence
14 end
```

Perl RESTful client

```perl
1  use strict;
2  use REST::Client; # These modules can be installed easily with 'cpan'
3  use XML::Simple;
4  use Data::Dumper;
5
6  my $client = REST::Client->new();
7  my $xs = XML::Simple->new(NoAttr=>1,KeyAttr=>[]);
8  $client->setHost("http://current.mirmaid.org");
9
10 # 1) Get the 'comment' attribute for the cel-let-7 precursor
11 $client->GET('/precursors/cel-let-7.xml');
12 my $precursor = $xs->XMLin($client->responseContent());
13 print $precursor->{'comment'}."\n";
14
15 # 2) Get the mature sequences for the hsa-mir-21 precursor
16 $client->GET('/precursors/hsa-mir-21/matures.xml');
17 my $matures = $xs->XMLin($client->responseContent())->{'mature'};
18 foreach my $m (@$matures) { print $m->{'sequence'}."\n" }
```

Command-line RESTful client
(Retrieves the 157 C. elegans mature miRNA sequences in fasta format)

```
> curl current.mirmaid.org/species/cel/matures.fa
```

R RESTful client
(Retrieves the 157 C. elegans mature miRNA sequences in fasta format)

```
> Library(Biostrings)
> read.RNAStringSet(url(http://current.mirmaid.org/species/cel/matures.fa),
                    format="fasta")
```

Figure 4. RESTful clients. RESTful clients can be implemented in most programming languages. Listed above are two examples in the Ruby and Perl programming languages. Both programs perform the same tasks: getting the 'comment' attribute for the cel-let-7 miRNA precursor and getting the mature miRNA sequences (hsa-miR-21 and hsa-miR-21*) for the hsa-mir-21 miRNA precursor. Both programs use standard libraries to issue HTTP GET requests and to parse the resulting XML documents. The final two examples demonstrate how miRMaid's FASTA sequence rendering capability can be used. We use the R statistical framework [21] and the 'curl' command-line program to issue a HTTP request to retrieve all C. elegans mature sequences in FASTA format.

Local Ruby Clients with Direct Access to Data Models

The second leg of miRMaid is the object oriented model layer. With a local miR-Maid installation data can be accessed efficiently through a Ruby program without the overhead of HTTP protocol and network communication that is associated with the REST interface. miRMaid uses the RoR object-relational mapping library called ActiveRecord. This library provides an intuitive way to find objects, retrieve attributes and to navigate between associated models. In Figure 5, we provide an example of how the models can be queried interactively in a Ruby IRB session. We start out by retrieving all 8 human precursors in the mir-17 precursor family. Next, we identify all precursors in a neighborhood of +/- 1000 nucleotides. These nearby precursors are finally grouped into mir-17 family members and non mir-17 family members. This is a very simple example yet it illustrates how the data models can be queried swiftly in an intuitive manner.

```
## Start interactive ruby environment with 'script/console production'
>> mir17_members = PrecursorFamily.find_by_name('mir-17').precursors
=> # got 145 mir-17 family precursors
>> mir17_hsa_members = mir17_members.select{|x| x.species.abbreviation == 'hsa'}
=> # got 8 human mir-17 family precursors
>> mir17_neighbours = mir17_hsa_members.map{|prec| prec.nearby_precursors(1000)}
=> # got the neighbours within 1000 nt of all mir-17 family precursors
>> mir17_neighbours.flatten!.uniq!
=> # removed duplicates
>> (mir17_neighbours & mir17_hsa_members).map{|x| x.name}.sort.join(", ")
## mir-17 family members less than 1000 nt away from each other
=> "hsa-mir-106a, hsa-mir-106b, hsa-mir-17, hsa-mir-18a,
    hsa-mir-18b, hsa-mir-20a, hsa-mir-20b, hsa-mir-93"
>> (mir17_neighbours - mir17_hsa_members).map{|x| x.name}.sort.join(", ")
## other precursors less than 1000 nt away from mir-17 family precursors
=> "hsa-mir-19a, hsa-mir-19b-1, hsa-mir-19b-2, hsa-mir-25,
    hsa-mir-363, hsa-mir-92a-1, hsa-mir-92a-2"
```

Figure 5. Ruby data models. In a local miRMaid installation, the data models can be queried directly without the overhead of the HTTP protocol and network communication. The figure lists an interactive Ruby IRB session where the data models are queried to analyze the genomic clustering of human mir-17 family members.

miRMaid Plugins

As detailed earlier, data and functionality in miRMaid can be extended by plugins. We have developed a proof-of-concept plugin using data from the miR2-Disease web service [22]. The plugin extends miRMaid with two data models and RESTful resources: diseases and disease links. A disease link associates a mature miRNA and a disease and it carries information about the association, for example PubMed reference and target genes. A specific disease instance can be reached using the URL,/m2d_diseases/DOID, where DOID is the Disease Ontology identifier. Disease links are identified by a concatenation of DOID, mature miRNA name and PubMed ID. Figure 3 demonstrates how the plugin connects with miRMaid to integrate the disease link model and resource with the miRMaid mature model and resource. The plugin should also define HTML representations for the resources that are being introduced. These plugin HTML representations are accessible from a web browser and are automatically integrated in the menu layout of the miRMaid web site. The net effect is a complete integration of miRMaid and plugin in both the web site and application interface. We host a public version of miRMaid with example plugins activated at http://plugins.mirmaid.org.

Conclusion

First of all, miRMaid is a software framework aiming at easing the manual workload for researchers when doing computational analyses involving miRNA data. miRMaid provides a uniform, intuitive and flexible application interface that is independent of programming language. miRMaid is designed to live as a public service as well as being installed locally. The public service should be used when doing a simple and quick analysis and for integration with other web services. The local installation (using the Ruby data models) is recommended when a more data extensive analysis is needed. miRMaid is open-source software and users can contribute to the framework through the public source code repository or they can develop a miRMaid plugin that can be shared with the rest of the community. Furthermore, individual users or labs can integrate private data as miRMaid plugins or they can couple existing information systems loosely to miRMaid using the RESTful API.

We believe that the miRMaid platform can pave a new and exciting way for scientists to share data and programs that involve miRNAs. miRMaid follows a design philosophy that web services and resources should be able to integrate: web services should participate in the web instead of merely living on the top of it. We envision that if new data resources are released as miRMaid plugins, or at least follow the RESTful design principles for web services, then this would be a big step towards a global integration of miRNA data. By developing miRMaid we hope that such an effort can be coordinated not only by huge centralized software development teams at Ensembl and the UCSC genome browser, but also by a community that shares a common scientific interest.

Availability and Requirements

- Project name: miRMaid
- Project home page: http://www.mirmaid.org.

- Operating systems: Server software: Linux and Mac OSX, Client software: Platform independent.

- Programming language; Server software: Ruby. RESTful clients: most modern programming languages.

- Other requirements; Database management system: PostgreSQL, MySQL or SQLite. Other minor requirements are detailed at http://www.mirmaid.org.

- License: Free for academic and commercial users under the GNU Lesser General Public License (LGPL).

- Public servers: A public server running the current miRMaid release can be found at http://current.mirmaid.org and a server instance with example plugins activated can be found at http://plugins.mirmaid.org.

Competing Interests

ML and SK are employees of Santaris Pharma A/S, a biopharmaceutical company developing RNA-based medicines.

Authors' Contributions

AJ designed and implemented most of the software and drafted the manuscript. ML conceived of the project, designed and tested the software and helped draft the manuscript. All authors read, helped draft and approved the final manuscript.

Acknowledgements

AJ was funded by grants from the BioSys Innovation Network and the Novo Nordisk Foundation.

References

1. Bartel DP: MicroRNAs: Genomics, Biogenesis, Mechanism, and Function. Cell 2004, 116:281–297.

2. Chekulaeva M, Filipowicz W: Mechanisms of miRNA-mediated post-transcriptional regulation in animal cells. Current Opinion in Cell Biology 2009, 21:452–460.

3. Medina PP, Slack FJ: microRNAs and cancer: an overview. Cell Cycle 2008, 7:2485–2492.

4. Petri A, Lindow M, Kauppinen S: MicroRNA silencing in primates: towards development of novel therapeutics. Cancer Res 2009, 69:393–395.

5. Griffiths-Jones S, Saini HK, van Dongen S, Enright AJ: miRBase: tools for microRNA genomics. Nucleic Acids Res 2008, 36:D154–158.

6. Ambros V, Bartel B, Bartel DP, et al.: A uniform system for microRNA annotation. RNA 2003, 9:277–279.

7. Gerlach D, Kriventseva EV, Rahman N, Vejnar CE, Zdobnov EM: miROrtho: computational survey of microRNA genes. Nucleic Acids Res 2009, 37:D111–117.

8. Megraw M, Sethupathy P, Corda B, Hatzigeorgiou AG: miRGen: a database for the study of animal microRNA genomic organization and function. Nucleic Acids Res 2007, 35:D149–155.

9. Taccioli C, Fabbri E, Visone R, et al.: UCbase & miRfunc: a database of ultraconserved sequences and microRNA function. Nucleic Acids Res 2009, 37:D41–48.

10. Levy A, Sela N, Ast G: TranspoGene and microTranspoGene: transposed elements influence on the transcriptome of seven vertebrates and invertebrates. Nucleic Acids Res 2008, 36:D47–52.

11. Lewis B, Burge C, Bartel D: Conserved seed pairing, often flanked by adenosines, indicates that thousands of human genes are microRNA targets. Cell 2005, 120:20. 15.

12. Hsu S, Chu C, Tsou A, et al.: miRNAMap 2.0: genomic maps of microRNAs in metazoan genomes. Nucleic Acids Res 2008, 36:D165–169.

13. Betel D, Wilson M, Gabow A, Marks DS, Sander C: The microRNA.org resource: targets and expression. Nucleic Acids Res 2008, 36:D149–153.

14. Wang X: miRDB: a microRNA target prediction and functional annotation database with a wiki interface. RNA 2008, 14:1012–1017.

15. Xiao F, Zuo Z, Cai G, et al.: miRecords: an integrated resource for microRNA-target interactions. Nucleic Acids Res 2009, 37:D105–110.

16. Papadopoulos GL, Reczko M, Simossis VA, Sethupathy P, Hatzigeorgiou AG: The database of experimentally supported targets: a functional update of TarBase. Nucleic Acids Res 2009, 37:D155–8.

17. Jiang Q, Wang Y, Hao Y, et al.: miR2Disease: a manually curated database for microRNA deregulation in human disease. Nucleic Acids Res 2009, 37:D98–104.

18. Papadopoulos GL, Alexiou P, Maragkakis M, Reczko M, Hatzigeorgiou AG: DIANA-mirPath: Integrating human and mouse microRNAs in pathways. Bioinformatics 2009, 25:1991–1993.

19. Nam S, Li M, Choi K, et al.: MicroRNA and mRNA integrated analysis (MMIA): a web tool for examining biological functions of microRNA expression. Nucleic Acids Res 2009, 37:W356–362.

20. Fielding RT, Taylor RN: Principled design of the modern Web architecture. ACM Trans Internet Technol 2002, 2:115–150.

21. R Development Core Team: R: A Language and Environment for Statistical Computing. Version 2.10.1 2009.

22. Jiang Q, Wang Y, Hao Y, et al.: miR2Disease: a manually curated database for microRNA deregulation in human disease. Nucleic Acids Res 2009, 37:D98–D104.

Some Attributes of a Language for Property-Based Testing

Matt Bishop and Vicentiu Neagoe

ABSTRACT

Property-based testing is a testing technique that evaluates executions of a program. The method checks that specifications, called properties, hold throughout the execution of the program. TASpec is a language used to specify these properties. This paper compares some attributes of the language with the specification patterns used for model-checking languages, and then presents some descriptions of properties that can be used to detect common security flaws in programs. This report describes the results of a one-year research project at the University of California, Davis, which was funded by a University Collaboration LDRD entitled "Property-based Testing for Cyber Security Assurance."

Introduction

Property-based testing is a technique for testing the security of programs. Recall that secure means conforming to a security policy. The analyst doing the testing first specifies the properties she wishes the program to conform to. The program is then instrumented based on the specification of the properties. Consider the execution of the program as a state machine, where as each instruction is executed, the state of the program changes. Relevant changes affect only those portions of the state used in the properties. The instrumentation produces output whenever such a change occurs. The program is then executed under control of another program called the test execution monitor (TEM). The TEM is given the properties, and whenever the execution enters a state forbidden by the specified by the properties, it reports a security error.

These properties are written in a little language (called TASPEC) with constructs designed to aid testing. These include location specifiers (which specify specific places in the program where the properties hold, or where the state of the executing program will change), assertion statements (which assert that a certain property now holds), retraction statements (which assert that a certain property no longer holds), and temporal relationship operators (which specify whether something occurs before or after something else, or should occur and hold for the rest of the execution).

This report first compares TASpec to other specification languages. We then examine some of the temporal operators used in TASpec in considerable detail. We analyze their precise meaning and show how to capture some of the notions in model checking and temporal logic languages using TASpec constructs. We conclude by presenting specifications of properties of programs that attackers commonly exploit in order to compromise the program (and, usually, the system on which the program runs).

A word about motivation will clarify the goals of this report. The software life cycle, in terms of assurance, is usually described using the Waterfall Life Cycle Model. The relevant stages of that model are:

1. Requirements definition and analysis, in which the specifications of the program or system are created and validated;

2. Design, during which the program or system is architected, and the design is validated;

3. Implementation, in which the program or system is created and tested;

4. Integration and system testing, in which a set of programs are brought together and their union is tested and validated; and

5. Operation and maintenance, in which the program or system is deployed and used.

TASpec fits into the life cycle at steps 3 and 4, because it is a language tied to the implementation of the program or system. However, the properties it must validate are often the same as, or derived from, properties that the design must meet. The design properties may be stated using a model checking language such as LTL. This naturally leads to the question of whether TASpec can describe the properties that LTL can describe, although at an implementation level. This is the reason for the analysis of the operators in TASpec.

That said, there are vulnerabilities specific to an implementation that may have no counterpart to design flaws. For example, buffer overflows arise from a failure to check bounds. Models of systems and software usually do not have states in which the failure to check bounds causes a transition, unless that failure is necessary for some reason. The model is at a level of abstraction in which this detail of checking is not relevant, and so is omitted. But it cannot be ignored at the implementation level. Hence, TASpec must be able to express these properties.

The next section reviews TASpec very briefly to provide background. The third section discusses the temporal operators of TASpec with an emphasis on aspects found in LTL, a model checking language. The fourth presents some common implementation vulnerabilities and the TASpec properties that detect them

TASpec and Property-Based Testing

The goal of property-based testing is to validate that a program satisfies a set of specifications, called "properties." The program to be validated is called the "target program."

As with formal methods, we do not discuss the derivation of requirements or, from them, specifications. We simply assume that the specifications are known. We also assume they are written in a low-level specification language (called "TASpec") that describes the specifications in terms of the program being validated. We distinguish this type of specification from the higher-level specifications of formal methods by calling the former "properties."

The first step in property-based testing is instrumentation. The property file, which contains the properties, is analyzed to determine which variables and functions will affect the properties. A program called the slicer eliminates all code in the target program that does not affect the properties. After slicing, the only paths of control and of data flow in the program are those that could affect the program.1 The resulting program satisfies the properties if, and only if, the original program satisfies the properties. Next, a second program called the instrumenter adds instructions to the target program to emit special directives describing changes of program state whenever a change of state occurs that could affect the desired properties. For example, suppose the property were "x > 5." The following fragment:

if (y > 6) then x := 3; else x := 6

would be instrumented to output the value of x after each part of the statement:

if (y > 6) then begin

 x = 3; print "assert x = 3";

end else begin

x = 6; print "assert x = 6";

end

The directives will be saved in a file called the "state file" for later analysis.

The next step is execution. The program is executed with appropriate test data. Ideally, all paths of execution should be tested. In practice, this number is too large, so some fraction of those paths are executed. Failure to test all paths means that some flows of control have not been validated. This illustrates the difference between validation and verification (in which all paths would be shown to be correct) as well as the need for careful test data generation. The inputs to each run are saved with the corresponding state file.

The final step is analysis. A third program, called the test execution monitor or TEM, takes the property file and the state file, and tests whether the directives show that the properties have been violated. If so, the precise property violated, and the location at which the property was violated, will be printed.

These steps differ from those for formal verification in two key ways. First, formal verification is primarily an a priori technique for developing correct code, although it can be used to prove an existing program correct. Property-based testing is strictly an a posteriori testing technique. It requires an existing program to use. Secondly, the focus of property-based testing is on the implementation rather than the higher-level layers of abstraction such as design. The properties are written in a little language similar to that of the target program. In formal verification, design is to be verified as well as implementation. So the language of specification is more abstract.

How TASpec Works

A brief description of the mechanics of TASpec and the TEM will be helpful in what follows. When the instrumented target program emits directives describing changes of program state, those changes have the form of assertions or retractions of particular predicates (called facts). The desired properties are expressed in terms of these predicates. As each assertion is emitted, the predicate being asserted is added to a database; as each retraction is emitted, the predicate being retracted is deleted from that database. At each step, the TEM ensures that the facts in the database do not violate any of the properties.

Basically, the state of the program execution is encapsulated in the set of facts in the database.

TASpec and Model Checking Languages

Our first question is the relationship between the language constructs in TASpec and the logic languages used to do model checking, as discussed earlier. For our purposes, we focus on the temporal operators.

Taxonomy

We use the taxonomy described in [3] to categorize TASpec as a hybrid approach between a history-based and a state-based specification language.

State-based specification has been traditionally used for sequential programs while history-based specification with temporal logic has been traditionally used for concurrent programs.

In history-based specification, time can be either linear or branching. Linear time makes assertions about paths and at each moment, there is only one possible future. Branching time has a treelike nature. Assertions are made about states and at each moment time may be split into alternate courses representing differ-ent possible futures [2]. Branching time views events as concurrent "alternative universes" [1, p. 954].

TASpec implements a form of "history" that describes preconditions such as "predicate A must be true before predicate B becomes true." It does not keep track of events that happened in the past.

TASpec is a state-based specification language that focuses on functional re-quirements describing what the software is expected to do. Aside from the state-based paradigm, it borrows temporal logic from history-based specification lan-guages. While the temporal operators do not increase its capability to express properties of programs, the temporal logic does allow some security properties to be expressed easily and clearly. History-based specification languages were de-signed for dealing with concurrent systems and systems that simulate real-time. TASpec is unique in using temporal logic because it deals with single threaded programs, and therefore linear time. TASpec fits into the discrete time paradigm because each state represents a discrete point in time.

If not designed carefully, specification languages can be cumbersome for expressing certain properties. Temporal logic does not enhance ease of expression when dealing with single threaded programs. It may make coding specifications easier and clearer, therefore reducing greatly the chances of introducing error in a specification. But even with temporal operators, simple specifications can require complex expressions. For example, consider a simple ordering property for moving an elevator. Between the time an elevator is summoned to a floor, and the time it opens its doors at that floor, the elevator can arrive at that floor at most twice [4]. This simple property requires "six levels of operator nesting in linear temporal logic" [3].

But without temporal operators, expressing temporal relationships between states and events becomes unnatural. Extra variables need to be added to indicate whether certain events happened, thereby making writing the specification more complex. Z is an example of a commonly used state-based specification language that lacks temporal operators.

Branching and Linear Time

Branching and linear time has more to do with how a person views reality. In the case of TASpec, we are only handling the case of single threaded programs, so the discussion about concurrent programs in [Lamport80] does not apply. We think the concept of linear and branching temporal logic can be applied in the following way. If a program has all information which it needs to run, before the program starts (such as a calculation intensive program), we consider that linear time logic is the more appropriate paradigm because we have all the information before the program starts to determine what the final result will be. If a program takes external input as it is running, we consider branching logic to be more appropriate because at any input state in the program, the next state depends upon the external input that may not be known when the program started.

Time and Before and Until Temporal Operators

In specification, there is a notion of "strong" and "weak" versions of the before and until temporal operators. Let A and B be states of the program. For the strong version of before, A before B means that if the execution enters state A, then the execution will enter state B at some point before the execution terminates. If the execution enters state A and thereafter never enters state B, then the expression is false. The expression becomes true only if state B is entered, and state A was entered before state B was entered. By comparison, for the weak version of before, A before B means that if the execution entered state A, it may or may not enter state B. As soon as state A is entered, the expression becomes true whether or not state B is entered subsequently. This expression is false if state B is entered before state A is entered.

However, the fundamental difference between checking specifications in TASpec and in logic creates a problem with mapping operators. Consider the before operator in (most) temporal logics. If A happened in the past, but is no longer true when B, then A before B would be true. Now consider the same operator in TASpec, and recall TASpec considers states A and B as facts in a database. These facts may be asserted (added to the database of current facts) or retracted (removed from the database of current facts). All checking is done over the set of current facts in the database. This means that if state A is entered, then left, then state B is entered, there is no indication that when state B is entered (and the fact corresponding to B is in the database), that state A held earlier (because as state A holds no longer, the fact corresponding to state A has been retracted from the database and is not there).

The TASpec interpretation of the before temporal operator actually states a precondition. So, A before B means "fact A is asserted before fact B is asserted, and must be asserted when B is asserted." Because multiple assertions are allowed, this definition needs to be made more precise. With multiple assertions, it is possible that A could be retracted in the same event that asserts B, in which case A before B would be false. So we should say that A must be asserted when B is first asserted. This means that the TASpec equivalent of "strong before" is:

A implies ((A before B) and eventually B)

But what if fact A needs to remain asserted throughout the whole time that B is asserted? For example, for the fact Authenticated(user) (meaning the user is authenticated) and the fact LoggedIn(user) (meaning the user has logged in), we want the property that Authenticated(user) is asserted before LoggedIn(user) is asserted, and Authenticated(user) remains asserted while LoggedIn(user) is asserted. How can we express that? We might use two properties to express this:

A before B

(A and B) until (not B)

In terms of strength, the TASpec before operator is weak, and the TASpec until operator is strong. The reason for this choice is simply that the security properties found so far were easier to express using this arrangement. An alternate arrangement would work equally well.

Expressibility

There is a tension between how easily a property can be expressed and how powerful the language is. It is the same tension that is found between high level and low level programming languages. Programming in a high level language like Modula makes high-level tasks easy, but the programmer loses the ability to access the machine architecture directly, as she can do when programming in assembly language. But the effort to write an accounting system (for example) in assembly language is much higher than in Modula, and the programmer is more prone to make a mistake.

Intuitively, we would like to be able to express every kind of property in one language. Someone may create a language in which this is possible. But, as [Lamport80] mentions, "this approach is based upon the misguided notion that the more expressive a system is, the better it is." We have high level languages to create an abstraction in order to hide the irrelevant details of the specific model we are working with.

TASpec has some limits that make expressing certain types of properties difficult. For example, consider the issue of "bounds", where one wants to say that between states P and R, the system is always in state Q. In many logics, this could be expressed as:

(P before Q) and (Q before R)

In TASpec, because of the representation of states as facts in the database, this is more complex:

(not P) implies (not Q)

P implies Q

Q and not R

Taking these three properties together, we have:

- If fact P has not been asserted, then if fact Q is asserted, the first property fails;

- If fact P has been asserted and fact Q has not been asserted, the second property fails;

- If fact R has been asserted and fact Q remains asserted, the third property fails

Combining these three statements, we have the desired result.

Now consider an "after" operator. This is more complex, because the TASpec before operator is weak. Expressing "A before B and ~A after B all the way to the end of the execution" would require converting the "after" operator to some expression using the before operator. A strong before operator would do this nicely, but the TASpec before operator is weak. So, this expression takes two steps:

1. Convert the "after" operator into a form using the strong "before" operator. This gives:

(A before B) and not ((B before not A) "strong before" A)

2. Express the strong "before" operator using the weak before operator, as described above.

This demonstrates the difficulty of mapping model checking specifications to TASpec. The reason for the difficulty is that the languages are fundamentally different, in that TASpec uses the model of facts in a database and logic languages use events. An event occurs. A fact is in the database or not in the database, but in TASpec's model one can record that a fact was in the database but is no longer there only by entering another fact in the database. This makes the underlying model of TASpec more like an assembly language, and the model-checking languages more like higher level languages. Intuitively, this makes sense, as TASpec deals with a much lower level of detail than is found in most models.

Common Vulnerabilities

Four common vulnerabilities are the escalation of privileges before authentication, buffer overflows, race conditions involving file accesses, and the ability to access files using a web server because the server does not adequately check the path name of the requested file. In this section, we present descriptions of how to write properties that will handle these problems. We assume a UNIX-like environment (this includes Linux), and present the first three properties for C programs, and the fourth for Java programs.

Privilege Escalation without Authentication

The problem of escalating privileges when a user has not properly authenticated herself arises because of programming flaws in most cases. In the UNIX world, consider the following program fragment:

```
/* get user name */
if (fgets(stdin, uname, sizeof(uname)–1) == NULL)
 return(FAILED);
/* get user password */
typedpwd = getpass("Password: ");
/* now get information about user with that name */
if ((pw = getpwnam(uname)) != NULL){
 /* generate user's password hash */
```

hashtp = crypt(pw->pw_passwd, typedpwd);

/* compare this to stored hash;

if match, grant access */

if (strcmp(pw->pw_passwd, hashtp) == 0){

/* match -- grant access */

setuid(pw->pw_uid);

return(SUCCESS);

}

/* didn't match -- fall through to deny access */

}

return(FAILED);

This fragment reads a user's name into a buffer, obtains the password from the user, and then validates it. If the password is correct, the user acquires privileges (the setuid system call). If not, an error code is returned.

Although this segment of code is straightforward, the escalation often occurs long after the authentication. If the programmer errs, the escalation may occur despite a user's having incorrectly authenticated herself. A bug in an FTP server illustrated this. The program authenticated the user, and set a "correct authentica-tion" flag. If the user then tried to change to a new login (say, root), but entered an incorrect password, the authentication would fail but the flag would not be reset. As obtaining privileges was contingent on the flag being set, the user would promptly acquire root privileges without authorization.

We define a set of properties to capture the various states. The authentication process begins when a name is mapped to a set of privileges (pwent->pw_uid) and a password. This property is described as:

location func getpwnam(name) result pwent

{ assert user_password(name,

pwent->pw_passwd, pwent->pw_uid); }

This instructs the instrumenter to add code to assert the predicate

user_password(name, password, UID)

with name, password, and UID the values stored in the variables name, pwent->passwd, and pwent->pw_uid, respectively.

The next state occurs when the cleartext password is hashed to produce the stored password. This property is described as:

location func crypt(password,salt) result encryptpwd

{ assert password_entered(encryptpwd); }

This instructs the instrumenter to add code to assert the predicate

password_entered(hash)

where hash is the value returned by the function crypt, which is in fact a hash computed in the same way that a stored password is derived from the correct cleartext password.

The next state is entered when the computed hash is compared to the stored password:

location func strcmp(s1, s2) result 0

{ assert equals(s1, s2); }

At this point, the user would enter the authenticated state if the following holds:

password_entered(pwd1) and

user_password(name, pwd2, uid) and

equal(pwd1, pwd2)

{ assert authenticated(uid) ; }

Note this property is not tied to any function in the program. If, at any point, the three assertions joined by "and" in the above property hold, the predicate

"authenticated(uid)" becomes asserted—and the "uid" corresponds to that of the predicate "user_password."

Finally, when privileges are escalated, we need to indicate this change of state. The relevant property is:

location func setuid(uid) result 1

{ assert access_acquired(uid); }

Note this includes the UID to which privileges are given.

To tie all this together, we require that one authenticate as a particular user before being given privileges of that user:

check authenticated(uid) before access_acquired(uid)

Now, let us consider two executions of this program. In the first, all proceeds as expected. The user "me" with UID 917 provides the correct password. During execution of the code fragment, after the setuid system call, the set of facts in the database is:

user_password("me", "xyz", 917)

password_entered("xyz")

equals("xyz", "xyz")

authenticated(917)

access_acquired(917)

At this point, the predicate

authenticated(917) before access_acquired(917)

holds, and no violations are found. But now the same user tries to become root, and supplies an incorrect password. After this (second) execution of the setuid system call, the database contains:

user_password("me", "xyz", 917)

password_entered("xyz")

equals("xyz", "xyz")

authenticated(917)

access_acquired(917)

user_password("root", "abc", 0)

password_entered("xyz")

equals("abc", "xyz")

access_acquired(0)

Now the property

authenticated(0) before access_acquired(0)

is false, and the TEM would report a violation.

File Creation Race Condition

This flaw arises when two actions, in this example file creation and changing file ownership, are sequential and a third action can occur between the two. Consider a program executing as root that performs the following sequence of actions:

Create file

Read data from another program, adding it to file

Close file

Change ownership of file from root to user

If reading the data takes long enough for someone else to change the binding of the file name (used for the "create" and the "change ownership") to the file object, then the file whose ownership is changed will not be the one that was created. This can allow an unprivileged user to create a privileged program without authorization.

The relevant code fragment is:

```
/* create the file */
if ((fd = creat("xyz", O_WRITE) >= 0){
/* read input and copy it to the
created file */
while(read(buf, 1000, finp) > 0)
write(buf, n, fd);
/* close it */
close(fd);
/* change ownership from root to
user 917 group 10 */
chown("xyz", 917, 10);
}
```

The race condition is exploited by a second program (one that does the rebinding). But as noted earlier, TASpec does not deal with concurrent programs. So, we look for system calls and functions that can block execution, such as the "read" function. Then a window of time during which the race condition can be exploited can be detected.

This involves two states. The first is access(file), in which the named file is being accessed. The second is block(file), in which the race condition exists. They work together as follows.

When the file is created, the process enters the access(file) state, and is not in the block(file) state. This is expressed as:

```
location func creat(file){
 assert access(file); retract block(file);
}
```

When the file is read, if the process is in the access(file) state, it then enters the block(file) state. The relevant property is:

```
location func read(){
```

if access(file) { assert block(file) };

}

Note here the file name carries over from the last creat system call. When the file's ownership is changed, the process must not be in the block(file) state. That is expressed as:

location func chown(file, user, group){

check not block(file);

}

Consider the database when the above code fragment is executed. After the creat, the database contains:

access("xyz")

After the while loop, the database contains:

access("xyz")

block("xyz")

...

where the block("xyz") predicate is repeated as many times as the loop is executed. When the chown system call is executed, the property

not block("xyz")

is tested, and fails. So this reports that a race condition exists.

Buffer Overflows

Buffer overflows are pernicious. A common source of buffer overflows is in the redaction of command line arguments. For example, in the fragment:

int main(int argc, char *argv[])

{

char pname[1024];

for(i = 0; argv[0]; i++)

pname[i] = argv[0][i];

pname[i] = '\0'

there is an implicit assumption that the name of the program (argv[0] will not be more than 1023 characters long. If it is, a buffer overflow will result.

First, we need to define a property that describes buffer overflow. It occurs when an array reference is out of bounds. Every array has an upper bound (for pname, 1023) and a lower bound (for pname, 0). Our property will say that when an array reference to element i occurs, and the array's bounds are l (lower) and u (upper), then l _ i and i _ u must both hold.

We define the predicate array(pname, 0, 1023) to mean that the array pname was declared with upper bound 1023 and lower bound 0. We define the predicate arrayref(pname, i) to mean that element i of array pname was referenced. The property to be tested is then:

check array(aname,lower,upper) and arrayref(aname,index)

implies (lower <= index and index <= upper)

Note that we need not explicitly name the array in the property. The TEM will validate all array references when checking the property.

Next, we must instruct the instrumenter to put these predicates, and the property, into the source file appropriately. We use location specifiers to do this. The property file is:

location decl pname[1024] {

assert array(pname, 0, 1023); }

location variable pname[i] {

assert arrayref(pname, i);

check array(aname,lower,upper) and

arrayref(aname,index)

implies (lower <= index and index <= upper);

}

Unlike the property, the "pname" and "i" in the first two lines must match the variables in the program. The instrumenter will transform the code fragment above into the following (conceptually; several implementation-level details and error checking are omitted):

int main(int argc, char *argv[])

{

char pname[1024];

tf = open("directivefile", WR_ONLY);

fprintf(tf, "assert array(pname, 0, 1023)\n");

for(i = 0; argv[0]; i++){

fprintf(tf, "assert arrayref(pname, i)\n");

fprintf(tf, "check ...\n");

pname[i] = argv[0][i];

}

fprintf(tf, "assert arrayref(pname, i)\n");

fprintf(tf, "check ...\n");

pname[i] = '\0'

(The "check ..." refers to the entire check in the property file; it is elided for clarity.) The program containing this code fragment can now be compiled and executed.

Assume the program is given a name of 1025 characters. When the run is complete, the state file will contain:

assert array(pname, 0, 1023);

assert arrayref(pname, 0);

check array(aname,lower,upper) and arrayref(aname,index)

implies (lower <= index and index <= upper);

...

assert arrayref(pname, 1024);

check array(aname,lower,upper) and arrayref(aname,index)

implies (lower <= index and index <= upper);

assert arrayref(pname, 1025);

check array(aname,lower,upper) and arrayref(aname,index)

implies (lower <= index and index <= upper);

(the ellipsis indicates 1023 lines elided). When the TEM is run over this state file, the property will be checked at every arrayref, because both predicates hold. At the next-to-last check above, the antecedents are true, but the consequent is false, as index is 1024. Hence the TEM will report a violation of the property.

Improper Web Server Restriction

The next bug is one common to older web servers. When a web browser connects to a web server, the web server gives the browser access to a hierarchy of files. The area accessible to the browser is to be restricted to the top-level directory of this hierarchy, and its descendents. Hence an attempt to access the file "../../../../../ etc/passwd" should fail if made from the top-level directory. The ".." means to access the parent directory. That directory exists on the web server, but the software should block access to it. Unfortunately, many web servers do not restrict this type of access. In this case, attackers can read system and other files not in the web hierarchy.

As a test of the Java implementation of property-based testing, we obtained a Java web server and had a student delete the checks for this flaw. We then used property-based testing to determine whether the flaw existed.

The basic structure of the relevant parts of the web server are as follows. A method called HttpWorker.doit() is given the URL from the browser. If the URL is illegal in any way, the web server throws an exception with that URL passed as a parameter.

First, we define the property. For this example, we will assume there are no subdirectories of the hierarchy. This simplifies the statement of properties without changing the basic ideas. Again, we define two predicates. The first, hasDotDot(url), asserts that the URL url has the ".." in it. The second, causedException(req), asserts that the URL req caused an exception to be thrown. Then the property of interest is:

check hasDotDot(url) implies causedException(url);

because if hasDotDot(url) is true, and causedException(url) is true, the URL referred to the parent directory and was caught. But if hasDotDot(url) is true and causedException(url) is not asserted, then the invalid URL is not caught and the property was violated.

We next instrument the server. The assertion for a URL referring to the parent goes, as indicated, at the beginning of HttpWorker.doit():

location assign HttpWorker.doit()::req result r

if "r.getRequestURI.indexOf(\.".\/\") > -1" {

assert hasDotDot(r);

}

This says to check whenever something is assigned to the variable req in the function doit() in the class HttpWorker. If the new value of req contains ".." (the "if" part) then the program will output the appropriate assertion. Similarly, the assertion for exceptions is output when the reply function in the exception part of the class is called:

location funcall HttpException::reply(HttpRequest req,

HttpResponse res){

assert causedexception(req);

}

This binds the assert to the call to the reply function in the class HttpException. Note the URL is output; the specific response sent is irrelevant to the property.

When the instrumented web server was run, and a browser requested an illegal URL, the state file contained:

check hasDotDot(Areq) implies causedException(Areq);

assert hasdoddot("/../../../../../etc/passwd");

check hasDotDot(Areq) implies causedException(Areq);

The first line is vacuously true, as hasDotDot(Areq) has not been asserted. The last line, however, is false, because hasDotDot("/../../../../../etc/passwd") is asserted, but the corresponding causedException("/../../../../../etc/passwd") has not been asserted.

As a control, the same sequence of URLs was requested from an instrumented but correct version of the same web server. The state file for that version of the program contained:

check hasDotDot(Areq) implies causedException(Areq);

assert hasdoddot("/../../../../../etc/passwd");

assert causedException("/../../../../../etc/passwd");

check hasDotDot(Areq) implies causedException(Areq);

Both hasDotDot("/../../../../../etc/passwd") and causedException("/../../../../../etc/passwd") have been asserted when the final check is made.

Summary

This section presented four examples of programs with common flaws. We showed the properties that described each, and the instrumenting necessary to enable the TEM to detect changes of state that affect the truth of the properties as the program runs. These examples demonstrate the usefulness of this testing methodology.

Conclusion

Although it is used to specify properties that programs must satisfy, TASPec is different from logic languages used to do model checking. The key difference comes from TASpec's model of events (state changes are represented as facts in a database), which differs from the notion of state changes used in model checking.

TASpec's lack of history constructs increases the complexity of expressing some temporal events. Fortunately, as shown by the description of several common vulnerabilities above, these do not affect the use of TASpec to describe many common implementation flaws.

References

1. M. Bishop, Computer Security – Art and Science, Addison Wesley, Boston, MA (2003).

2. L. Lamport Leslie, "'Sometime' Is Sometimes 'Not Never': On the Temporal Logic of Programs", Proceedings of the 7th ACM SIGPLAN-SIGACT Symposium on Principles of Programming Languages pp. 174–185 (Jan. 1980).

3. A. van Lamsweerde, "Formal Specification: a Roadmap", Proceedings of the Conference on The Future of Software Engineering, pp. 147–159 (June 2000).

4. M. Dwyer, G. Avrunin, and James C. Corbett, "Property Specification Patterns for Finite-State Verification", Proceedings of the Second Workshop on Formal Methods in Software Practice, pp. 7–15 (Mar. 1998).

5. M. Dwyer, "Spec Patterns", athttp://patterns.projects.cis.ksu.edu/documentation/patterns.shtml.

6. G. Fink and M. Bishop, "Property Based Testing: A New Approach to Testing for Assurance," ACM SIGSOFT Software Engineering Notes 22 (4) pp. 74–80 (July 1997).

7. G. Fink, Discovering Security and Safety Flaws using Property-Based Testing, Ph.D. Thesis, Dept. of Computer Science, University of California, Davis, CA 95616–8562 (1996).

Copyrights

Index

Printed and bound by CPI Group (UK) Ltd, Croydon, CR0 4YY

23/10/2024

01777692-0004